Unintended Consequences
of Constitutional Amendment

Unintended Consequences
of Constitutional Amendment

Edited by David E. Kyvig

The University of Georgia Press
Athens & London

Library of Congress Cataloging-in-Publication Data

Unintended consequences of constitutional amendment /
edited by David E. Kyvig.
    p.   cm.
Includes bibliographical references and index.
ISBN 0-8203-2188-5 (alk. paper)—
ISBN 0-8203-2191-5 (pbk. : alk. paper)
1. Constitutional amendments—United States.
2. Constitutional history—United States.
I. Kyvig, David E.
KF4555.U55   2000
342.73'029—dc21   99-053078

British Library Cataloging-in-Publication Data available

Portions of "The Unintended Consequences of the
Nineteenth Amendment: Why So Few?" originally
appeared in *Women's Suffrage and the Origins of
Liberal Feminism in the United States, 1820–1920* by
Suzanne M. Marilley copyright © 1996 by the President and Fellows of Harvard College. Excerpts used by
permission of Harvard University Press.

Paperback ISBN-13: 978-0-8203-2191-2
2017 hardcover reissue ISBN-13: 978-0-8203-5269-5

Contents

Contents

Unintended Consequences
of Constitutional Amendment

Introduction

David E. Kyvig

Government involves an act of faith regarding the future. The adoption of laws, establishment of services, and enforcement of regulations all presume results that will somehow produce a benefit for someone sometime ahead. This is true whether the form of government is authoritarian, republican, or purely democratic, that is, whether the effective responsibility for decision making rests in the hands of an oligarchy, a representative body, or the mass of citizens. Even if the motive of the policy maker is totally self-serving or corrupt, the intention is to achieve some positive future outcome from government action. In this respect all government is rooted in predictive activity.

Governments, therefore, face a constant challenge to make policy choices based upon sensible estimates of what the future will hold. Regardless of its procedures or preferences, a government must be able to forecast rationally the situation that lies ahead in order to have any reasonable chance of dealing with it successfully. Envisioning what is yet to occur is, without question, a task of surpassing difficulty. To confirm the importance, not to mention the difficulty, of anticipating the consequences of policy decisions, one need look no farther than the scattered relics of myriad governments that failed to do so and fell as a result.

Fortunately for governments, not all of their failures to forecast accurately the results of their own decisions are immediately fatal. Sometimes, in fact, the unanticipated consequences of governmental actions turn out to be highly beneficial. Certainly that has been true on occasion of the United States of America and not simply because, as once suggested, "God looks after fools, drunkards, and the United States." Nevertheless, the more often the effects of government action are unforeseen and unintended, the more likely it is that difficulty will arise and damage will be done. Reducing the risks of policy choices to a minimum becomes increasingly problematic as political, economic, technological, and cultural conditions evolve and as society grows progressively more complex, but making sound decisions as circumstances change is always the specific burden confronting governments.

Constitutions can be looked at as hedges against the unintended consequences of public policy decisions. Constitutions define standards of government responsibility and conduct as well as limits to authority, thus confining the range of possible outcomes resulting from policy choices. In order to perform their functions effectively, the United States Constitution and others of its type set requirements for the definition and alteration of their own terms that are much more demanding than for the ordinary adoption of policy. The rules for making the rules are relatively inflexible by design so that the structure of government will remain stable even if a particular policy of that government has unanticipated results. Therefore, even more significant than the adoption of legislation, bureaucratic policy, or judicial rulings that turn out to have unintended consequences is the establishment of constitutional provisions with unexpected outcomes. Once a formal constitutional change is put in place its removal presents an exceptional challenge.

The notion has become popular in some circles that the United States Constitution can be fundamentally changed without following the formal procedure of amendment as long as a large majority of the polity appears over a span of years to agree with a judicial, legislative, or executive initiative. This theory flies in the face of both historical experience and constitutionalism's essential commitment to procedural definition. If there can be no certainty as to whether or not a provision has been adopted or what it formally states (even if implied meanings may be in question), the very essence of constitutionalism evaporates. Arguments to the contrary are interesting and intellectually challenging but not ultimately persuasive. "Due process" has a bedrock importance not only in terms of individual rights but also as regards the overall right of the polity under a constitutional system. The character of constitutionalism itself renders vitally important the consequences of constitutional change, especially if they are unintended.

The essays in this volume devote attention to the unanticipated outcomes of constitutional formation and alteration. The successes and failures of those with constitution-making responsibilities to foresee the possible results of their actions carry profound consequence for constitutionalism. Exploring such matters may foster a better understanding of the importance and limitations of constitutions. Among other things, these essays reveal the fundamental difference between evolutionary, informal understandings of what is constitutionally permissible and formal constitutional amendment. The latter has proven a much more effective restraint than the former on subsequent public policy decisions with their own unintended consequences. To argue, as some have, that enduring transformative constitutional change can be achieved without resort to Article V seems a foreshortened misreading of the long sweep of American experience.

Predicting the outcomes of government initiatives, whether administrative, legislative, judicial, or constitutional, has never been an easy task. Those who attempt to make such forecasts tend to find that looking at what has taken place in the relevant past serves as the best means of gaining a sense of what is likely to occur in an equivalent span of time ahead. A pattern that has held for only a few months or years does not become a likely guide for more than a short term, whereas a pattern that has persisted for decades or centuries can probably be relied upon much farther into the future. Historical insight, especially when focused on two centuries or more, can, therefore, serve as a helpful guide for the policy maker.

Just as human memory is a useful if imperfect guide for individual action, history can similarly serve society. Honesty requires acknowledgment that memory can be incomplete, distorted, or ambiguous and thus must be employed with care. Like memory, historical understanding can be flawed. Only a partial record may survive; the observer's perspective may cause a development to be interpreted in a particular fashion; preoccupation with one situation may lead others to be overlooked; and various contradictory explanations may seem equally valid or at least plausible. Human historical reconstructions can make no legitimate claim to infallibility, no more than can human memory. By and large, however, a careful examination of the manner in which individuals, institutions, and processes have performed in the past (acknowledging and compensating for an incomplete record, limited perspective or range of attention, and alternative interpretations) provides the best available means of estimating how the same individuals, institutions, and processes are likely to function in the future.

A great difference looms between drawing insight from the past and simply finding comfort there. Of late some critics of certain governmental policy choices have argued that since some consequences of those policies were unforeseen, they should never have been made in the first place. Some U.S. policy choices made during the 1960s, especially in the area of racial and social welfare policy, have since been heavily attacked along these lines. The existence of such critical views does not mean, however, that anyone who examines the unanticipated consequences of policy decisions is philosophically conservative, much less an advocate of retrograde public policy. The very concept of examining the intentions and the unintended consequences of policy judgments is much older, less ideological, and more useful than recent neoconservative agendas imply. As a method of policy analysis, appraising the intentions of designers and instigators in historical context has special merit. As a means of assessing proposed constitutional reforms that will subsequently be unusually difficult to overturn, this approach gains even greater value.

Attention to examples of the unintended consequences of public policies can, in the hands of fair-minded analysts, illuminate some of the complexities of the policy-making process. Such studies can remind policy makers, and those who advise them, of substantive and procedural matters deserving attention as well as patterns of result from previous choices. Raising the issue of unintended consequences of policy decisions no more leads inevitably to conservative conclusions than raising the issue of social responsibility leads necessarily to liberal ones. Addressing such questions can, however, provide insight on how policy decisions have been made, how flaws or benefits crept in unexpectedly, and how both related and unrelated matters might be better handled in the future.

Governments make no policy determinations any more critical to their ultimate success or failure than judgments as to their fundamental form, obligations, and limitations, in other words, their constitutional terms. Thus no policy choices are fraught with more peril in terms of unanticipated consequences than decisions to define or alter constitutions. When constitutional change is formalized in the process and language of amendment, rather than the more malleable claims of judicial, executive, or legislative interpretation, the significance and risk of unintended outcomes escalate. Once in place, a constitutional amendment becomes devilishly difficult to dislodge. Only once in the entire course of U.S. constitutional history since 1787 has an amendment been overturned once adopted. In terms of both the breadth and the persistence of their effect, therefore, constitutional changes may be unrivaled in their consequences.

An understanding of the policy implications of constitutional amending for the United States requires examination of the procedures for change established in the Articles of Confederation and revised in Article V of the 1787 Constitution. It demands as well specific scrutiny of the amending process over the course of the more than two centuries since the system for constitutional policy formation was first established. The interaction of scholarship considering the general process of amendment with investigations of specific instances thereof can shed considerable light on the history of constitutional policy making. In particular, such an exploration can illuminate causes and effects when unintended consequences crop up in constitutional reform.

This volume offers the first focused and extended consideration of the unintended consequences of constitutional amendment. It incorporates the varied approaches and perspectives of several mature and accomplished scholars. It is presented with a desire to aid the understanding of past constitutional practices and therefore improve the quality of future constitutional decision making.

A June 1997 conference sponsored by the Bowling Green (Ohio) State University Center for Policy History launched the discussion reflected in this volume. At the Bowling Green conference Richard Aynes and David Kyvig of the University of Akron, Richard Hamm of the State University of New York at Albany, and Suzanne Marilley of Capitol University addressed various aspects of the topic in two sessions chaired by Kermit Hall, dean of the College of Humanities at Ohio State University. Subsequently, David Bodenhamer of Indiana University, David Currie of the University of Chicago, and Mary Farmer and Donald Nieman of Bowling Green State University joined the discussion, taking up the unintended consequences of other amendments in essays prepared especially for this volume. While Bowling Green State University deserves credit for launching the discussion, the authors and editor of this volume have extended it considerably beyond its original scope. They are solely responsible for their individual judgments presented herein.

The essays in this volume address the entire sweep of U.S. constitutional development and illuminate, sometimes quite starkly, aspects of its stability and discontinuity. The collection begins with essays examining the late eighteenth century during which the American constitutional system was first elaborated. Essays follow that deal with the Reconstruction and Progressive eras of substantial constitutional reform. A number of the essays as well as an afterword refer to the late twentieth century, when new consequences of old as well as not so old amendments continued to reveal themselves. The range of issues addressed in this volume underscores the continuing relevance of the topic throughout the course of the American constitutional experience.

The collection opens with my discussion of the framers' intentions to articulate a definite though revisable set of governmental structures, obligations, and limits when they created the Constitution. The establishment of an innovative formal mechanism for amendment was a vital, though subsequently undervalued, element in their constitutional design, intended to provide a means of judging whether a binding constitutional change had been legitimately adopted. The essay offers an implicit challenge to the current theory that constitutional change of an enduring nature can occur outside the formal system specified by Article V of the Constitution.

Thereafter, David Bodenhamer considers, against the backdrop of the First Congress's initial use of the amendment mechanism to articulate a Bill of Rights, the manner in which conceptions of criminal procedure evolved and changed, particularly during the twentieth century. He compellingly describes the intentions of the architects of the Bill of Rights to restrain the power of government over individual liberty. Their preeminent interest in protecting the rights of the accused led to their insistence that government observe rules of due process in criminal proceedings. Bodenhamer sees that long-neglected intention resurfacing in Supreme Court rulings of the 1960s but slipping from view once again in the 1990s. Tension persists between the framers' desire to protect the individual and modern preferences to punish the guilty. In any case, Bodenhamer's essay helps in evaluating which modern criminal procedures represent the intentional and which the unintentional consequences of early constitutional amendments.

David Currie sheds light on the surprising significance for the authority and influence of the vice president of the apparently quite simple and straightforward Twelfth Amendment, which ostensibly only recast procedures for electoral college balloting for the presidency and the vice presidency. By examining closely the drafting of the Twelfth Amendment, Currie shows that its framers were not oblivious to the possibilities of outcomes they did not intend. However, he suggests, the difficulty of drafting and securing adoption of constitutional language increased the likelihood that unintended consequences would actually occur.

Richard Aynes moves the discussion farther ahead with an examination of the intentions and consequences of the Fourteenth Amendment, anomalous because of its multiple facets. As he considers the amendment's various provisions and results, Aynes raises the interesting question of its framers' intention to persuade the country, and in particular the South, to accept constitutional provisions they might not desire to embrace. This essay raises significant questions about the subtlety and complexity of intentions in the adoption of one of the most important of all constitutional amendments.

Mary Farmer and Donald Nieman subsequently take a careful look at the Fifteenth Amendment as it impacted both black and woman's rights and shaped partisan American politics for more than a century thereafter. The intention of the framers of the Fifteenth Amendment to extend suffrage rights to black males was, Farmer and Nieman point out, carefully and cautiously phrased out of concern to avoid alienating northern whites. The subsequent southern effort to disfranchise blacks was unanticipated, as was the widespread disfranchisement of poor whites. Both resulted from the resort to literacy tests and poll taxes to evade the legal requirements imposed by the Fifteenth Amendment. An additional unintended consequence of the Fifteenth Amendment was the wedge driven between advocates of black rights and the previously closely allied supporters of woman's rights. Finally, the Fifteenth Amendment, in ways that its drafters did not anticipate, empowered an expanded population of northern blacks nearly a century later and gave impetus to the post–World War II civil rights movement. Farmer and Nieman conclude that, in an ironic twist, through unintended consequences the fundamental intentions of the Fifteenth Amendment's framers were in fact ultimately achieved.

A wave of constitutional amendments during the Progressive era had unintended consequences of their own. Focusing on the most notorious of these reforms, Richard Hamm addresses the overestimated influence of the Eighteenth Amendment on drinking behavior. He directs notice as well to the underestimated, and underappreciated, effect of national prohibition on the federal government's involvement in local law enforcement and policing procedures. Finally, he draws attention to the Twenty-first Amendment's little-noticed and largely unintentional enduring power beyond its primary function of ending national prohibition.

Suzanne Marilley thereafter offers insight into how consciousness that amendments might have unintended consequences and a desire to avoid such outcomes in order to achieve the primary goal limited the scope of yet another important measure, the Nineteenth Amendment for woman suffrage. Marilley stresses the breadth of political consensus necessary to achieve amendments and thus the restrictions on reform possible through amendment. Her essay suggests that in fact the requirements of Article V tend to shape the language of amendments as reformers pursue the supermajorities needed for serious consideration of their proposal. The quest to obtain the broad support necessary for congressional adoption and state ratification, she argues, serves to reduce the likelihood of unanticipated consequences of constitutional amendments.

My brief afterword examines some unanticipated consequences of the Twentieth Amendment of the early 1930s, the post–World War II Twenty-second Amendment, and the Twenty-fifth Amendment adopted in the 1960s. Repercussions of these amendments were still coming to light at the end of the century. While drawing some general conclusions about two centuries of experience with constitutional amending in the United States, the afterword should suggest to the attentive reader that the overall topic deserves further attention.

In addition to illuminating its primary subject, each of the essays in this volume contributes to the general discussion of unintended consequences of constitutional amendment. Not all of the essayists view the issue in the same manner, but all treat it insightfully. Collectively, they substantially advance constitutional understanding. In an era when constitutional amendments are being proposed with unprecedented frequency, this exploration might suggest a new basis for assessing both the proposals and their advocates: has the possibility of unintended consequences been seriously and thoroughly considered and explained? If so, what potential might the proposed innovation have for producing results other than the obvious ones? If not, what does that oversight, acknowledged or otherwise, suggest about the judgment, not to mention the motives, of the sponsors?

The authors and editor trust that this volume will encourage such civic reflection. Better historical understanding of the United States Constitution and further study of its implications ought to result in wiser approaches to future policy choices concerning the fundamental terms of government. No more valuable outcome of this scholarly endeavor could be imagined, and none would be more gratifying to the eight of us who offer it for public consideration.

1 Arranging for Amendment: Unintended Outcomes of Constitutional Design

David E. Kyvig

In the first six months of the 105th Congress no fewer than five constitutional amendments came to a vote in one or the other of its chambers. The House of Representatives during the spring of 1997 addressed amendments to set term limits for members of Congress, require a two-thirds vote of Congress to raise taxes, and prohibit desecration of the American flag. The first two measures lost, while the third won two-thirds approval. The Senate meanwhile defeated measures to require an annually balanced federal budget and permit Congress to regulate campaign contributions and election spending. Members of Congress also seriously considered but did not bring to a vote in either chamber other amendments to elevate the standing of crime victims in criminal proceedings and assert a right to practice religion in schools and on government property.[1] While none of these individual propositions gained sufficient support to obtain two-thirds approval in both houses of Congress and thus be sent on to the states for ratification, the overall burst of activity raised questions about the consequences of decisions to alter the terms of the Constitution, designed to be a stable, relatively inflexible defining framework for government. Particularly relevant when such a flurry of public policy initiatives is under way is the issue of whether constitutional amendments may have unintended consequences, outcomes other than those anticipated, or at least acknowledged, by their architects and proponents.

Constitutional changes demand the highest degree of political consensus of any formal actions of the U.S. government. Article V of the United States Constitution requires that amendments be proposed by two thirds of Congress or a constitutional convention requested by two thirds of the states, then ratified by three fourths of the states through legislative or convention action. In contrast, most important U.S. policy decisions require only the concurrence of simple majorities in each house of Congress or two thirds in the face of presidential objection; in the special case of the ratification of treaties, two-thirds approval is required, but only of the Senate. The threshold for formal alteration of the Constitution is unrivaled. Arguments that amendment ratification was coerced from some southern states during Reconstruction cannot obscure the fact that their approval was nevertheless required nor that it was sometimes withheld. Likewise, arguments that constitutional understandings sometimes shift without amendment, as in the late 1930s, ignore the relative insecurity and impermanence of such changes, as the reaction against federal authority and New Deal activism during the 1980s and 1990s makes clear. Unless they comply with Article V's requirements, innovations in constitutional understanding have limited weight.[2]

While they require a far greater degree of political consensus than legislation to be implemented, constitutional decisions thereafter demand a much greater reversal of sentiment to be overturned. Removing an amendment from the Constitution requires the same supermajority approval as its initial adoption, thus a reversal of political sentiment of enormous magnitude. Only once, in the case of the acceptance and then repeal of prohibition, has such a reversal ever occurred. In sharp contrast, ordinary legislation can be reversed by simple majority vote. A small shift of opinion, in fact, can often turn a majority into a minority or vice versa. Awareness of this political reality has more often than not kept major national political parties and leaders close to the middle of the road.

Given the requirements of Article V, it is no wonder that only one amendment to the Constitution has ever been repealed. The national prohibition of alcoholic beverages established by the Eighteenth Amendment had consequences that were unquestionably unanticipated and proved highly unpopular, and yet its reversal remained problematic until nearly the last moment.

One of the prohibition amendment's Senate sponsors thought the possibility of it being overturned so unlikely that he scoffed, incorrectly as it turned out but with considerable justification, "There is as much chance of repealing the Eighteenth Amendment as there is for a hummingbird to fly to the planet Mars with the Washington Monument tied to its tail."[3]

The demands of the amending process certainly explain why there have been relatively few constitutional amendments in the nation's history, merely twenty-seven in 210 years. The same considerations, however, may help account for amendment's retention of considerable political appeal. The difficulty of undoing such measures once adopted has induced caution about their adoption in the first place but under some circumstances has, for the same reason, encouraged dedicated reformers to undertake the struggle to obtain them. On the other hand, cynics may well conclude that the very obstacles to success allow advocacy of a particular reform without the need to take responsibility for its implementation, that is, permit proponents to strike a politically useful symbolic posture without a risky measurable result. Whatever the case, the possibility exists of constitutional amendments being adopted and then turning out to have unintended consequences. Given the enormous obstacles to the correction of perceived mistakes, this eventuality deserves thoughtful consideration whenever U.S. constitutional changes are proposed.

By their very nature constitutions are acknowledgments that public policy decisions may have unanticipated and unintended consequences that need to be restrained. The great effort put into the creation of constitutions since the seventeenth century in Britain, North America, and elsewhere represents a wide recognition of that fact. In their establishment of parameters of government authority and responsibility, constitutions represent attempts to keep unintended outcomes of public policy decisions within acceptable bounds.[4]

Written constitutions originated in a desire for formal requirements to confine and channel public policy making, not a quest for all-encompassing strictures to define every aspect of the policy process. As long as they conducted themselves according to constitutional guidelines, policy makers enjoyed considerable latitude even if an outcome proved unexpected. If the unanticipated result proved disquieting, the constitutional system allowed for the possibility of corrective legislative or judicial action or even further constitutional restriction. This eighteenth-century system of constitutional amendment functioned for 150 years in the United States more or less as designed. In the 1930s, however, the traditional mechanism was abandoned for a less formal method of sanctioning constitutional redefinition. The result has been a governmental structure both more flexible in dealing with unanticipated shifts in public policy and less reliable as a statement of government obligations and limitations.[5]

Never has a more sustained effort to eliminate unintended consequences from public policy making taken place than occurred in the initial process of U.S. constitution making and amendment. The acknowledged purpose of a unitary written constitution was to prevent government from undertaking actions that its creators did not desire. Yet as any student of American constitutional history well knows, various features of the nation's system of government were not addressed in the Constitution; some were certainly not what the framers had in mind. In this regard, the rise of political parties to link forces in different states as well as in separate branches of the federal government has received the greatest attention. At the other end of the spectrum, anticipating the unexpected but itself often overlooked, stands Article V, the framers' device to remedy unintended and unacceptable consequences of constitutional policy making. This mechanism for constitutional correction confirms that the framers recognized that in public policy making unintended consequences are virtually unavoidable.

As they sat in Philadelphia during the summer of 1787, the drafters of the United States Constitution gave considerable thought to the question of whether and, if so, how such an instrument ought to be altered. The notion that a government's powers and responsibilities should be defined and limited by a specific law of greater weight than all others had emerged in England and North America during the previous century and a half. The importance of a written constitution was well accepted in the nascent United States by 1787. Only during the previous decade, however, had a corollary to the idea of written constitutionalism emerged, the notion that a specific procedure for constitutional reform should also be articulated as a part of the fundamental law. In Philadelphia the framers worked out a policy regarding constitutional amendment and articulated it in Article V of the Constitution.

Over the course of the next two centuries Article V operated along lines notably different from what the framers expected. Furthermore, the amendments adopted under the system often had consequences unexpected by their various designers. With two layers of possibly unintended results, each of which had extraordinary legal strength and durability, constitutional amendments provide striking examples of policy choices in which at least some of their consequences were unforeseen.

Constitutionalism, the authoritative articulation of the general principles, structures, and functions of government, is rooted in one of the oldest concerns of Western political culture: the felt need to define and limit the power of government so that it will carry out those tasks and only those tasks that the society wishes it to perform. Constitutions embody the agreements that communities have reached through one means or another as to the general form they want their governments to take, the manner in which they wish power to be apportioned therein, and the boundaries of governmental practice they find acceptable. English constitutionalism, first articulated at the great gathering of barons at Runnymede in 1215, was rooted in a desire to limit the arbitrary power of monarchs.

Far more elaborate and modern theories of constitutionalism emerged four centuries later during the English Civil War. The Levelers of the 1640s, one of the most radical factions on the English political landscape of the time and an influential element within the Puritan movement, opposed not only the absolutism of the Stuart monarchy but also what they saw as arbitrary tendencies on the part of Parliament. The Levelers insisted that sovereignty, the ultimate authority to define and direct government, rested with the people. They went on to argue that the best means for the sovereign power to establish the terms under which not only the monarch but also the Parliament would function was through a written constitution setting forth the terms of government for all to see. Such a clearly articulated and non-contested set of rules seemed to the Levelers far preferable to the prevailing imprecise and occasionally contradictory mix of natural law, custom, and statute.[6]

John Lilburne, the leader of the Levelers and a constant advocate of "the rights of the people," in 1647 offered the first written constitution for England. This Agreement of the People evolved through much discussion and several versions but rested upon bedrock Leveler principles. Most fundamental was the concept of sovereignty as belonging to the people, the entire community, rather than to the monarch, as proponents of natural law proclaimed, or Parliament, as the Levelers' Puritan rivals asserted. From the outset the question of how the will of the people was to be articulated represented a major stumbling block for the theory of popular sovereignty.

The Levelers contended that Parliament possessed only delegated authority. The actual human beings who composed the nation had the natural right to determine the fundamental laws even if they normally allowed Parliament to act for them. Rejecting the traditional English notion that Parliament represented the great "interests" such as land, corporations, and church, the Levelers offered the original conception that Parliament represented all Englishmen equally and directly. Such views drew the Levelers inexorably toward advocacy of universal manhood suffrage and equality of representation in Parliament. More immediately, however, these ideas led them to assert the power of the people themselves to establish a constitution that would define every individual's inalienable rights against his or her representatives.

The Levelers' Agreement of the People set forth a bill of fundamental individual rights that Parliament was not to violate. Accordingly, Parliament was not to interfere with the operation of law, exercise power over religion, impress men for the army or navy, destroy rights of personal liberty or property, repudiate debts, or modify any of these rights. Furthermore, the Levelers wanted to convene a special body representing the sovereign people to refine the Agreement, to act as a sort of constitutional convention to establish the foundation for government and fix the limits of Parliament's legislative prerogative. Thereafter the Agreement was to achieve regular sanction from the sovereign power by being endorsed and signed by voters and candidates at every election. Such a specific, familiar, and frequently reconfirmed document would effectively define and limit the powers of government. The Agreement of the People would serve evermore as a measure of the government's legitimacy.

The Levelers quickly faded from the scene after 1649. Once Charles I was dispatched, Puritan army leaders no longer regarded Leveler support as crucial. However, Leveler ideas of popular sovereignty, law as protection of individual rights against unrestrained government, and written constitutionalism did not fade with them. The Puritans soon put into effect the first written constitution, the 1653 Instrument of Government. Although not every Leveler idea made its way into the 1653 Instrument, and unitary written constitutionalism itself did not survive the Restoration in Britain, the open flow of political ideas across the Atlantic assured that the Levelers' constitutional notions would not be altogether forgotten.

In the British colonies of North America, the notion had been present from the outset that a written framework should explicitly define and limit government. The authority to found and rule a colony originated in every case in a grant from the throne, the terms of which were made quite specific. Enthusiasm for written frames of government spread throughout Britain's American colonies as turmoil in the mother country created political uncertainty. The English Civil War forced the colonists to be more self-reliant and enabled their representative assemblies to be more assertive in establishing instruments of government. The articulation of constitutions grew more common in the proprietary colonies established during the Restoration period, although these instruments were clearly concessions on the part of proprietors rather than compacts among people. James II's 1686 decree establishing the Dominion of New England provided a stark reminder to the colonies that their constitutional arrangements rested ultimately on arbitrary royal authority. Although the upheavals of 1688 in Britain soon undid James's changes, the Glorious Revolution nevertheless compelled all colonies to seek reconfirmation of their authority from Britain's new sovereign power. These events gave renewed and ringing notice to the colonies that, in the eyes of Britain, they did not possess sovereignty. Accordingly, their sense grew steadily that great importance rested in sovereign power, authority that could define the terms of government and that could not be overridden.

The 1776 Declaration of Independence rested squarely upon a general conception, articulated in various ways by local governments, colonial legislatures, and ultimately the Second Continental Congress, that governments should be defined, limited, and bound by written agreements entered into by the people who ultimately established and validated them.[7] The nation brought into being in 1776 was as yet, in its own eyes, unformed. The task still loomed ahead of turning abstract concepts of constitutionalism, especially fixed yet flexible written constitutionalism, into a workable system of government.

Throughout their first decade of separation from Britain, Americans engaged in a great continuous laboratory experiment in constitution making. Along with the evolution of fixed and specific written instruments to frame state and federal governments emerged a recognized need for suitable procedures for altering the terms of those constitutions to prevent their becoming ineffective or obsolete. A constitution to be effective could not afford to become oppressively restrictive or inadequately expressive of expectations for government. Constitutional thinking evolved rapidly to meet the demands of the moment. At the same time, a foundation was being created upon which later American constitutionalism would remain, for better or worse, firmly planted.[8]

By 1780 the notion had been fully developed and cast in concrete form that a constitution was the sovereign people's means to define their preferred system of government, authorizing or limiting that government's actions as they chose. The terms of the 1780 Massachusetts Constitution expressed this vision of constitutionalism by specifying the particular tasks of the legislative, executive, and judicial components of the state's government. As such the Massachusetts Constitution offered a marked contrast to the 1776 Pennsylvania Constitution, which placed primary authority with a unicameral legislature and relied upon a review of government operations every seven years by a council of censors to assure that the constitution was observed. The Massachusetts Constitution gave the executive and judicial branches standing equal to the legislature and restrained the representatives from doing whatever might please them or their constituents at the moment.

Using the constitution to confine government was certainly the intent of John Adams, its principal architect, but he was far from alone in wanting to prevent legislative construction of a constitution, require popular review of the convention-designed instrument, and insist upon more than a simple majority consensus for implementation or alteration of the fundamental law.

A dramatic break from British ideas of sovereignty and constitutionalism, the Massachusetts model nevertheless made perfect sense to Americans. As state after state wrestled with constitution making, methods emerged for turning popular sovereignty from a vague abstraction into a workable system for setting forth the terms of government. As a result, legislatures lost their status as absolute and therefore unrestrainable representatives of the people. Instead, there emerged a distinctively American conception of legislatures as finite powers operating within a defined framework.

The British understandably found it difficult to comprehend the American view of constitutionalism. Mid-eighteenth-century Britons, whose thinking had been shaped by William Blackstone, regarded a constitution as simply an assemblage of laws, customs, and institutions that collectively defined the proper form and functions of government. As the concept of parliamentary supremacy emerged in Great Britain from notions that sovereignty belonged to the people rather than the monarch and that Parliament legitimately represented the sovereign will, any thought of limiting Parliament's power to alter the terms of government faded away. Despite assertions from Sir Edward Coke that acts of Parliament against reason would be void, no court or other institution laid consistent claim to a right to exercise review of such reason. Therefore, no significant or effective check on the British Parliament, other than its own sense of propriety, served to restrain it.

Americans considered a constitution to be higher law than ordinary legislation.[9] As an expression of the sovereign will of the people, a constitution stood on a more elevated plane than an act of legislation. The higher constitutional law set the terms under which the government routinely functioned and which that government had no authority to alter. Thus, Americans came to believe that constitutions, if they were to serve their purpose of defining and limiting government, must be explicit, written instruments. Only concrete, articulated constitutions provided the necessary clear standard against which to measure other laws.

In British eyes any act of government that Parliament supported was, by definition, constitutional. From the American viewpoint, the Parliament as well as a government ministry was quite capable of overstepping its bounds and should properly be restrained by a constitution. The Declaration of Independence argued that the British monarch, by failing to stay within the terms of his contract with his colonial subjects, had thereby nullified it. Parliamentary complicity in the long list of constitutional violations was implied, if unstated, in the Declaration.

In the course of devising constitutions, the newly independent American states wrestled with myriad problems. One was fundamental to the very notion of written constitutions. Given a dedication to concepts of higher law embodied in specific instruments endorsed by supermajorities, what was a sovereign people to do if it felt the need to change the terms of its government? Only by providing for a means of its own amendment, the Lexington, Massachusetts, town meeting declared in 1778, could a constitution "give satisfaction to the people; and be a happy means, under providence, of preventing popular commissions, mobs, bloodshed and civil war." A constitution, if it was to survive, must make provisions "to rectify the errors that will creep in through lapse of time, or alteration of situation," concluded the town meeting of Essex, Massachusetts, the same year. John Dickinson of Pennsylvania called attention to the advice of Machiavelli that "a state to be long lived, must be frequently corrected, and reduced to its first principles."[10]

Unwilling to accept the notion that the terms of government were unchangeable except by revolution yet indisposed to treat the fundamental directives to and limitations upon government as ordinary law susceptible to reform by simple parliamentary majority, some states began working out arrangements by which their new constitutions could be changed. They sought amendment systems that would render revolution unnecessary yet avoid periods of unstable government. Although methods varied, most states sought to insure that amendment could be achieved only when a broad consensus, a supermajority of the sovereign people or their representatives, agreed to a change. Articulating a plan for amendment grew to be seen as an essential part of defining a constitution as a higher law while avoiding its becoming a rigid and unduly confining structure.

The Articles of Confederation that the Congress eventually managed to fabricate took far longer to formulate and adopt than most of the initial state constitutions. Creating an amendment mechanism was a significant part of this undertaking, although certainly not the central focus. The inevitability of amendment was evident to the congressional delegates who approved the Articles of Confederation. In stipulating state unanimity for amendment, they clearly assumed that the consensus finally achieved regarding the Articles themselves would prevail again when their amendment became necessary, as many thought would soon be the case. Most assuredly, they never intended the Articles of Confederation to be unamendable.

The requirement of unanimous state agreement to congressionally initiated proposals for amendment of the Articles of Confederation was, from the outset, the defining characteristic of the first U.S. government. The confederation proved unwieldy in practice from the very moment of its birth. Changes in its structure were constantly being suggested. However, the unanimity requirement gave every state an absolute veto power over any alterations. Unexpectedly, each state felt encouraged to insist upon acceptance of its position rather than seek a compromise of differences. Several widely supported proposals for modification of the Articles were ultimately frustrated. Sometimes the objection of a single state was all that blocked change in the Articles. Consequently, the confederation rapidly came to be seen as not only unsatisfactory in practice but also impossibly difficult to reform.

The framers who met in Philadelphia between May and September 1787 and crafted a second constitution for the United States did not, as the often-used collective label for them implies, engage in an altogether original act of creation. Instead, as they themselves acknowledged, they revised a plan of government "to form a *more perfect* union." It is reasonable to argue, in fact, that the 1787 Constitution was both the first and the greatest act of U.S. constitutional amendment.

The framers rejected the prescribed amendment procedure of the Articles of Confederation in favor of a less rigorous standard for implementing their proposed substitute. More than any other step the framers took, this procedural departure helped to obscure the amendatory character of the 1787 convention and fostered its image as an initial act of creation. Indeed, the ratification plan for the new constitution was arguably the most revolutionary act of the Philadelphia convention, overturning as it did the previously agreed upon method of sanctioning constitutional change. Nevertheless, the Philadelphia convention sought approval of its work from the existing Congress and state legislatures, a decidedly amendatory rather than extralegal procedure.

A dozen years of experience with state and national written constitutions that specified procedures for their own amendment led to a consensus at Philadelphia on the sanctioning of constitutional arrangements significantly different from what had prevailed when the Articles were drafted and ratified. The new amending process dealt boldly with the unintended consequences of the Articles. Both the ratification provision of the 1787 Constitution and the arrangements for further amendment contained in Article V represented significant adjustments of thinking about the process of obtaining sanction for constitutional change but by no means a complete abandonment of earlier ideas. The proposed new arrangements for constitutional alteration subsequently gained the approval of state conventions called upon to ratify the

Constitution. Ultimately, every one of the thirteen states accepted these provisions in the course of embracing the new Constitution. Thus, not only did state ratification meet the requirement of the 1787 Constitution for constitutional reform but it also conformed to the stricter standards of the Articles of Confederation.

The Article V delineation of an amendment process reflected the framers' quintessential thinking about constitutionalism: the necessity for written constitutions to define, direct, and delimit the powers and processes of government in a fashion that was responsive to the sovereign power of the people, stable enough to endure through a crisis, and yet flexible enough to adjust to new and unexpected circumstances. While the arrangements specified for putting the proposed constitution into effect represented a complex amalgam of principle and practical consideration, the prescribed method for further amendment was a purer statement of the framers' ideal of constitutional change.

The Article V amendment instrument embodied the framers' concept of federalism. Individual states retained an important voice but not controlling authority over broadly supported central government. The national legislature could propose change, but any reform would have to be approved by most states; and if the national legislature declined to act when a substantial number of states wished it to do so, the latter could compel the calling of a convention to circumvent the former. Change binding on all required the assent of a preponderant majority of the states, though not their unanimous consent.

The late-eighteenth-century inclination toward representative government was likewise evident in Article V. Elected representatives, whether assembled in legislatures or conventions, were regarded as best equipped to draft proposed constitutional reforms. The final sanctioning of changes in the name of the sovereign people could be carried out either by state legislatures, where representatives were left to make their own judgments, or conventions, where delegates chosen to reflect particular principles by voters of each state would prevail.

Whatever else they might have felt about the emerging plan of government, most Philadelphia delegates in 1787 subscribed to John Locke's notion that a constitution rested on the sanction of the people. The most direct expression of popular approval feasible was desirable. The initial proposal to submit the new constitution to state legislatures for ratification went down to defeat seven to three. Thereafter, a resolution that the measure be sent to conventions chosen by the people then gained nine-to-one approval, with only Delaware opposed. The measure did not suffer from its appearance as the most likely path to success in the upcoming contest over ratification. It is nevertheless notable that a convention willing to accept indirect selection of senators and an even more indirect process of presidential election stood steadfastly for popular endorsement of the basic frame of government.

In discussing ratification, several Philadelphia delegates insisted upon the possibility of putting the new constitution into effect without the unanimous consent of the states required by the Articles of Confederation. One or two states should not be able to block the entire enterprise, as the delegates were well aware had happened to delay the initial ratification of the Articles and stop altogether their proposed amendment in 1782. Rhode Island, which had on the latter occasion frustrated the action of the other twelve states, had not even sent delegates to Philadelphia and seemed likely to reject its results. North Carolina delegate Richard Dobbs Spaight was in agreement with many of his colleagues when he wrote privately that one or two states should not "prevent the Union from rising out of that contemptible situation to which it is at present reduced."[11]

By the time the convention, in the course of reviewing the proposed draft clause by clause, got around to discussing ratification on the last two days of August, it was clear that support for the emerging constitution was, while substantial, less than unanimous. James Wilson of Pennsylvania instantly proposed that ratification by seven states be deemed adequate to put the Constitution into effect, "that being a majority of the whole number & sufficient for the commencement of the plan." Gouverneur Morris suggested that if the ratifying states were contiguous a smaller number should be sufficient to introduce the new government than if they were dispersed. Roger Sherman, willing to accept less than unanimous agreement, thought, however, that at least ten states should concur. Edmund Randolph proposed nine as "a respectable majority of the whole" and a level of concurrence frequently used in the confederation. Wilson offered to compromise on eight.[12]

As the debate over state ratification went forward, James Madison worried that if seven, eight, or nine were the number agreed to, the Constitution could conceivably be put into operation "over the whole body of the people though less than a majority of them should ratify it." Wilson offered his understanding that only states that actually ratified it could be bound by the new constitution. He appealed for feasible ratification arrangements in light of the urgency of the current situation. "We must," he said, "in this case go to the original powers of Society. The House on fire must be extinguished, without a scrupulous regard to ordinary rights."[13]

The debate continued into the next day. Pierce Butler of South Carolina, revolted by the idea that one or two states might restrain the rest, declared himself in favor of a minimum of nine ratifications. Rufus King moved to make specific that the new constitution would only apply to those states ratifying it, and all but Maryland agreed. However, only James Wilson and George Clymer of Pennsylvania supported Madison's formula requiring ratification not only by a majority of states but also by states that together contained a majority of the people. When the convention finally got down to deciding how to fill in the blank on the number of states required for ratification, only Maryland voted for a unanimous thirteen. Connecticut, New Jersey, and Georgia then joined Maryland in supporting ten, while seven states opposed. All, except for Virginia and the Carolinas, which presumably preferred a lower number, accepted nine. By this process of groping toward compromise, the delegates agreed upon the ratification standard.[14]

The question of whether ratification should be considered in state legislatures or conventions was also at issue on Friday, 31 August. Gouverneur Morris moved to strike out the draft's requirement of conventions and leave the states to choose their own means of ratification. Rufus King equated giving up conventions to surrendering the possibility of gaining approval. "Conventions alone, which will avoid all the obstacles from the complicated formation of the Legislatures, will succeed," he predicted, "and if not positively required by the plan, its enemies will oppose that mode." Morris protested that he only meant to facilitate adoption of the Constitution. However, James Madison agreed with King, noting that the power being given the central government was being taken from the state governments; state legislatures were more likely than conventions to oppose this and, if so, "could devise modes apparently promoting, but really thwarting the ratification." In response to concerns that state constitutions already specified modes of ratification, Madison asserted that "the people were, in fact, the fountain of all power, and by resorting to them, all difficulties were got over. They could alter constitutions as they pleased." Morris's motion was put to a vote and defeated six to four.[15] Carl Van Doren properly called the adoption of these ratification arrangements "one of the most revolutionary decisions in the whole convention."[16]

Provision for amendment, assumed from the outset to be a necessary part of the new constitution but not settled until almost the end of the Philadelphia convention, evolved along with ideas about ratification procedure. Experience with unforeseen flaws in the Articles of Confederation reinforced the delegates' beliefs that the new constitution should provide for further amendment. This same background persuaded them of the desirability of establishing amending rules different from the Articles' rigid requirements that Congress initiate amendments and the states unanimously approve them. The members of the Philadelphia convention clearly wanted to create an amending system that, without rendering the Constitution unstable, would allow generally agreed upon change to take place. They certainly did not intend to re-create the combination of constitutional inadequacy and inflexibility that had produced the governmental crisis they were confronting.

The Virginia plan presented at the outset of the Philadelphia convention contained a resolution that "provision ought to be made for the amendment of the Articles of Union whensoever it shall seem necessary, and that the assent of the National Legislature ought not to be required thereto." When the subject of an amendment provision came up again on 11 June, a few delegates said they failed to see the necessity of it at all. Nor did they comprehend the propriety of making congressional consent to amendments unnecessary. George Mason quickly rose to the defense of the Virginia proposal:

> The plan now to be formed will certainly be defective, as the Confederation has been found on trial to be. Amendments therefore will be necessary, and it will be better to provide for them in an easy, regular, and Constitutional way than to trust to chance and violence. It would be improper to require the consent of the Natl. Legislature, because they may abuse their power, and refuse their consent on that very account. The opportunity for such an abuse may be the fault of the Constitution calling for amendmt.

Without further discussion, the convention responded by approving the Virginia resolution without dissent, although it postponed consideration of the congressional role in amendment.[17]

Little more was said about amending, not to mention the amendment process, until the waning days of the convention. The committee on detail, having been told to provide for amendment, drafted an extremely simple mechanism: "On the application of the Legislatures of two-thirds of the States in the Union for an amendment of this Constitution, the Legislature of the United States shall call a Convention for that purpose." When it came before the convention on 30 August, Gouverneur Morris suggested that the Congress should be free to call a constitutional convention whenever it chose, but no more was said as delegates adopted the committee proposal without dissent.[18] Procedures for initial ratification rather than subsequent amendment were still the focus of procedural discussions.

Not until 10 September did the convention specifically address the issue of amendment. On that day, Elbridge Gerry asked for reconsideration of the proposed amending article. He expressed concern that it would allow two thirds of the states to obtain a convention that in turn could bind the union to innovations that might subvert state constitutions altogether. Alexander Hamilton replied that he did not object to such a possibility, seeing no greater evil in making the people of the entire country subject to a majority than making the people of a particular state subject to one. He observed that many wished for an easier mode of amending the Articles of Confederation. An easy means of remedying defects in the new system was equally desirable. Under the proposed method, Hamilton believed, state legislatures would only seek alterations to increase their own powers. The national legislature would first perceive the need for amendments and thus ought also to be empowered, whenever two thirds of each branch concurred, to call a constitutional convention. Hamilton saw no danger in this if the people retained ratification power. After Madison added that he found the terms of the proposed article vague, the delegates voted nine to one for Gerry's motion to reconsider the amending provision.[19]

Roger Sherman, responding to Hamilton's complaints, sought to overturn the Virginia and committee on detail plans to exclude Congress from the amending process. He moved to add to the article "or the Legislature may propose amendments to the several States for their approbation, but no amendment shall be binding until consented to by the several States." James Wilson, conscious that this language would restore the Articles of Confederation requirement of unanimous state ratification of amendments, promptly moved to specify two-thirds state approval. The two-thirds ratification standard, in effect the same requirement of approval by nine states that had already been agreed upon for the implementation of the new constitution, was narrowly defeated by a vote of six states to five. Wilson immediately proposed to raise the threshold to three fourths, meaning that the endorsement of ten current states would be needed before the new constitution could be altered. The delegates accepted without dissent this higher standard for change than for initial approval.[20]

After several days of silence on the subject, George Mason on 15 September expressed general unhappiness with the amending plan. It was, he charged, "exceptionable & dangerous." Mason pointed out that both means of proposing amendments required the approval of Congress and expressed his fear that "no amendment of the proper kind would ever be obtained by the people, if the Government should become oppressive, as he verily believed would be the case." Should Congress become oppressive, he had written in the margin of his copy of the 12 September printed draft, "the whole people of America can't make, or even propose alterations to it; a doctrine utterly subversive of the fundamental principles of the rights and liberties of the people." Gouverneur Morris and Elbridge Gerry, sharing Mason's concern, proposed that the article be revised to require that a convention to consider amendments be held on the application of two thirds of the states, thereby circumventing the Congress. Madison thought Congress would feel as compelled to propose amendments as to call a convention at the request of two thirds of the states but did not object to providing for such a convention. Thereupon the delegates unanimously adopted the Morris-Gerry motion.[21]

The amending system worked out in the Philadelphia convention reflected the beliefs of most delegates regarding a reasonable process of constitutional revision. Like the rest of their creation, Article V evinced the essential compromise struck between the proponents of a strong central government and the advocates of retained state power. Although Congress was granted a powerful role in the process, constitutional ratification and amendment were not to be achieved solely by the central government nor merely with the concurrence of some majority of an undifferentiated national population. States, as distinct entities with separate populations and political institutions, occupied as significant and unavoidable a position in the process as did the national government; majorities in the legislatures or conventions of individual states would ultimately decide the fate of constitutional reform proposals. The possibility of the states in concert initiating constitutional change as well as checking congressionally originated reform emerged as notable characteristics of the amending system. Although the Constitution's preamble proclaimed that "We the People of the United States" were ordaining and establishing a constitution, it was the people acting through their individual states who would do this and later be empowered to revise the instrument. The federal compromise of the 1787 Constitution could be found in no more pure a form.

In the eyes of the Philadelphia delegates, it was not the general principle of concurrence between the central government and the states but rather the state unanimity requirement of the Articles of Confederation that had represented the chief defect of the preceding amendment method. Their proposed alternative of three-fourths concurrence seemed to them to prevent a tiny minority of states from obstructing widely desired reform while establishing an adequate requirement of consensus to avoid the constitutional instability inherent in simple majoritarianism. Their experience with the Articles of Confederation had shaped their belief that a government with the support of two thirds of the states could be successfully put into effect and that a constitutional reform with the endorsement of three fourths of those states would not unreasonably endanger any individual state. After the previous decade, two-thirds state approval for ratification and three-fourths for amendment seemed a moderate standard, neither an unduly lax nor an impossibly difficult one.

Article V as finally set forth represented a compromise between the contending republican faiths of the era, often characterized as Whig versus Federalist.[22] Both rested squarely on the belief that authority ultimately lay with the sovereign people and, therefore, that government must operate by consent of the governed. They agreed that the people, holding final authority over the terms of their government, were free to set those terms as they wished and establish new ones if they desired. Whigs and Federalists alike deemed it proper to ignore the existing set of rules for government and appeal to the sovereign people to establish a new framework. The Philadelphia convention did so in circumventing the Congress and state legislatures to rest ultimate approval of the new Constitution with its altered set of ratification standards in popularly elected state conventions. If the sovereign people approved, the Constitution would meet the highest standard of legitimacy.

Whigs and Federalists shared the Enlightenment's optimistic belief that it was possible to determine which course in human affairs was proper and virtuous, in other words, "the good." Whigs tended to be more sanguine than Federalists about the ease of perceiving the good, but both assumed that a high degree of community agreement could eventually be achieved in recognizing and supporting the good. Neither Whigs nor Federalists were opposed, therefore, to requiring a high level of consensus on fundamental matters. They did not conceive of supermajorities as thwarting democracy. Indeed, if only a slender majority could be formed, the good was not yet in focus. Once the good had been distinguished, on the other hand, an overwhelming majority would choose to support it. On something as important as defining a constitution, a supermajority of two thirds or three fourths was neither unreasonable, unattainable, nor undemocratic.

However, fundamental differences between the two political philosophies did exist. Whig political theory in the 1780s rested on a belief in the homogeneity of legitimate political communities. Its members shared a capacity and willingness to identify and support the best interests of the community, Whigs believed. Thus, they reasoned, it was desirable to provide direct popular involvement in government through frequent election of representatives. Legislatures, so chosen, should then possess great latitude in carrying out the popular will. Constitutions, devices that alone could define and limit legislatures, should be shaped and ratified by means that most closely reflected the public will, in other words, by popularly elected conventions. The decision to require ratification of the 1787 Constitution by state conventions marked a triumph of this viewpoint, though it was obviously based on political practicalities as well as philosophy.

The Federalist view, in contrast, assumed that people's interests varied and that government served as an arbiter among them. In the presence of competing heterogeneous factions, deliberative mechanisms removed from popular passions were preferable. This meant, among other things, entrusting constitution making to legislatures, bodies composed of representatives chosen for their general merit, rather than conventions with delegates selected to uphold a specific position.

The evolution of Article V involved a balancing of Whig and Federalist preferences. The initial Virginia plan was vague on the mechanism to be employed but specific on the point that the national legislature should not be involved. Midway through the Philadelphia deliberations, the committee on detail proposed that a national constitutional convention be called when two thirds of the state legislatures requested it. By September, however, the delegates were ready to give the Congress more power, first the right to call a convention on its own initiative, and then, at the last minute, to propose amendments itself. The compromise, allowing either the national legislature or a national convention to offer amendments, was then echoed in Madison's draft language providing for state ratification by either legislatures or conventions as the Congress chose.[23] This maintained the balance between the Whig preference for conventions and the Federalist inclination toward legislatures. It avoided undermining the already agreed upon initial ratification method as well. Madison did, however, tilt the balance in the favor of legislatures by placing in the hands of Congress the crucial decision as to which ratification alternative would be used in the states.

The Philadelphia delegates first thought to specify that all constitutional action be taken by conventions, but when a nonexclusive alternative legislative role was suggested, no real resistance arose to its use at either the national or state level. The amending system as finally drawn, with its legislative and supermajority elements, contained Federalist checks on democratic impulses. It likewise possessed Whig features with its mechanisms to outflank legislatures at both state and national levels through the device of conventions. The convention system was indeed employed to design the amendment procedure and give it the sanction of state ratification. Thereafter, however, it would scarcely be used. Battles over constitutional change would be fought within and between representative bodies, while the struggles among legislative bodies and populace anticipated by the framers did not materialize.

"The Americans of the Revolutionary generation believed that they had made a momentous contribution to the history of politics," Gordon Wood has observed. Specifically, "they had for the first time demonstrated to the world how a people could diagnose the ills of its society and work out a peaceable process of cure. They had, and what is more significant they knew they had, broken through the conception of political theory that had imprisoned men's minds for centuries and brilliantly reconstructed the framework for a new republican polity, a reconstruction that radically changed the future discussion of politics."[24] The concept of written constitutionalism lay at the heart of the republicanism that Wood and others have regarded as the eighteenth century's most notable political innovation. In turn, constitutionalism had at its core the dynamic device whose presence enhanced the chances of republican agreements on government achieving stability and lasting success: a mechanism for formal amendment. Wood did not cite, though he might have, a well-known contemporary assessment of the 1787 Constitution, George Washington's farewell address of 1796. Washington spoke for the founding generation as well as himself when he said that the Constitution

> till changed by an explicit and authentic act of the whole people, is sacredly obligatory upon all. . . . This Government, the offspring of our own choice, uninfluenced and unawed, adopted upon full investigation and mature deliberation, completely free in its principles, in the distribution of its power, uniting security with energy, and containing within itself a provision for its own amendment, has a just claim to your confidence and your support.[25]

Neither procedurally nor substantively did the Article V amendment process work out exactly as the framers seemed to have in mind. They had every reason to anticipate that the amending system they established would make altering the Constitution relatively easy. They expected, therefore, that the Constitution would be kept quite current with contemporary needs and preferences. Furthermore, they presumed that when change was instituted, conventions would often, if not always, be employed as amending devices at both the initiation and ratification stages. Except for the latter, these expectations were at first fulfilled. Gradually, however, as the late eighteenth century's preoccupation with the articulation of constitutional terms faded, the framers' intent that amendment be used as a device to keep the statement of U.S. government authority and responsibility specific and up-to-date was honored only intermittently.

Such was assuredly not the desire of those who crafted Article V in Philadelphia during the summer of 1787. It does, of course, reflect the way that the Constitution has functioned in the American governmental system as a set of general guidelines and principles rather than, as the framers at first appeared to intend, more regularly honed and decidedly more exact specifications for the operation of the state. The gap between intention and consequence resulted in no small part from the early experience of putting into operation a mechanism that had been laid out hastily and only in bare-bones form. A considerable amount of time and effort was devoted to constitutional amendment in the early republic, leading the framers and their successors as U.S. policy shapers to retreat from the position that Article V should again be called upon every time a matter not spelled out with absolute clarity in the Constitution needed resolution.

During the inaugural session of the Congress, Article V was first put to the test. Both its great value and the reasons it would not be used excessively became evident. James Madison offered a package of amendments to the Constitution that his colleagues in the House of Representatives, after lengthy discussion, approved and later the Senate, after consolidating the seventeen House provisions into twelve, endorsed. While formally initiated by Congress, the Madison amendments reflected proposals offered only a few months earlier by state conventions called to ratify the original Constitution. The First Congress, in which not only Madison but also a number of the other framers sat, accepted ratification by state legislatures as a speedy and convenient embodiment of the recently held state conventions. The manner in which the states quickly ratified ten of these amendments, those that came to be popularly known as the Bill of Rights, and gave a lukewarm reception to the other two occasioned little comment at the time. This was, after all, exactly the manner in which the two-stage amending process had been intended to operate to insure that only measures very widely agreed upon would become part of the fundamental instrument of government.[26]

However, the framers had clearly not anticipated questions regarding procedural details of constitutional reform that arose in the course of the First Congress's debates over amendments. In the House, the issue of where in the Constitution amendments should be placed came up for the first time and proved to be considerably less trivial than it might initially appear. Madison began the controversy by innocently proposing that amendments be inserted at appropriate locations throughout the text of the Constitution. Roger Sherman of Connecticut was instantly on his feet to object vigorously. "This is not the proper mode of amending the constitution," he asserted. "We ought not to interweave our propositions into the work itself, because it will be destructive of the whole fabric."[27] He quickly moved that, instead, amendments be appended to the original document.

Sherman raised a fundamental question about constitutional amendment that the framers had apparently not thought about and certainly not deliberated. Should a constitution be kept "uniform and entire," as Madison preferred, or should amendments remain "separate and distinct"? The latter, Madison believed, might cause "a very considerable embarrassment." With supplementary amendments, he contended, "it will be difficult to ascertain to what part of the instrument the amendments particularly refer; they will create unfavorable comparisons, whereas if they are placed upon the footing here proposed, they will stand upon as good foundation as the original work." [28] John Vining of Delaware concurred, likening supplementary amendments to "a careless written letter, [with] more matter attached to it in a postscript than was contained in the original composition." [29]

Other representatives disagreed. They insisted that, unless amendments stood separate from the original Constitution, the authority of the initial instrument and the intentions of its creators would be obscured. Michael Jenifer Stone of Maryland worried about making it appear that "George Washington, and the other worthy characters who composed the convention, signed an instrument which they never had in contemplation." Stone regarded the incorporation of amendments into the original text to be the equivalent of substituting a new Constitution for the old one.[30]

Elbridge Gerry scoffed at the amendment location debate as "trifling about matters of little consequence." Amendments, if adopted, would, wherever placed, be, in the words of the Constitution, "valid to all intents and purposes, as part of the constitution." As for the argument that incorporating amendments would virtually repeal the Constitution, the same could be said for supplementary amendments, Gerry pointed out. "Consequently the objection goes for nothing, or it goes against making any amendment whatever." [31]

The House found itself forced to resolve a previously unaired difference of opinion between two of the Constitution's drafters. At first the House deferred to the judgment of the much respected constitutional thinker Madison and defeated Sherman's motion. After six days of further thought, however, the House reversed itself and adopted the plan to have amendments follow rather than interweave the Constitution.[32] For once rejecting Madison's preference, representatives set a precedent for all amendments to come: they would follow the original text of the Constitution. The 1787 document would, in turn, be left untouched.

Although some arguments advanced for and against Sherman's motion may have been inconsequential, the decision was not the trifle that Elbridge Gerry considered it. Free-standing additions to the Constitution did not have to be reconciled with prevailing language to the extent required of incorporations into the existing text. Any question of the amending power being confined to modification of existing provisions was clearly answered in the negative: Article V could be used to address matters not treated in the 1787 document. Judging from discussion in the First Congress, the expectations of the framers about the amending process were confirmed, not altered.

As Madison wrote less than a week after the vote on amendment placement, "It is already apparent I think that some ambiguities will be produced by this change, as the question will often arise and sometimes be not easily solved, how far the original text is or is not necessarily superseded, by the supplemental act."[33] William Loughton Smith and others were equally well aware of the increased potential for conflict between sections of the Constitution. All realized that the decision to make amendments supplementary increased the need for an arbiter of disputes over constitutional interpretation. The role of the judiciary in American constitutionalism would assume greater prominence.

The outcome of the previously unanticipated dispute over placement of amendments helped shape the subsequent image of the United States Constitution. The determination of the First Congress to treat the 1787 text as inviolate helped foster the later impression that it was a work of perfection. Amendments might properly deal with matters not addressed at the Philadelphia convention, but the core of the system articulated by the founders was inviolate. The conservatism of American constitutional arrangements rests, in some part, upon this perception. Only rarely, most notably after the Civil War, have provisions of the Constitution's original text been tampered with, and then merely by the addition of a superseding amendment, not by substitution and erasure of original language. The increasing sanctification of the framers' definition of the U.S. government's structure, powers, and limits, the so-called doctrine of originalism, appears, in this light, less a result of the framers' conscious intent than a consequence of the decision of the First Congress as to where to locate amendments.

Likewise unforeseen by the framers was a controversy over a protracted life for amendments adopted by Congress but not promptly ratified by the necessary number of states. The delegates to the Philadelphia convention thought in terms of short periods of political empowerment in the democratic republic they were constructing. Representatives of the people were to be elected for only two-year terms, a president merely four years, and even the legislative officials most protected from popular whim, members of the Senate, a scant six. The framers certainly did not anticipate that after the First Congress's amendment proposals were reviewed by the states, the two unratified measures would remain alive. Had they contemplated the possibility of the situation that would develop, they most assuredly would have addressed it in some fashion. It seems likely, however, that their shared assumptions about the republican process blinded them to the need to anticipate what turned out to be a consequence of their oversight.

The second of the twelve amendments adopted by the First Congress, a prohibition on a Congress raising its own salary, was presumed dead after it failed to win full ratification with the ten amendments that became the Bill of Rights in December 1791. The amendment was ratified by six states between 1798 and 1791 and by Kentucky as a part of its entrance into the Union in 1792. The measure then lay largely forgotten until an Ohio legislature, outraged by the so-called salary grab of 1873, decided to ratify it. The validity of that ratification went untested as the amendment, still far short of the necessary proportion of state endorsements, again fell into obscurity. More than a century later, a fresh wave of hostility toward Congress inspired a host of ratifications by states that, like Kentucky and Ohio, had not even existed when the pay raise amendment was first proposed. In 1992 the ratification of the Twenty-seventh Amendment by three fourths of the current states was completed, 203 years after James Madison first set it before Congress. Surely the framers had not intended that the amending process be so attenuated that the country, not to mention its government, would be fundamentally changed between congressional and state action. In the climate of distrust of government prevailing in 1992, however, Congress was not inclined to raise the objections to ratification that a series of Supreme Court rulings had judged to be its right.[34]

The Supreme Court clarified the Article V process in the 1939 cases of *Coleman et al. v. Miller, Secretary of the Senate of the State of Kansas* and *Chandler, Governor of Kentucky v. Wise* along lines consistent with but expanded from an earlier 1921 decision, *Dillon v. Gloss*. The Court ruled that the efficacy of ratifications by state legislatures should be regarded as a political question pertaining to the political departments, with the ultimate authority resting with the Congress. On the question of whether the proposed amendment had lost vitality through the passage of time, Chief Justice Charles Evans Hughes noted that Congress had not set a time limit for its ratification. Referring to the *Dillon v. Gloss* holding that recently imposed time limits were reasonable, he said that it did not follow that the Court should set one when Congress had not done so. There were no constitutional or statutory criteria for judicial determination of time limits. These were political questions that Congress possessed the power to decide, regardless of whether it acted when an amendment was submitted or ratification by three fourths of the states had been completed, and its choices were not reviewable by the Court. Justice Hugo Black, in a concurring opinion signed as well by Felix Frankfurter, William O. Douglas, and Owen Roberts, went even further. "The Constitution grants Congress exclusive power to control submission of constitutional amendments," Black wrote. "Final determination by Congress that ratification by three-fourths of the States has taken place 'is conclusive upon the courts.'"[35]

The long-delayed adoption of the Twenty-seventh Amendment was definitely an unintended but substantively a fairly minor consequence of the failure of the framers to be more explicit about the amending process. The effect of this amendment is merely to delay a pay raise desired by Congress until after a subsequent election, never more than two years away. This is certainly the most inconsequential constitutional amendment ever adopted. Only a modest amount of advance planning is required to keep congressional pay raises marching steadily ahead despite the restrictions of the Twenty-seventh Amendment. However, the unpremeditated effect of this use of Article V could have much greater significance. The potential still exists for the implementation of the last of James Madison's 1789 amendment proposals. This would vastly overshadow the 1992 Twenty-seventh Amendment as an unintended consequence of the amending process.

The first of the dozen amendments adopted by the First Congress in 1789 was, like the second, not immediately ratified thereafter by the states. It remains alive, however, by the precedent of the Twenty-seventh Amendment and the failure of Congress in 1992 or after to take any action to terminate its viability. What is this eighteenth-century proposal for governmental reform? It reads:

> After the first enumeration required by the first article of the Constitution, there shall be one Representative for every thirty thousand, until the number shall amount to one hundred, after which the proportion shall be so regulated by Congress, that there shall be not less than one hundred Representatives, nor less than one Representative for every forty thousand persons, until the number of Representatives shall amount to two hundred, after which the proportion shall be so regulated by Congress, that there shall not be less than two hundred Representatives, nor more than one Representative for every fifty thousand persons.

This measure reflected the late eighteenth century's understanding of the maximum feasible ratio between the public and its representatives in a democratic republic. Designed to insure that members of the House would remain in touch with those they represented by limiting constituencies to what was considered a reasonable size, thirty to fifty thousand people, this proposal made sense in a nation of four million people in 1790. One doubts whether any member of the First Congress intended to create the House of fifty-two hundred representatives that the measure could be interpreted to require by the last decade of the twentieth century.

Despite the radical change in the shape of Congress that the Madison amendment would now entail, in 1997 voices were raised in support of completing its ratification. The amendment gained fresh support on the grounds that Congress had ceased to function well and needed radical reform to put representatives in closer touch with their constituents.[36] Perhaps a Congress of more than five thousand members would bring forth a wider range of ideas on governance; on the other hand, individual voices might be drowned out in the roar of the crowd. Perhaps the larger Congress would be more unruly and less responsible; to the contrary, it might be required to accept greater regimentation and discipline in order to function at all. No doubt residentially clustered populations that presently find themselves minorities within much larger congressional districts would be able to elect representatives to Congress without the extreme gerrymandering of districts that in the 1990s the Supreme Court at first approved but later disallowed. Smaller congressional districts would presumably eliminate the feelings of unfair denial of congressional representation that sizable populations were left with after each Court ruling, but whether representation would translate into influence is much less clear. About the only certain result of the adoption of the final 1789 amendment would be the need to revise the architecture of the U.S. Capitol. Just as the amendment would have consequences unintended by the First Congress if adopted now, it would very likely have outcomes unanticipated by those who suggest that it finally be embraced.

The substantive unintended consequences of the ten amendments ratified in 1791, the Bill of Rights, could be explored at length. The stack of books and essays discussing the intentions and consequences of the First Amendment alone threatens to block out the sun, and heated debate over the Second Amendment is not lacking. In this volume's next essay, David Bodenhamer offers a thoughtful discussion of unanticipated developments involving the criminal procedure amendments. In terms of amendment procedure itself, however, the unintended consequences of the Bill of Rights were comparatively few and certainly comparatively obscure. They have been, nevertheless, extremely important.

Besides the matter of amendment placement, the most consequential procedural precedent established with the Bill of Rights amendments was the employment of state legislative ratification.[37] The framers clearly intended that the highest authority, the sovereign people, be able to directly express its views on adoption of new constitutional arrangements. Action by delegates chosen by the electorate to express their views on the proposed constitution in conventions assembled for this purpose alone was stipulated as the sole means of ratification of the original instrument. Ratification conventions were designated as one of two equally acceptable means for states to endorse subsequent constitutional changes. Madison did not explain publicly why he altered preliminary draft language on the amending process that mandated ratification by state legislatures, nor was such an explanation necessary. In polishing the draft, Madison added a provision specifying that conventions could be employed for ratification. His fellow delegates did not need to be told that Madison was making provision for an alternative amending mechanism to work along lines they had already embraced for initial state ratification of the Constitution.

The framers made it quite clear that they definitely intended to provide a means for the electorate to pass final judgment on constitutional amendment rather than leave such a decision entirely in the hands of state legislators. Elbridge Gerry, who did not share the general enthusiasm for popular sovereignty in constitutional matters, attempted to regain for state legislatures the exclusive right to ratify amendments. He proposed elimination of Madison's provision giving Congress the authority to choose between state legislative or convention ratification. Gerry's motion was supported only by Connecticut, however, and not even his fellow Massachusetts delegates. Ten state delegations opposed the motion, a resounding indication of the framers' preferences. By the final days of the Philadelphia convention when this vote was taken, few doubts remained among the delegates that conventions provided an attractive alternative to legislatures when constitutional issues were to be decided.[38]

Nevertheless, when James Madison initially proposed the Bill of Rights to the First Congress, he stipulated legislative ratification. He did so in the context of repeated requests for a bill of rights by recent state conventions held to ratify the Constitution. Allowing state legislatures to ratify the Bill of Rights appears to have been viewed by Madison and his colleagues as not worthy of debate. Their enthusiasm for conventions was on record, and legislative ratification of the proposed amendments was nothing more than an expedient means of completing a procedure on which conventions in practically every state had shortly before expressed themselves. There is no indication that the First Congress acted from any conscious, long-term desire to distance amending from the electorate.[39]

The same process used for ratifying the Bill of Rights was soon thereafter employed in the adoption of the Eleventh and Twelfth Amendments. Once again, short-term correction of constitutional flaws rather than long-term precedent seems to have been the prime consideration. In neither case was much attention devoted to procedure, certainly not what the framers had intended when giving Congress a choice of ratification alternatives. The perceived need in both cases for speedy correction of constitutional flaw led to what was apparently a completely unreflective decision to use the now familiar and evidently quick approach of state legislative ratification.[40] Thereafter, the legislative method of amendment ratification became firmly entrenched as the normal means of state participation in the Article V process. The framers' intentions to the contrary were, in effect, obliterated by neglect rather than by deliberate choice. Direct public involvement in setting the terms of the Constitution virtually vanished.

Thomas Jefferson wrote to James Madison late in 1789 that he believed each generation (which he reckoned as having a life span of nineteen or twenty years) should thoroughly reexamine the constitutional arrangements it inherited by holding a convention that would return to first principles and decide fundamental matters for itself. Seeking to balance the right of each generation to set its own standards for government and its responsibility to pass on undiminished that which it held in trust for later generations, he declared that "the earth belongs in usufruct to the living."[41] Madison, in a rare disagreement with his close friend, replied politely but firmly that destructive upheaval would be the likely result of such frequent constitutional reconsideration. He was no doubt reflecting on the stress and tumult generated by the 1887 constitutional convention, the 1788 Virginia ratifying convention, and the just-completed first use of Article V by the First Congress, all events in which he played a central role. Jefferson, by contrast, missed all three while serving as ambassador to France. Rather than compel full and formal constitutional reconsideration so frequently, Madison argued that "a tacit assent may be given to established Constitutions and laws, and that this assent may be inferred, when no positive dissent appears."[42] Madison's more conservative and, one suspects, more weary view prevailed. Constitutional reform would become occasional, as-needed repair rather than the once-a-generation thorough renovation Jefferson advocated.[43]

The less frequent use of Article V than Jefferson envisioned and the framers may have at first expected no doubt suited the vast majority of Americans who could remember the constitutionally unsettled early years of the republic. They were understandably disinclined to undergo again, much less regularly schedule, the political crises that defined the 1780s. Further reflection by framers such as Madison on the extent to which amendment was needed no doubt had some influence on evolving constitutional practice. So, too, did the acceptance by even Jefferson that amendment was not inevitably required in cases where government authority was not altogether clear, such as when there arose an opportunity to purchase the Louisiana Territory. Most important, Americans subsequent to the founding generation appeared less concerned about and even less aware of the framers' understanding of the Constitution as a specific, organically evolving statement of the society's desires in governance.

Sectional conflict defined constitutional amending for the following century, with the requirements of supermajority consensus impeding it for sixty years, then determining the approach used to secure amendments in the late 1860s. The framers had hardly anticipated the Civil War or the circumstances in which a triumphant majority of states would insist upon acceptance of amendment by defeated and militarily occupied states as the price of their restoration to a normal place in the federal union. The reconstructed southern state legislatures decided for themselves whether to ratify the Thirteenth, Fourteenth, and Fifteenth Amendments, and indeed several declined to do so for a time, but ultimately they felt they had little choice but to accept the verdict of the battlefield and ratify. Thus the requirement of supermajority agreement for amendment was formally observed, although the framers' intention of achieving broad consensus on constitutional matters was certainly strained. The lack of amendment during the next forty years stemmed in part from a prevailing sense that it was no longer possible in an enlarged and increasingly diverse nation to achieve the degree of consensus mandated by the framers.

A wave of four progressive amendments during the 1910s demonstrated that pessimistic assessments of Article V were mistaken. The framers' insistence on supermajority consensus could be met, even in a much enlarged republic and on highly charged issues. The establishment of a federal income tax, direct election of U.S. senators, national prohibition of alcoholic beverages, and woman suffrage all gained more than the necessary level of both federal and state approval. In other respects, however, the framers' intentions would be disappointed.

The Progressive era amendments demonstrated that the desire of Congress to keep the drafting of amendments in its own hands was stronger than the framers had anticipated. After it had for years resisted efforts of the House of Representatives to provide for direct popular election of senators rather than their selection by state legislators, the Senate quickly agreed to such an amendment in 1911 when it became clear that otherwise enough states would soon petition for a constitutional convention to compel one to be held. The Seventeenth Amendment proved easier for senators to swallow than the prospect of a constitutional convention that might seize the opportunity to initiate other fundamental reforms. Then and later, Congress displayed a notable lack of enthusiasm for constitutional conventions, which it perceived as unpredictable and uncontrollable, despite the framers' intention that conventions be available as an alternative avenue to constitutional amendment. Of course, if the framers could have seen how the mere threat of a convention could prod Congress into submitting for ratification an amendment with widespread support, they might well have concluded that the unanticipated result of providing amendment options had not in any fundamental sense violated their intent to allow amendment proposals to be put to the mandated test of ultimate acceptability, state ratification, whenever a sufficiently substantial supermajority requested.

The Eighteenth Amendment in particular badly upset the framers' expectation that the level of supermajority consensus they established for amendment passage by Congress and ratification by states was high enough to ensure that any amendment adopted would enjoy general acceptance. Even though beverage alcohol prohibition gained the approval of forty-five state legislatures, it did so through a then-unprecedented volume of special interest agitation. The efforts of the Prohibition party, the Woman's Christian Temperance Union, the Anti-Saloon League of America, and their allies helped produce the desired constitutional victory but did not create an all-encompassing social consensus of support for the liquor ban.[44] National prohibition, therefore, failed to achieve the anticipated public compliance. Widespread prohibition violation raised questions as to how the amending process could have failed. The fact tended to be overlooked that the prohibition amendment established a particular policy rather than merely an authority to act in an area of policy making and thus in a sense constitutionally restricted rather than enlarged the federal government's range of authority. On the other hand, much attention focused at the time on prohibition's use of legislative ratification, the procedure employed with the first seventeen amendments, as opposed to the mechanism regarded as closer to a direct expression of popular will: a convention of delegates chosen to address the specific issue.

When an Ohio referendum overturning the state legislature's ratification of the Eighteenth Amendment was declared unconstitutional by the U.S. Supreme Court in 1920, the impression grew that prohibition had been established contrary to public preference rather than as its reflection. As the drive for a repeal amendment accelerated, staunch antiprohibitionists insisted that any such measure be submitted to convention ratification. The so-called wets persuaded Congress to respect their demand, and between April and December 1933 conventions in thirty-seven states ratified an amendment providing for prohibition repeal.[45] It is noteworthy that the convention process of amendment ratification has not been used again or even given much consideration. The almost unbroken preference of federal legislators for the familiar and predictable process of state legislative ratification may seem unexceptional from a late-twentieth-century perspective. It would, however, most assuredly not have been expected by the eighteenth-century framers.

Although the various deviations from intended amendment procedures have been significant and the unanticipated outcomes of individual amendments likewise, as other essays in this volume will confirm, without question a most notable unintended consequence of the Constitution's amending provision has been the avoidance altogether of constitutional amendment when change was being sought in the fundamental terms of government. Here the mid-1930s confrontation between Franklin Roosevelt and a Supreme Court majority unfriendly to the New Deal proved the great turning point. The framers clearly expected formal sanctioning of basic redefinitions of federal obligation and power. Whether or not they would have agreed with the decisions of the Court before 1937 is irrelevant. They would have found unsatisfactory FDR's decision to eschew amendment when the country faced a fundamental choice regarding alteration of the limits of federal authority.

The framers would neither have anticipated nor approved Roosevelt's political calculation that he could successfully substitute for amendment an effort to influence the Supreme Court into reversing its recent rulings on commerce and general welfare clause cases. They most assuredly would have found appalling Roosevelt's judgment that he should circumvent amendment precisely because he could not obtain the supermajority needed for a constitutional mandate—an excessively pessimistic estimate in light of the extraordinary dimensions of his triumph in the just-completed 1936 election.[46] Even FDR's champions in this instance argue that the 1936 election returns were the functional equivalent of constitutional supermajority support for confirming federal government responsibility for national economic and social well-being, a mandate confirmed when Roosevelt was reelected in 1940.[47] Pivotal justices on the Supreme Court clearly reached that conclusion, and one suspects that Congress and state officials would have done likewise.

The framers would, however, have expected the long-term outcome of the so-called Court-packing episode. They had found no substitute for formal constitutional language as a means of setting durable expectations and limitations upon government. They provided Article V because of their belief that it was the right of those who would follow them, if they found the Constitution's terms inadequate, to articulate new constitutional language. The framers would not have been surprised to learn that the New Deal conception of the federal government as ultimately responsible for the social and economic well-being of its citizens, though it prevailed for thirty years, eventually faded. New Deal principles, whatever their merits, lacked the stability of formal constitutional sanction that would have helped them endure. Because of that weakness, those once seemingly secure understandings of federal responsibility and authority have steadily eroded since the beginning of the Nixon administration. Absent a formal declaration of federal obligation and power, both ebbed in an era of widespread criticism of the federal government. A series of leaders brought different governmental visions to the fore, often for transitory political advantage and always supported by far less than Article V supermajorities. They prevailed, at least momentarily. The success of all the presidents elected during the final third of the twentieth century in reducing the scope of the federal government was facilitated by the fact that they did not find themselves thwarted by contrary constitutional requirements.

It should hardly be surprising that Richard Nixon, Ronald Reagan, George Bush, and their congressional supporters achieved, in the absence of constitutional restraint, so much success in their determined efforts to undo the New Deal. Even the alleged heirs to the Roosevelt mantle, Jimmy Carter and Bill Clinton, lacked the support in difficult times of a constitutional obligation to uphold the New Deal view of federal social responsibility. Clinton, the one-time constitutional law professor, might have been particularly well served by constitutional guidance to resist signing the retrograde 1996 Welfare Reform Act. In light of executive and legislative developments from the 1970s to the 1990s as well as a growing number of Supreme Court decisions returning to a pre-1937 reading of federal authority under the Constitution, it is becoming harder and harder to accept the argument prevailing for the first few decades after the New Deal and still being advanced that informal constitutional transformations such as occurred in the 1930s serve as the functional equivalent of constitutional amendments. The so-called third American constitutional revolution of the 1930s was built on far less secure foundations than the first in 1787 or the second after the Civil War, both of which were set in formal language and ratified by a procedure widely accepted as representing the endorsement of sovereign authority.

Whenever it was employed, the amendment mechanism served the framers' underlying intention: the terms of the Constitution should be adjusted to suit the contemporary preferences of a supermajority consensus of the American nation. Achieving supermajority consensus is difficult, but the founders believed—and experience has generally demonstrated—that it is an effective means of balancing the individualism so highly valued in the American polity and the assumptions of authority and responsibility needed to maintain community. The framers certainly did not intend that when faced with a compelling desire to alter the terms of the federal government, responsible officials would turn toward intimidation of the Court rather than constitutional amendment. The apparent success of the 1937 Court-packing battle reduced the felt need to win adoption of an amendment, an admittedly formidable task, in order to shift the terms of government. The ultimate consequence has been a government less sure of its obligations and authority and a people less certain of what it can count on from government. At the end of the twentieth century, the founders' expectations for the amending process of Article V deserve renewed consideration, as do the results of modern departures from those intentions.

NOTES

1. *New York Times,* 13 February 1997, 5 March 1997, 19 March 1997, 16 April 1997, 9 May 1997, 13 June 1997.

2. A contrary view has been presented by Bruce Ackerman in *We the People: Foundations* (Cambridge, Mass.: Harvard University Press, 1991) and *We the People: Transformations* (Cambridge, Mass.: Harvard University Press, 1998). Ackerman finds far less to distinguish informal shifts in constitutional culture from formal amendments than I do.

3. Senator Morris Sheppard, quoted in Charles Merz, *The Dry Decade* (Garden City, N.Y.: Doubleday, Doran, 1931), 297. The complex and unlikely story of prohibition repeal is examined in detail in my *Repealing National Prohibition* (Chicago: University of Chicago Press, 1979).

4. Unless otherwise noted, information on the evolution of constitutional theory and practice in this essay is drawn from my *Explicit and Authentic Acts: Amending the U.S. Constitution, 1776–1995* (Lawrence: University Press of Kansas, 1996).

5. Two of the most interesting discussions of the constitutional revolution of 1937, both more positive assessments than my own, are Ackerman's *We the People* volumes, mentioned above, and William E. Leuchtenburg, *The Supreme Court Reborn: The Constitutional Revolution in the Age of Roosevelt* (New York: Oxford University Press, 1995).

6. An insightful discussion of the Levelers and the impact of their ideas on the evolution of popular sovereignty can be found in Edmund S. Morgan, *Inventing the*

People: The Rise of Popular Sovereignty in England and America (New York: W. W. Norton, 1988).

7. A recent exploration of the Declaration of Independence's broad underpinnings, often misattributed to Thomas Jefferson's singular genius, is Pauline Maier, American Scripture: Making the Declaration of Independence (New York: Knopf, 1997).

8. Early state constitutions are extensively and thoughtfully explored in Marc W. Kruman, Between Authority and Liberty: State Constitution Making in Revolutionary America (Chapel Hill: University of North Carolina Press, 1997).

9. The classic exploration of this idea is Edward S. Corwin, The "Higher Law" Background of American Constitutional Law (Ithaca, N.Y.: Cornell University Press, 1955).

10. Quoted in Willi Paul Adams, The First American Constitutions: Republican Ideology and the Making of the State Constitutions in the Revolutionary Era, trans. Rita and Robert Kimber (Chapel Hill: University of North Carolina Press, 1980), 141–43.

11. Spaight to James Iredell, 12 August 1787, in Max Farrand, ed., The Records of the Federal Convention of 1787, 4 vols. (New Haven, Conn.: Yale University Press, 1937), 3: 68.

12. Ibid., 2: 468–69.

13. Ibid., 2: 469.

14. Ibid., 2: 469, 475–77.

15. Ibid., 2: 475–77.

16. Van Doren, The Great Rehearsal (New York: Viking, 1948), 159.

17. Farrand, ed., The Records of the Federal Convention, 1: 22, 202–3.

18. Ibid., 2: 468.

19. Ibid., 2: 557–58.

20. Ibid., 2: 558–59.

21. Ibid., 2: 629–30.

22. Illuminating discussions of these contending systems of political thought can be found in Gordon S. Wood, The Creation of the American Republic, 1776–1787 (Chapel Hill: University of North Carolina Press, 1969), and Donald S. Lutz, Popular Consent and Popular Control: Whig Political Theory in the Early State Constitutions (Baton Rouge: Louisiana State University Press, 1980).

23. Farrand, ed., The Records of the Federal Convention, 2: 559.

24. Wood, Creation of the American Republic, 614.

25. George Washington, Farewell Address, 17 September 1796, in James D. Richardson, ed., A Compilation of the Messages and Papers of the President, 1789–1897, 20 vols. (New York: Bureau of National Literature, 1897), 1: 200, 212.

26. Robert Rutland, The Birth of the Bill of Rights, 1776–1791, rev. ed. (Boston: Northeastern University Press, 1983) remains a valuable study of the topic.

27. Congressional Register, 13 August 1789, in Helen E. Veit, Kenneth R. Bowling, and Charlene Bangs Bickford, eds., Creating the Bill of Rights: The Documentary Record from the First Federal Congress (Baltimore: Johns Hopkins University Press, 1991), 117.

28. Ibid., 118.

29. Ibid., 120.

30. Ibid., 120–21.

31. Ibid., 121–22.

32. *Congressional Register,* 19 August 1789, in ibid., 197–98.

33. James Madison to Alexander White, 24 August 1789, in Robert A. Rutland et al., eds., *The Papers of James Madison* (Chicago: University of Chicago Press, 1962–), 12: 352.

34. See my *Explicit and Authentic Acts,* chap. 19.

35. Ibid., 310–12.

36. Jeff Jacoby, "Fed Up with Congress? Fine, Let's Make It Bigger," *Akron Beacon Journal,* 20 February 1997, All, reprinted from the *Boston Globe.*

37. In Robert Rutland's classic work *The Birth of the Bill of Rights,* the matter of choice in ratification procedure is not even mentioned. See esp. 215.

38. Farrand, ed., *Records of the Federal Convention,* 2: 630.

39. Veit, Bowling, and Bickford, eds., *Creating the Bill of Rights.*

40. Useful studies of these amendments are John V. Orth, *The Judicial Power of the United States: The Eleventh Amendment in American History* (New York: Oxford University Press, 1987), and Tadahisa Kuroda, *The Origins of the Twelfth Amendment: The Electoral College in the Early Republic, 1787–1804* (Westport, Conn.: Greenwood, 1994).

41. Thomas Jefferson to James Madison, in Julian P. Boyd et al., eds., *The Papers of Thomas Jefferson,* 24 vols. to date (Princeton, N.J.: Princeton University Press, 1950–), 15: 392–97.

42. James Madison to Thomas Jefferson, 4 February 1790, in Rutland et al., eds., *Papers of James Madison,* 13: 18–21.

43. Two insightful examinations of Jefferson's ideas on this subject are David N. Mayer, *The Constitutional Thought of Thomas Jefferson* (Charlottesville: University Press of Virginia, 1994), chap. 12, and Herbert Sloan, "The Earth Belongs in Usufruct to the Living," in Peter Onuf, ed., *Jeffersonian Legacies* (Charlottesville: University Press of Virginia, 1993).

44. Richard F. Hamm, *Shaping the Eighteenth Amendment: Temperance Reform, Legal Culture, and the Polity, 1880–1920* (Chapel Hill: University of North Carolina Press, 1995) is an insightful exploration of the topic.

45. See my *Repealing National Prohibition,* as well as Clement E. Vose, "Repeal as a Political Achievement," in David E. Kyvig, ed., *Law, Alcohol, and Order: Perspectives on National Prohibition* (Westport, Conn.: Greenwood, 1985), 97–121.

46. Franklin Roosevelt's reasons for this controversial decision are explored in David E. Kyvig, "The Road Not Taken: FDR, the Supreme Court, and Constitutional Amendment," *Political Science Quarterly* 104 (1989): 463–81.

47. See particularly Ackerman, *We The People: Transformations,* pt. 3.

2 Lost Vision: The Bill of Rights and Criminal Procedure in American History

David J. Bodenhamer

In our mythic past, the framers captured the essential rights of Americans in the first ten amendments to the Constitution. We treat the Bill of Rights as a national icon, claiming its protections proudly and believing that its meaning is both self-evident and settled. These rights, we imagine, have grown organically with the nation, assisted by judges who can legitimately imply new protections only by reference to the original text.

The truth, of course, is far messier. Throughout American history, rights have been invented and repudiated, fought over and striven for, expanded and violated. The contest over rights has been a constant theme in our past. Scarcely was the ink dry on the Bill of Rights when debates began about what its words meant. Rarely have these struggles produced a neat consensus; more often, intemperate rhetoric and bitter division have been their hallmark. An angry clamor over rights, one scholar noted, "is one of the basic noises of our history."[1]

Still, it would be misleading to feature conflict too prominently in the story of American rights. One need not adopt a progressive view of history to see how consistently rights have expanded over time in number, scope, and practice. Freedom of speech, for example, is more extensive today than at any time in the nation's past. The rights of assembly and press are so well fixed in the public imagination that they are scarcely objects of notice. Challenges to religious belief and practice exist within a narrow compass compared to previous decades.

Until recently, rights of the accused could be viewed in the same frame as First Amendment guarantees. For much of their two-hundred-year history they received a liberal reading from the U.S. Supreme Court, although until the 1960s they applied primarily to federal, not state, actions. When the Warren Court bound the states to their provisions in the due process revolution, few people protested—at least until the justices extended the rights to pretrial police procedures. Even then, the guarantees quickly became part of popular culture. Police dramas on television gave them public notice, ultimately making them appear traditional. These protections also fit common notions of fairness, especially at a time when civil rights and antiwar protests heightened general sensitivity to unfairness.

This concern for fair procedure was not new to American history. It had been present since before the framers outlined the terms of fairness in the Bill of Rights. Frequently violated in practice and often under sharp dispute, the due process guarantees of the Fourth, Fifth, Sixth, and Eighth Amendments nonetheless remained central to most conceptions of American liberty.[2] Revealed through them was a core belief that freedom could not exist without restraints on the power of government. The guarantee of rights for the accused served to balance the scales of justice between the individual and the state. It made a fair trial possible, and it was this goal, not the suppression of crime, that was central to criminal justice in a democratic society.

This fundamental value came under sharp and sustained attack beginning in the late 1960s, when presidential candidate Richard Nixon charged that the Warren Court's decisions "let guilty men walk free from hundreds of courtrooms." His first appointment to the Supreme Court, Chief Justice Warren Burger, shared the new president's views. While still an appellate judge, Burger wrote that the Court's actions made guilt or innocence "irrelevant in the criminal trial as we founder in a morass of artificial rules poorly conceived and impossible of application."[3] Election after election saw politicians trot out variations of this theme, often with great success. The criticism remained politically potent during the Reagan-Bush years because it appeared to explain urban disorder and the dramatic increase of violent crimes.

Yet throughout the 1970s and 1980s the Warren Court reforms remained essentially intact. Even with a more conservative cast the Burger Court trimmed some newfound rights, but it did not repudiate the due process revolution. Even the Rehnquist Court followed suit initially, despite the new chief justice's view that the Warren Court had erred by deciding cases without constitutional justification.

In the 1990s the Court suddenly switched direction. Bolstered by the appointment of a conservative majority, the justices signaled a reversal on defendants' rights. They abandoned several precedents, some established only a few years earlier. More significant was a different tone to the Court's opinion, a determination to ensure that rights of the accused did not prevent a successful prosecution of guilty suspects.

This shift bore a striking, though perhaps circumstantial, resemblance to a series of reports on criminal procedure released in 1987 and 1988 by the Justice Department's Office of Legal Policy. Under the title "Truth in Criminal Justice," the reports challenged "a judicially created system of restrictions of law enforcement that has emerged since the 1960s" and sought a return to the "ideal of criminal investigation and adjudication as a search for truth." According to this view, the Warren Court had abandoned the discovery of truth, the traditional goal of criminal justice and the object of the criminal trial, in a misguided and harmful expansion of defendants' rights. The rights enabled criminals to escape punishment—and worse, to continue a life of crime—not through a trial determination of guilt or innocence but rather on some technicality that bore little relationship to what actually happened. Convicting the guilty was the primary mission of the criminal justice system, the report claimed, so "if truth cannot be discovered and acted upon, the system can only fail in its basic mission." As Attorney General Edwin Meese argued in his preface to the reports, above all else "criminal justice must be devoted to discovering the truth."[4]

After two decades of conservative electoral success, political power and constitutional law had converged. The politics of the shift are clear, but what about the interpretation of the past on which it rests? The Warren Court's decisions on criminal procedure were not as revolutionary, far-reaching, or even consequential as critics have maintained. Arguably, they were well within the framework of rights established by the framers. The new emphasis on convicting the guilty, however, departs significantly from this legal tradition, and a belief that a criminal trial is a search for truth is at odds with American constitutional experience.[5] The counterrevolution may be not only more radical than the revolution itself but also starkly at odds with the vision of the framers who gave formal expression to the American conception of rights of the accused.

It is always useful to read the Bill of Rights afresh. What often surprises even knowledgeable students is how much it focuses on rights of the accused. Numerous guarantees of fair criminal process appear in the Fourth, Fifth, Sixth, and Eighth Amendments. This result was no accident. Their framers viewed such safeguards as central both to individual freedom and the new nation's great experiment in liberty. They considered these and other rights expandable; indeed, as revolutionaries they had identified new protections for individuals against the overweening power of government. They also expected rights of the accused to gain meaning from experience, always in the direction of greater freedom. Their vision of rights, like their theory of government, was liberal. At the end of the twentieth century, it is this vision that we have lost.

A fundamental article of faith about our constitutional heritage proclaims that liberty and rights cannot exist without due process of law. Procedural fairness and consistency are touchstones of due process. They are, as Justice Robert Jackson argued, "what it most uncompromisingly requires."[6] In no other branch of the law is a proper concern for fairness more important than in criminal law. Government holds enormous power over individuals. It alone has the legitimate authority to accuse, prosecute, and punish, so any criminal trial between the government and a citizen is by its very nature unequal. Due process of law helps to redress this imbalance of power and make individuals less vulnerable to arbitrary governmental actions. And, as legal scholar Zechariah Chafee Jr. noted, the freedom from official capriciousness is essential to all other human rights.[7]

The framers of the Bill of Rights gained their understanding of due process by hard experience. Colonists entered the struggle for independence with a seventeenth-century view that rights restrained the exercise of governmental power by protecting the community against unwarranted interference with its affairs by agents of a distant, central authority. Rights did not free the individual from community norms or change the local character of justice. Indeed, the good order of society took precedence over the liberty of the individual. In this sense, colonists were closer to medieval ways of thinking than to modern ones. Their rights were an ancient legacy, setting forth duties and obligations, extending to communities and corporate bodies as well as individuals, and reflecting class distinctions.[8]

Significantly, these rights had no precise meaning. Colonial charters of settlement did not define the rights they guaranteed migrating Englishmen, even in rudimentary form. Nor did many of the documents such as the Magna Carta that formed the cornerstone of the British constitution. Most rights were customary and found in common law, not in statutes or royal decrees. Yet much custom was merely local and of limited value to provinces housing immigrants from all parts of England and beyond. So colonial lawmakers used their authority under the charters to transfer law selectively and innovate where necessary, putting it in written codes to make it accessible to every citizen. It is noteworthy that they used such discretion, in part, to make the rights of defendants under due process more extensive than in the mother country, even though these protections varied from colony to colony.[9] Not all rights fell within the wide embrace of written documents, moreover. There were certain inalienable natural rights—life, liberty, and property—that stood outside codes of law. Individuals could not renounce these rights, nor could governments abrogate them.

Trial by jury was the bedrock principle of Anglo-American liberty. Without it all other rights would fail. Only a jury from the neighborhood, unfettered in its judgments, formed an impregnable shield against arbitrary government. The presence of jurors precluded secret trials and protected citizens from venal judges, purchased testimony, threatening officials, and other abuses. The power of the jury to judge both law and facts and its use of the general verdict—a reply of innocent or guilty to an accusation—were the people's most effective weapon against tyranny. The local jury was, quite simply, the best method available for assuring justice and protecting liberty.[10]

Changes in eighteenth-century British political theory threatened the traditional view of inalienable, community-based rights. The successful assertion of parliamentary power over the king during the previous century led to a belief that the constitution was malleable and that rights existed at the pleasure of the legislature. With enforcement of new imperial policies in the 1760s and 1770s fear grew that the demands of power would soon require the sacrifice of English rights in America. By 1776 the rebelling colonists had developed a litany of grievances to support their claim that Great Britain had abandoned the constitution and their rights in an arrogant quest for power. The series of charges made by Americans were, in fact, a schedule of rights they considered vital to liberty. Rights of the accused were prominent on the list.

Protections for the criminally accused were also central to the revolutionary catalog of rights that followed separation. The new state documents that contained these safeguards drew liberally from English antecedents and colonial charters and statutes. The Virginia Declaration of Rights, the first and leading charter of these protections, took its injunction against cruel and unusual punishment directly from the Bill of Rights of 1688. A pledge of due process used language reminiscent of the Magna Carta, as did the right of trial by jury from the vicinage. But Virginians were not content simply to crib rights from history. Their experience had taught them the value of spelling out carefully and completely the penumbras of liberty. The privilege against general warrants received special attention. So did protection against self-incrimination. The right to trial by jury, long deemed the essential bulwark against tyranny, also took on additional coloration: trials must be speedy; defendants had to be confronted with their accusers and witnesses; defendants could call for evidence in their favor; and jury verdicts must be unanimous. Here were the requirements of procedural justice that the Bill of Rights would later incorporate.

Virginia was not alone in its desire to place these rights beyond the reach of government. Nine of the revolutionary constitutions contained separate bills of rights, while the other four incorporated certain rights into the frame of government. Some of these documents provided safeguards not mentioned in the Virginia Declaration; others extended new rights or decorated the criminal process with carefully elaborated protections for defendants.

Clearly, something was happening to expand previous conceptions of rights of the accused. Revolutionaries began to endorse guarantees that until 1776 had received scant notice or that went well beyond precedents at common law. The right to counsel is a striking example of how far the founders were willing to advance individual rights. Both in Great Britain and the colonies a person charged with a felony had no right under common law to the advice or representation of counsel. Only for a misdemeanor was counsel permitted. Several revolutionary state constitutions extended the right to all criminal defendants, as did the Sixth Amendment, an action not taken by Great Britain until 1836. What is most instructive about this change is its rationale. Unlike their English cousins, Americans viewed judges as an arm of the government, not as neutral protectors of a defendant's rights. They chose to create a barrier for government prosecutors to overcome, even though they recognized the ability of lawyers to delay or deny conviction and punishment.[11]

The newness of their enterprise took the framers beyond history in specifying the protections required by liberty. As one scholar has remarked, what was most impressive about the American rights was "not their derivative but their creative character."[12] Significantly, both revolutionary republicanism and the Enlightenment provided the philosophical and symbolic context for the identification of rights. Republicanism was not so much a coherent philosophy as it was a series of warnings about the abuse of power. Liberty inhered in the people, and only a morally responsible citizenry could protect it. Yet reliance on the civic virtue of people had in the past proven inadequate to resist the encroachments of power. Only written constitutions with carefully circumscribed limits on government provided sufficient guarantees, and even then citizens had to remain vigilant. An Enlightenment attitude encouraged an optimistic belief that people were rational and would respond positively to humane and intelligent government. This circumstance lessened the need for strong governments and encouraged the possibility of creating a new order, especially in areas such as criminal law where the power of the state was revealed most dramatically. The message from both republicanism and enlightened thought was mutually reinforcing: restrain power, trust liberty.

By 1780 the revolutionary canon of defendants' rights was part of the common language that framed issues of power and liberty for Americans. Yet the Constitution, drafted in 1787, contained no enumeration of these guarantees. Framers gave two reasons for the omission. First, the national government could exercise only the powers given to it. Without the power to legislate—and Congress had no such authority over individual liberties—there could be no threat to the rights of the people. Another reason for the charter's silence was that under the federal system states, not the national government, were responsible for protecting civil rights.

These arguments were not persuasive, and defenders of the Constitution had to pledge to submit an amendatory bill of rights to the First Congress in order to gain ratification in key states. When James Madison, congressman from Virginia and the intellectual force behind the Constitution, fulfilled this promise in 1789, the debate over his proposed series of amendments centered not on the rights in question but on whether they achieved any good purpose without changing the nature of the Constitution. Four of the amendments addressed matters so completely that scholars have noted their character as a miniature code of criminal procedure.[13]

The language of the amendments could not have been more recognizable to the American people, who had seen or heard it used repeatedly over one and a half centuries. It was a vocabulary pregnant with meaning but without fixed bounds. What was an unreasonable search? The colonial and revolutionary experience left examples; it did not establish settled definitions. The same was true with double jeopardy, the only right now added that had not been included in the litanies of the period. Here, common law provided an incomplete guide that could not anticipate the federal system's dual power to accuse and try offenders. And what was the meaning of assistance of counsel or excessive bail or cruel and unusual punishments?

These questions provided a rich source for debate and litigation over the next two hundred years, beginning with the state courts and legislatures in the nineteenth century and expanding primarily to the federal courts in the twentieth. The founders would likely not have been bothered by the knowledge that these amendments would undergo challenges and shifts in meaning. They were practical politicians who constructed the Bill of Rights not from abstract political theory but from experience, and they anticipated that future generations would expand the scope of protected rights.

Neither did they expect that the Bill of Rights would prevent all injustices. James Madison, whose genius shaped the Bill of Rights and who remains the best guide to its interpretation, argued that the amendments, at a minimum, would serve as "good ground for an appeal to the sense of community" when threatened by arbitrary governments or oppressive majorities.[14] This claim expressed more hope than promise. In truth, Madison worried much about the tyranny of the majority and the inadequacy of the states to resist this threat to individual liberty. He recognized how easily communities could be seized by concerns for their safety. He also had seen how states, thought by many revolutionaries to be the governments most protective of individual rights, could act to deny even the fundamental rights of minorities. He hoped that a bill of rights would serve to instruct the American people in "the fundamental maxims of free government" and "counteract the impulses of interest and passion," but he doubted this result, so he sought to apply the amendments to the states and not simply the national government. Restraining all governmental power for the sake of protecting individual rights not only helped to preserve liberty but might serve as well to make government vigilant on behalf of the rights of its most marginal citizens.[15] The judiciary especially would, in Madison's view, be central to this purpose: they would come to consider themselves "in a peculiar manner the guardians of those rights." They would "resist every encroachment on rights expressly stipulated for in the constitution," forming an "impenetrable bulwark against every assumption of power in the legislative or the executive."[16]

Madison's concerns are doubly instructive for an interpretation of the Bill of Rights. While most of his contemporaries viewed the first ten amendments as a standard that enabled people to judge their governors, Madison saw a more sophisticated use for them. They could promote the cause of self-government, he believed, by enabling republican citizens to resist the impulses of passion and interest that posed the greatest threat to the Revolution's great experiment in liberty. And if these protections extended to the state governments as well, an objective that Madison sought but did not gain, they would give the central government through the judiciary the authority to mitigate the injustices that he expected to occur there. It took almost two centuries for this original vision to be realized.[17]

From the beginning, the states, not the central government, were primarily responsible for the integrity of criminal due process. Rights of the accused—indeed, most individual rights—were primarily attributes of state citizenship, which state constitutions and state courts defined and protected. The Bill of Rights applied only to federal trials. Even the passage of the Fourteenth Amendment with its language suggesting national oversight of due process did not change this division of responsibility. Well into the twentieth century the Supreme Court adhered to the position first announced in *Hurtado v. California* (1884), that the Fourteenth Amendment did not bind the states to the procedural guarantees of the federal Constitution. Criminal due process referred only to the procedures employed by the state. If criminal prosecutions followed the process required by state law, then the result by definition was justice.

Few people found the lack of national supervision troublesome, at least not if they were part of the white majority, because Americans shared a common set of legal values, institutions, and procedures. Chief among them was a commitment to due process of law, which in ideal form pledged procedural fairness in all actions from indictment to trial and punishment. Underlying this notion of fairness was the continuing belief that the primary purpose of criminal justice was to protect the innocent, not to convict the guilty. The mid-fifteenth-century English maxim remained a guide for nineteenth-century Americans: it was better for twenty guilty persons to escape punishment than one person to suffer wrongly.[18]

Even as nineteenth-century Americans celebrated their commitment to due process, criminal justice was taking new and different shape. The grand jury came under sharp attack in the midcentury, and by the 1880s almost twenty states, mostly western, allowed the prosecutor to charge a person directly through an information rather than the traditional indictment.[19] Newly created police departments shifted the focus of law enforcement from reacting to citizen complaints to detecting crime by patrols and investigations. But it was the trial, long the centerpiece of the criminal process, that experienced the most dramatic challenge. Not only did bench trial, or trial by the judge alone, begin to rival jury trial in several jurisdictions as an acceptable means of trying a case, but most defendants avoided trial altogether by pleading guilty in exchange for less severe punishment. State surveys in the 1920s revealed a heavy dependence on plea bargaining, especially in big city courts: in Chicago, for example, 85 percent of all felony convictions resulted from a guilty plea. The percentages in other cities were almost as high or higher.[20]

Plea bargaining changed the face of American justice. It made efficient prosecution and conviction of the guilty, not protection of the innocent, a primary goal of the legal system, at least in practice. There were informal, subterranean, and highly particularistic standards for fixing guilt and innocence; confessions became the desired end and police interrogations the preferred means for obtaining them. State supreme courts often protested the departure from constitutional ideals: plea bargaining was a perversion of due process; it represented the sale of justice; and its secrecy mocked the pledge of neutral justice in a public trial. Other critics characterized plea bargaining as an auction, and legal scholars denounced it as a license to violate the law.[21] But the practice continued. Public concerns about order, especially in the face of rapid urbanization and a flood of immigration from Eastern Europe and Asia, made the control of crime paramount.[22]

Despite this public concern, the Supreme Court in the nineteenth and early twentieth centuries generally adopted an expansive interpretation of rights for federal defendants. Dramatic examples came in two Fourth Amendment cases. In *Boyd v. United States* (1886), the Court rescued the amendment from becoming "a dead letter in the federal courts" by tying it doctrinally to the Fifth Amendment's promise that no person "shall be compelled in any criminal case to be a witness against himself." A warrantless seizure of evidence, in this case by compelling the disclosure of an invoice in a customs dispute, deprived the accused of the Fifth Amendment's protection. The Court clearly saw its role as a watchdog of defendants' rights: "Unconstitutional practices get their first footing . . . by silent approaches and slight deviations from legal modes of procedure. . . . It is the duty of courts to be watchful for the constitutional rights of the citizen, and guard against any stealthy encroachments thereon."[23] A quarter-century later, in *Weeks v. United States* (1914), the Court went further, breaking with common-law precedents and excluding from federal trials any evidence obtained through an illegal search. Protection from crime, wrote Justice William Day, "is not to be aided by the sacrifice of these great principles established by years of endeavor and suffering which have resulted in their embodiment in the fundamental law of the land."[24] What is most striking about these judgments is that until 1886 American courts at all levels routinely admitted all relevant evidence of crime, even if illegally obtained, yet two Courts considered conservative in other respects found a constitutional obligation to rule otherwise, thereby boldly expanding the rights of defendants.[25] The decisions marked an especially Madisonian moment in American jurisprudence.

Dissatisfaction with the lack of national oversight in matters of criminal justice eventually persuaded the Supreme Court to extend the protection of the Bill of Rights to criminal defendants under the Fourteenth Amendment, as it had begun to do for the rights of free speech and free press. The Red Scare following World War I demonstrated the need as states failed to protect even the most basic rights of defendants, especially ethnic and racial minorities. During the 1920s, studies of criminal justice, including a major national investigation by the Wickersham Commission, revealed the open contempt many police departments held for the rights guaranteed by state and federal constitutions. And the wholesale lynching of blacks in the South finally became a national disgrace.[26]

By the 1930s numerous organizations, notably the American Civil Liberties Union and the National Association for the Advancement of Colored People, pressed for nationalization of the Bill of Rights. In 1932 they scored an initial success. *Powell v. Alabama*, the famous Scottsboro case, established that the due process clause of the Fourteenth Amendment guaranteed the assistance of counsel to defendants charged with capital crimes in state courts.[27] Even so, the Supreme Court continued to resist attempts to incorporate the protections of the Fourth, Fifth, Sixth, and Eighth Amendments into a national standard. The Fourteenth Amendment, the justices held in *Palko v. Connecticut* (1937), imposed on the states only rights essential to a "scheme of ordered liberty."[28] In criminal matters the assurance of fair trial alone was fundamental to liberty. States could employ widely different procedures without violating due process. Not even trial by jury was essential to fairness, even though the Founding Fathers had deemed it the bulwark of their liberties.

From the 1930s through the 1950s the Supreme Court grappled with the meaning of the phrase "due process of law." The fair-trial test meant that the Court would decide case by case which rights of the accused enjoyed constitutional protection. It also suggested that the values and attitudes of individual judges would determine which state procedures created such hardships or so shocked the conscience that they denied fair treatment. Still, the test provided a method for extending the Bill of Rights to the states, and the catalog of nationalized rights—provisions of the Bill of Rights binding on the states—grew extensively by the end of the three decades, although the list pales when compared to current practice. Fundamental rights included limited protection against illegal searches and seizures (Fourth Amendment); coerced confessions (Fifth); public trial, impartial jury, and counsel (Sixth); and cruel and unusual punishments (Eighth). Even so, the interpretation of these rights was not as far-reaching as later Courts would find, and some rights—double jeopardy, protections against self-incrimination, and jury trial, among others—remained totally under state control.[29]

The Court's continued reliance on the fair-trial test, although maintaining a theoretical line between state and federal power, led to much confusion regarding which criminal procedures were acceptable. Some state practices it permitted, others it rejected, but no clear standard emerged to guide law enforcement. Continued adherence to the test increasingly exposed the Court to charges that defendants' rights depended on judicial caprice. Such an "ad hoc approach," Chief Justice Earl Warren cautioned in 1957, "is to build on shifting sands."[30] It also was at odds with the Court's decisions on First Amendment freedoms. These rights applied fully and identically to central and state governments alike under the due process clause of the Fourteenth Amendment. Why should not the same standard govern rights of the accused? *Palko v. Connecticut*, progenitor of the fair-trial doctrine, Justice William Brennan reminded his colleagues, contained no "license to the judiciary to administer a watered-down subjective version of the individual guarantees of the Bill of Rights."[31]

By the late 1950s four justices—Warren, Hugo Black, William Douglas, and Brennan—were ready to abandon the fair-trial approach to the Fourteenth Amendment. The 1960s witnessed their triumph. Too much had changed nationally to continue an interpretation that defined rights in terms of state boundaries. State prosecutors and local police alike had grown weary of a tribunal in distant Washington deciding long after trial that state practices violated the Constitution. Law schools and bar associations desired more uniform rules. Commentators and legal scholars also questioned why Amendments 4, 5, 6, and 8 were not as fundamental as the freedom of speech and press.

In a nation where interstate highways collapsed distances and chain stores erased a sense of place, it was only a matter of time before national standards replaced local practice. For criminal law the shift came in a rush of Supreme Court decisions in the 1960s. In what was termed the "due process revolution," the Bill of Rights became a national code of criminal procedure. Suddenly, rights of criminal defendants became more real, more immediate, and, for many people, more threatening.

Between 1961 and 1969 the Supreme Court accomplished what previous courts had stoutly resisted: it applied virtually all of the procedural guarantees of the Bill of Rights to the states' administration of criminal justice. Adopting the strategy of selective incorporation, the justices explicitly defined the Fourteenth Amendment phrase, due process of law, to include most of the rights outlined in the Fourth, Fifth, and Sixth Amendments. The result was a nationalized Bill of Rights that dimmed the local character of justice by applying the same restraints to all criminal proceedings, both state and federal. The majority justices did not seek to diminish states' rights; they desired instead to elevate subminimal state practices to a higher national standard. But in the process the Court reshaped the nature of federalism itself.[32]

Leading the due process revolution was an unlikely figure, Chief Justice Earl Warren, a former California district prosecutor, attorney general, and governor whose pre-Court reputation was that of a crusader against corruption and for vigorous law enforcement. The judiciary scarcely entered into his calculus of what constituted proper government, and as a politician he certainly did nothing to challenge traditional meanings of due process. In fact, Warren led the campaign to intern Japanese-Americans during World War II, an action that denied, among other constitutional guarantees, the right to a fair hearing.

Warren's reputation took a sharp turn as chief justice, in large measure because he brought a different style and philosophy to the Court. His longstanding belief in active government challenged the majority justices' embrace of judicial restraint, which included deference to legislative actions, respect for federalism and the diversity of state practice, and reliance upon neutral decision making based on narrow case facts rather than broad constitutional interpretation. Warren specifically dismissed as "fantasy" the notion that judges can be impartial. "As defender of the Constitution," he wrote, "the Court cannot be neutral."[33] More important, Court decisions must reach the right result, a condition defined by ethics, not legal procedures. He firmly believed that the Constitution embodied moral truths that were essential to enlightened government. The Court had a duty to apply these principles, even if doing so contravened the expressed wishes of the legislature. And finally, its role was to champion the individual, especially those citizens without a meaningful political voice.[34]

By the 1960s the Court was ready to follow the chief justice's lead. Acting with unprecedented boldness, a majority on the Warren Court promoted policies it deemed essential to a just society. Equality joined individualism in the pantheon of modern liberal values. Liberty, long defined as the restraint of power, now required positive governmental action. Individual freedom rested upon the protection and extension to all citizens of the fundamental guarantees found in the Bill of Rights and the Fourteenth Amendment. In its emphasis on equality and national standards, the Court was not alone. Liberalism experienced a resurgence under the presidencies of John Kennedy and Lyndon Johnson, and the rhetoric of civil rights and social justice framed the agenda of the ascendant Democratic party. So for most of the decade, the justices drew support from a liberal political coalition that preached a similar message.

Popular memory has it that the Court's decisions on criminal justice were highly controversial and came only through the determined efforts of a bare majority of judges. This view distorts what actually happened. Take, for example, *Gideon v. Wainwright* (1963), which declared that the Sixth Amendment right to counsel applied to the states under the due process clause of the Fourteenth Amendment and that states had to provide a lawyer for felony defendants too poor to hire one. The decision was unanimous, even though it reversed a 1942 precedent *(Betts v. Brady)* that allowed a state to refuse such assistance in noncapital cases unless its refusal denied a fair trial.[35] More striking was the fact that twenty-three states filed amicus curiae, or friend-of-the-court, briefs asking the Court to mandate the assistance of counsel in serious criminal cases. Their assessment of the Court's previous deference to the states was damning. It had resulted only in "confusion and contradictions" that failed totally "as a beacon to guide trial judges."[36] The states themselves demanded the nationalization of this important guarantee of the Bill of Rights.

Other decisions affecting the conduct of state trials also met general acceptance, even when the justices divided narrowly. For example, the Court decided in *Malloy v. Hogan* (1964) that the privilege against self-incrimination was part of the due process clause of the Fourteenth Amendment.[37] And the next year, 1965, in *Pointer v. Texas*, the Court ruled that the Sixth Amendment right of an accused to confront a witness against him was a fundamental right that the Fourteenth Amendment required of all states.[38] Neither case occasioned much public comment, certainly not the storm of protests often depicted by opponents of the decisions.

In truth, there was never much objection to the Warren Court's restraints on state trial practices. News coverage of the landmark decisions was limited; few columnists discussed the changes. Most people undoubtedly viewed the trial as the centerpiece of American justice, especially when placed in contrast to totalitarian practices during the height of the Cold War. (The absence of a trial in the vast majority of criminal cases scarcely dented public awareness.) At least for trial rights they concurred with Justice Arthur Goldberg's opinion in *Pointer* that states had no "power to experiment with the funda-mental liberties of the people."[39] Diversity here denied equal justice.

The greatest protest against the Court's extension of federal trial rights came from state judges who considered the decisions an infringement of their prerogative. Conservative legal commentators also objected, claiming that the theory of selective incorporation used to justify the decisions was constitutionally incorrect, primarily because it undermined the federal sys-tem's division of authority between state and central governments.[40] But these criticisms were blunted by most states' acceptance of the Court's direc-tion. Uniform rules for trials did not threaten the core of state power, and they removed much of the uncertainty that accompanied numerous appeals.

Pretrial rights were a wholly different matter. The Court discovered early that any challenge of state police practices would be highly controversial. In *Mapp v. Ohio* (1961) the liberal justices narrowly (five to four) applied the federal exclusionary rule to the states. Even though the case facts revealed a blatant disregard of search and seizure guarantees, the Ohio Supreme Court had upheld the state law permitting the use of illegally seized evidence to convict Dollree Mapp of possession of obscene material. The Supreme Court disagreed. One of its earlier decisions, *Wolf v. Colorado* (1948), had extended the Fourth Amendment to the states but without the federal rule of proce-dure that required the exclusion of any evidence gained in violation of the amendment's guarantees. Now with the amendment's protection went the means to enforce it, the exclusionary rule. "To hold otherwise," Justice Tom Clark reasoned, "is to grant the right but in reality withhold its privilege and enjoyment."[41]

Clark, a former U.S. attorney general, did not believe the decision would impede law enforcement (although, he argued, the Constitution demanded it regardless), but critics of *Mapp* concluded otherwise. They condemned the Court as unrealistic: policemen were engaged in dangerous work that often required quick action; failure to follow the correct procedures should not doom the evidence of crime, especially when state law and state courts per-mitted it. Indeed, *Mapp* undermined state ability to maintain order, oppo-nents argued, by breaching the federal principle that left criminal matters to state control. The majority justices had overreached their authority and fashioned their decision not on constitutional precedent but on their sense of a right result.[42]

These criticisms surfaced with more force a few years later when the Court extended the right of counsel to the pretrial stages of criminal process, first in *Massiah v. United States* (1964) and then in *Escobedo v. Illinois* (1965) and *Miranda v. Arizona* (1966).[43] The justices concluded that Fifth Amendment guarantees against self-incrimination and coerced confessions and the Sixth Amendment's right to counsel were meaningless unless applied to a police investigation at the point where it focused directly on an individual suspected of a crime. Any information gained illegally by denying these protections was not admissible at trial. Significantly, the decisions affirmed and extended the precedents of earlier Courts, stretching back at least to 1945, that automatically overturned convictions achieved through coerced or involuntary confessions, even if the confessions were true and the guilty defendant went free as a result.[44] But for opponents of the decisions the Court had departed dramatically from past practice, impeding the investigation of crime and jeopardizing public safety.

Miranda was by far the most controversial decision, the one still cited as the premier example of a Court gone wrong. Chief Justice Warren's opinion extending the Fifth Amendment protection against self-incrimination to suspects under interrogation exemplified his ethically based, result-oriented jurisprudence. The opinion first detailed the unfair and forbidding nature of police interrogations. Police manuals and statements by law enforcement officers revealed that beatings, intimidation, psychological pressure, false statements, and denial of food and sleep were standard techniques used to secure the suspect's confession. For Warren, these tactics suggested that "the interrogation environment [existed] . . . for no other purpose than to subjugate the individual to the will of the examiner."[45] Ethics alone made reprehensible any practice that tricked or cajoled suspects from exercising their constitutional rights, leaving them isolated and vulnerable. But such police tactics also violated the Fifth Amendment protection against self-incrimination.

The longest part of the opinion was a detailed code of police conduct. The new rules quickly became familiar to anyone who watched television crime dramas: suspects must be informed of their right to remain silent; anything they say can be used against them; they have the right to have counsel present during questioning; if they cannot afford an attorney, the court will appoint a lawyer to represent them. These privileges took effect from the first instance of police interrogation while the suspect was "in custody at the station or deprived of his [or her] freedom in a significant way." And the rights could be waived only "knowingly and intelligently," a condition presumed not to exist if lengthy questioning preceded the required warnings.[46]

Warren's language vividly portrayed the unequal relationship between interrogator and suspect, an imbalance that the chief justice believed did not belong in a democratic society. "The prosecutor under our system," he commented later, "is not paid to convict people [but to] protect the rights of people . . . and to see that when there is a violation of the law, it is vindicated by trial and prosecution under fair judicial standards." [47] The presence of a lawyer and a protected right of silence created a more equal situation for the accused; thus, these conditions were essential to the constitutional conception of a fair trial.

Police officers, prosecutors, commentators, and politicians were quick to denounce the *Miranda* warnings. They charged that recent Court decisions had "handcuffed" police efforts to fight crime. This claim found a receptive audience among a majority of the general public worried about rising crime rates, urban riots, racial conflict, and the counterculture's challenge to middle-class values. The belief that the pretrial reforms threatened public safety even acquired a certain legitimacy from members of the Supreme Court itself. "In some unknown number of cases," Justice Byron White warned in his dissent from the *Miranda* decision, "the Court's rule will return a killer, a rapist or other criminal to the streets . . . to repeat his crime whenever it pleases him." [48]

These alarms were exaggerated. Numerous studies have since demonstrated that the decision, like the ones in *Mapp* and *Massiah*, did not restrain the police unduly and, in fact, had little effect on the disposition of most cases. Access to an attorney, usually an overworked and underpaid public defender, may have smoothed negotiations between suspect and prosecutor, but it did not lessen the percentage of cases resolved by plea bargains, nor did it result in lengthy delays, greater bureaucracy, or more dismissals of guilty suspects. [49]

Even as a matter of law, *Miranda* was not as revolutionary as critics claimed. The Supreme Court had held from the 1930s that voluntariness of a confession was essential for its acceptance as evidence, and since 1945 it automatically reversed convictions based on involuntary confessions, whether or not the confession was in fact true. Various terms were used to describe the voluntariness test: "free will" and "unconstrained choice" signified a voluntary confession; "breaking the will" and "overbearing the mind," an involuntary one. But as Justice John Marshall Harlan noted in his dissent in *Miranda*, the Court's gauge for determining whether or not a confession was voluntary had been steadily changing, usually in the direction of restricting admissibility. [50] *Miranda* scuttled this case-by-case determination. It established uniform rules of procedure and, equally important, accepted as constitutional any confessions gained under these rules. More significantly, the Court, in expanding the right beyond all precedent, did not exceed the Fifth

Amendment's historical spirit and purpose. Rather, it kept the amendment, in the words of its chief scholar, "as broad as the mischief against which it seeks to guard."[51]

Although controversial, the reforms in pretrial procedures gradually brought needed improvements in police practices. Police procedures came more fully into public view, resulting in heightened awareness of official misconduct and greater expectations of professionalism. In response, many police departments raised standards for employment, adopted performance guidelines, and improved training and supervision. The Court's actions had begun to bear fruit, much in the manner desired by the majority, who believed that hard work and respect for the law, not deception or law breaking, were the requirements of effective law enforcement.

The Court, ever aware of public criticism, made concessions to secure more widespread acceptance of its rulings. Most important was the decision not to apply new rulings retroactively. The justices acknowledged that this course denied equal justice to prisoners convicted under abandoned procedures, but they admitted candidly that wholesale release of prisoners was politically unacceptable. Another concession was the adoption of a "harmless error" test to determine the impact of an unconstitutional act at trial: constitutional errors would not void convictions if "beyond a reasonable doubt that error did not contribute to the verdict obtained."[52] The Court also hesitated to restrict the police unduly. It held in 1966, the same year as *Miranda*, that the government's use of decoys, undercover agents, and paid informants was not necessarily unconstitutional. The justices further approved the admissibility of evidence secured by wiretaps and sustained the right of police "in hot pursuit" to search a house and seize incriminating evidence without a warrant. Even *Miranda* itself represented a compromise response to concerns that the earlier *Escobedo* decision required the presence of counsel during the preliminary stages of a police inquiry, before the investigation centered on a suspect in custody.

These moderating decisions failed to quiet the Court's critics, but mounting pressure did not deter the justices from making further reforms in state criminal procedures. *In re Gault* extended certain due process requirements to juvenile courts. Several important cases incorporated the remaining Sixth Amendment guarantees—specifically, the rights to compulsory process, speedy trial, and trial by jury—into the due process clause of the Fourteenth Amendment as new restraints on state criminal process. The Court continued to insist that poverty should be no impediment to justice by requiring that the state furnish transcripts to indigent defendants. And it strengthened its long-established position that confessions be truly voluntary. Much more controversial were the continuing reforms of pretrial procedures. In 1967 several search and seizure decisions especially brought further protest from "law and order" advocates who accused the Court of coddling criminals, a charge that gained momentum during the 1968 election when two presidential candidates—Richard Nixon and George Wallace—made it a major theme in their campaigns.

Such cases, whether controversial or not, departed sharply from the decades-old tradition that defined criminal justice as a local responsibility. Each decision underscored the dramatically changed relationship between the federal Bill of Rights and the state's authority to establish criminal procedures. Earlier Courts had accepted state experimentation with any part of due process unless the justices considered it essential to a scheme of ordered liberty. This standard permitted states to define fairness in a variety of ways that might or might not include the guarantees of the federal amendments. But the Warren Court concluded that rights of the accused were rights of American citizenship. It rejected theory and diversity in favor of history and uniformity. In *Duncan v. White* (1968), which denied the right of a state to withhold jury trial in cases of serious crime, Justice White wrote for the majority: "State criminal processes are not imaginary and theoretical schemes but actual systems bearing virtually every characteristic of the common-law system that has been developed in England and this country." The issue, he continued, was not whether a procedure "is fundamental to fairness in every criminal system that might be imagined but is fundamental in the context of the criminal processes maintained by the American states."[53]

The next year, 1969, the Court reversed, fittingly, *Palko v. Connecticut*, the landmark case that had justified state experimentation with criminal procedures. The issue, as it had been in 1937, was double jeopardy. The question was, Did the Fifth Amendment restrain the states? This time the answer was yes. Writing for the majority in *Benton v. Maryland*, Justice Thurgood Marshall noted that recent cases had thoroughly rejected the premise in *Palko* that a denial of fundamental fairness rested on the total circumstances of a criminal proceeding, not simply one element of it. Once the Court decides a particular guarantee is fundamental to American justice, he continued, then failure to honor that safeguard is a denial of due process. Equally important, these essential protections applied uniformly to all jurisdictions.[54] Here, then, was the core of the due process revolution: rights of the accused did not vary from state to state; they were truly national rights, as James Madison had hoped they would be almost two centuries earlier.

By 1969 the Court's transformation of criminal procedure was at its end. Neither popular nor political opinion supported further reform. The previous year, stung by rioting in American cities and pressured to curb a recent sharp upturn in crime and violence, Congress had responded by passing the Omnibus Crime Control and Safe Streets Act, the most extensive anticrime legislation in American history. The measure contained a number of provisions designed to reverse recent Court decisions, especially the *Miranda* rule. And Richard Nixon appointed a new chief justice, Warren Burger, to redeem his campaign pledge to restore a conservative cast to the Supreme Court.

Contrary to expectations, there was no counterrevolution in the law governing defendants' rights, even after three conservative appointees replaced Warren Court justices. Upon Burger's retirement in 1986, the major criminal procedure decisions of the Warren Court remained intact. The lasting influence of the due process reforms owed little to the chief justice, who did not share his predecessor's concern with rights of the accused. Indeed, he had often attacked the Court's decisions while on the appellate bench. His announced goal was to shift the burden of reform to the state legislatures. "To try to create or substantially change civil or criminal procedure by judicial decision," he argued, "is the worst possible way to do it."[55]

The Burger Court did not renounce the due process revolution, but the justices were more tolerant of police behavior and less receptive to further expansion of rights of criminal defendants. Symbolic of the change was the Court's interpretation of the Fourth Amendment's requirement that search warrants be based upon probable cause. Previous decisions had challenged the validity of a warrant issued on the basis of rumors or even an anonymous informant's tip, yet in *United States v. Harris* (1971) a divided Court held that a suspect's reputation alone was sufficient to support a warrant application. Writing for the majority, Chief Justice Burger denounced "mere hypertechnicality" in warrant affidavits and urged a return to more practical considerations in actions against criminals.[56]

Subsequent cases confirmed the new direction. Not only did the Court lower the threshold requirements for a valid search, thus permitting police greater latitude, it redefined the exclusionary rule. Framers of the exclusionary rule, first announced in 1914, may have expected it to influence police behavior, but the principle itself, they believed, was part of the Fourth Amendment. Not so, concluded the Court in 1974. In ruling that grand jury witnesses may not use unlawful searches to keep them from testifying, the Court characterized the exclusionary rule as a "judicially created remedy designed to safeguard Fourth Amendment rights generally through its deterrent effect." It was not a "personal constitutional right," and its use presented "a question, not of rights but of remedies"—one that should be answered by weighing the costs of the rule against its benefits.[57]

This new cost-benefit analysis led ultimately to a good-faith exception to the exclusionary rule, announced in *United States v. Leon* (1984): evidence produced by an officer's reasonable or good-faith reliance on the validity of a warrant was admissible in court, even if the warrant later proved defective. The good-faith exception rested explicitly on a balancing of the costs and benefits involved: using evidence captured innocently under a defective warrant exacted a small price from Fourth Amendment protection when compared to the substantial cost society would bear if an otherwise guilty defendant went free.[58] Left unanswered was the question of whether the exception was necessary. Opponents of the decision argued that it was not; since *Mapp*, evidence was excluded or prosecutions dropped in fewer than 2 percent of all cases. Strict adherence to the exclusionary rule had resulted in better police work. If the good-faith exception invited a more casual approach to law enforcement, they feared, the Fourth Amendment would once again become a meaningless guarantee.

In most other areas of criminal procedure, the Court maintained but did little to advance the rights of the accused extended during the Warren era. Arguing that the law requires only a fair trial, not a perfect one, the Court upheld a conviction even though the police, when giving the required *Miranda* warnings, neglected to tell the defendant of his right to appointed counsel if he could not afford one. It also allowed admissions secured without the required warnings to be used to impeach defendants' credibility, though not to obtain their conviction, if they took the stand in their own behalf. In Sixth Amendment cases the Court guaranteed the right to counsel in all trials that could result in imprisonment, but, following the lead of Congress in the Crime Control Act of 1968, it refused to grant the protection to unindicted suspects in a police lineup. Similarly, the justices extended the guarantee of a jury trial to include all petty misdemeanors punishable by six months or longer imprisonment, yet allowed states to experiment with the size of juries and accepted ten-to-two and nine-to-three verdicts in noncapital cases.[59]

Initially, the Rehnquist Court followed its predecessor in cases involving rights of the accused. It declined to extend defendants' rights and insisted on balancing individual protections with the need for effective law enforcement, but it did not reverse Warren Court decisions. Law officers gained greater latitude in applying the *Miranda* rules when, in *Colorado v. Connelly* (1986), the Court adopted a less strict standard to determine the voluntariness of a confession. Police must give the required warnings and stop all questioning if a suspect demanded a lawyer, but they could use nonthreatening tactics, such as pretending sympathy with the suspect, to secure a valid confession.[60] Strengthening the ability of the police to fight crime was also the result in *United States v. Salerno* (1987), which upheld the Bail Reform Act of 1984.[61] It allowed the government to deny bail if release of a defendant would endanger lives or property. Even though an apparent departure from the presumption of innocence, the law itself provided numerous procedural safeguards, including representation of counsel. These protections, the justices concluded, provided a reasonable balance between the rights of the accused and the need for public safety.

This incremental rebalancing of societal and individual interests gave way to a more comprehensive reassessment of rights of the accused during the 1990s. For over two decades politicians' demands for a law-and-order judiciary had reaped electoral windfalls, but not until the appointment of three conservative justices—Arthur Kennedy, Antonin Scalia, and David Souter—did politics and constitutional law join so conclusively. Suddenly the calculus of decision making had changed, and it emboldened the new conservative majority to challenge Warren Court precedents.

Several cases signaled the new direction. The most dramatic departure came in confession law, long a bellwether of constitutional attitudes toward the defendant. Since the 1940s the Court had reversed convictions based in whole or in part upon an involuntary confession, even when there was ample evidence apart from the confession to support the conviction. In *Arizona v. Fulminante*, the five-to-four majority abandoned this precedent and applied instead the harmless error test to such evidence. This new approach classified evidence of a coerced confession not as an automatic violation of due process but simply as a trial error. Like other mistakes at trial, an involuntary confession must now be examined in the context of all the facts presented at trial to determine if its use was harmless or consequential to the verdict.

The dissenting justices claimed that the majority had misapplied the harmless error rule (first announced, ironically, by the Warren Court), which specifically noted three errors that could not be categorized as harmless error: depriving a defendant of counsel, trying a defendant before a trial judge, and using a coerced confession against a defendant. In his controlling opinion, Chief Justice William Rehnquist dismissed this argument. The first two errors, he concluded, were "structural defects affecting the framework within which the trial proceeds, rather than simply an error in the trial process itself."[62] An involuntary confession did not taint the entire trial; it was like other evidence and was subject to the same rules of admissibility. This argument was strained: it ignored the far-reaching effects of a coerced confession, which, unlike other types of evidence, cast a shadow over the entire case, both for prosecution and defense. But the chief justice ignored these distinctions. There was a more important reason to adopt the harmless error rule: it was essential to preserve the central truth-seeking purpose of the criminal trial.[63] The goal was to convict the guilty, not restrain the government. Settled constitutional interpretations of due process stymied that function; the harmless error rule would promote it. Not only had the Court shifted its doctrinal stance, but its very tone was markedly different. The dominant philosophy of the emerging conservative majority was clear: criminal justice existed to convict the guilty, and judicial decisions that frustrated this end were impermissible.

Judicial restraint and a respect for federalism were other key themes of the new jurisprudence. The first principle required deference to legislative authority; the second, to state practice. Judges could only interpret whether or not the law was constitutional in its form and application. Few jurists disputed this standard. Not even the Warren Court at the height of its rule making in *Miranda* believed that it had violated these bounds. But the Rehnquist Court made these concepts a touchstone of its philosophy. In practice, the justices retreated from broad constitutional decisions and determined case by case whether a practice was acceptable. This approach marked a return to the fair-trial standard that guided the pre-Warren Court. Fairness was the essential constitutional requirement of due process, and states might achieve this result in a variety of ways. Indeed, the justices concluded, the federal principle demanded that the Court respect the states' authority to control criminal process, Madison's warnings to the contrary.

By what measures did the justices determine fairness? Tradition and reason were the two criteria used in *Schad v. Arizona* (1991), a case involving the constitutionality of certain instructions to the jury. In determining what was due process, Justice Souter wrote for the majority: "History and current practice are significant indicators of what we as a people regard as fundamentally fair and rational . . . which are nevertheless always open to critical examination."[64] There was nothing unique in these standards (the Warren Court used similar language), and it still left much to judicial interpretation. Too much, according to Justice Scalia, along with the chief justice the dominant intellectual force on the high bench. In his concurring opinion he wanted to restrict the criterion of judgment to history alone: "It is precisely the historical practices that *define* what is 'due.' 'Fundamental fairness' analysis may appropriately be applied to *departures* from traditional American conceptions of due process; but when judges test their individual notions of 'fairness' against an American tradition that is broad and deep and continuing, it is not the tradition that is on trial, but the judges" (emphasis in original).[65]

The contrast with the Warren Court could hardly have been more dramatic. Earl Warren had called for the "constant and creative application" of the Bill of Rights to new situations. This process implied continual revision of the catalog of rights, leaving "a document that will not have exactly the same meaning it had when we received it from our fathers" but one that would be better because it was "burnished by growing use."[66] The framers, especially Madison, had embraced a similar calculus of rights. The Rehnquist Court rejected this emphasis. Historical continuity, not change, became the new guiding principle.

Federalism too was a lodestar for the Rehnquist Court. *Coleman v. Thompson* (1991), which with other recent decisions sharply restricted a state prisoner's access to federal courts, is illustrative. The first sentence in Justice Sandra Day O'Connor's opinion for the six-to-three majority ("This is a case about federalism") established the grounds for the denial of federal habeas review when the prisoner missed the filing deadline for a state court appeal because of his attorney's error. But the text scanted a discussion about the proper division of power and ignored any question of rights in favor of a cost-benefit analysis: "Most of the price paid for federal review of state prisoner claims is paid by the State . . . in terms of the uncertainty and delay added to the enforcement of its criminal laws." Habeas corpus, while a bulwark against unfair convictions, entails significant costs, "the most significant of which is the cost in finality in criminal litigation." And in overruling *Fay v. Noia* (1963), the Warren Court decision that expanded federal review of habeas petitions, "we now recognize the important interest in finality served by state procedural rules, and the significant harm to the States that results from the failure of the federal courts to respect them."[67]

Justice Harry Blackmun, joined by Justices Marshall and John Paul Stevens, rebuked his colleagues in a stinging dissent: "Displaying obvious exasperation with the breadth of substantive federal habeas doctrine and the expansive protection afforded by the Fourteenth Amendment's guarantee of fundamental fairness in state criminal proceedings, the Court today continues its crusade to erect petty procedural barriers in the path of any state prisoner seeking review of his federal constitutional claims." Where was the concern for the petitioner Coleman's rights, especially since he was under sentence of death? These rights are not an issue of federalism, they are constitutional guarantees and as such are superior to state interests. Federal review exists not to diminish state authority but "to ensure that federal rights were not improperly denied a federal forum." Most unsettling was the majority's "blind abdication of responsibility" and its willingness to replace "the discourse of rights . . . with the functional dialect of interests." The Court "now routinely, and without evident reflection, subordinates fundamental constitutional rights to mere utilitarian interests."[68] The goal of finality alone was not sufficient to compromise the protection of rights.

Federalism implies a diversity of practice, and the Rehnquist Court repeatedly demonstrated its willingness to accept different criminal procedures for different states, even if it meant reversing precedents only recently affirmed. Such was the case in *Payne v. Tennessee* (1991). Various states in the 1980s had enacted laws that permitted sentencing juries in capital cases to consider evidence about the victim when deciding whether or not to impose the death penalty. These statutes clearly represented a political response to public beliefs that the law favored the criminal and cared little for the victim of crime. In 1987 and 1989 the Court rejected victim impact evidence as a violation of the Eighth Amendment's ban on cruel and unusual punishment. *Payne* abruptly jettisoned these precedents.

Judicial opinions usually begin with a brief, dispassionate statement of the facts, but not so in this case. Rarely has a Court opinion made the description of a crime more vivid. Chief Justice Rehnquist, for the six-to-three majority, quoted extensively from the evidence at trial, emphasizing the bloody crime and the dissolute nature of the defendant: Payne appeared to be "sweating blood"; he had "a wild look about him. His pupils were contracted. He was foaming at the mouth." Rehnquist had set the stage for overturning *Booth v. Maryland* and *South Carolina v. Gathers*, the controlling precedents. These cases "unfairly weighted the scales in a criminal trial." Citing as authority the opinion of his fellow dissenting justices in the earlier cases, he rejected the notion that evidence about the victim leads to arbitrary decisions in capital cases, a result forbidden by the Eighth Amendment. In any event, the states must remain free "in capital cases, as well as others, to devise new procedures and new remedies to meet felt needs." Blind adherence to past mistakes would not accomplish these ends, especially when the precedents "were decided by the narrowest of margins, over spirited dissents."[69] Nowhere in evidence was the Warren Court's concern that due process protected the citizen from the overbearing power of the state. The new jurisprudence increasingly echoed the conservative politics of the past two decades. Now it was society that had to be protected from the effect of a citizen's constitutional rights.

The change in the Court's attitude and approach was painfully obvious to Justice Marshall, the sole holdover from the Warren era. "Power, not reason, is the new currency of this Court's decision making," he protested in dissent. "Neither the law nor the facts supporting Booth and Gathers underwent any change in the last four years. Only the personnel of this Court did." The admission of victim impact evidence, although unconstitutional in Marshall's view, was less consequential than the majority's disregard of stare decisis, or the doctrine that the Court will look to its precedent when deciding cases. Joined by Justice Blackmun, he charged that the Court had declared itself free to "discard any principle of constitutional liberty which was recognized or reaffirmed over the dissenting votes of four Justices and with which five or more Justices now disagree." The implications of this departure were radical and staggering: "the majority today sends a clear signal that scores of established liberties are now ripe for reconsideration."[70]

Marshall's view was more than the lament of an isolated liberal justice. The Court's recent decisions foreshadowed an end, if not a reversal, of the due process revolution. Justice Scalia's concurring opinion in *Payne*—and the majority's actions throughout the 1991 term—suggested that the Court in future cases would be less inclined to continue or extend constitutional protection to what it now viewed as mere procedural rules. "Considerations of *stare decisis* are at their acme in cases involving property and contract rights, where reliance interests are involved; the opposite is true in cases such as the present one involving procedural and evidentiary rules."[71] If so, then the Court was rejecting a legacy that far predated the Warren Court. It was, after all, Justice Felix Frankfurter, one of the century's staunchest advocates of judicial restraint, who over fifty years earlier cautioned that "the history of American freedom is, in no small measure, the history of procedure."[72]

Much more certain was the Court's new direction, at least for rights of the accused. Federalism and the diversity of state practice it implies had once again become a touchstone for the conservative majority, which saw it as a return to the framers' first principles. But this constitutional scheme of dividing power had not protected individual liberties as the first generation had intended. The due process revolution of the 1960s occurred in large measure because the states failed to protect the minimal liberties guaranteed by their own constitutions.

One consequence of this deference to the states would be a diminishment of the notion of equal justice. But it is questionable, as the Warren Court realized, whether local standards of due process are appropriate or meaningful in a highly mobile national society, especially when states have repeatedly created artificial distinctions between their citizens. It is also instructive to recall Madison's concern that the states ultimately could not protect individual rights in the face of public pressure to abridge them: "The invasion of private rights is *cheifly* [sic] to be apprehended, not from acts of Government contrary to the sense of its constituents, but from acts in which the Government is the mere instrument of the major number of the constituents."[73]

What may be most troubling, however, is the suggestion that the goal of criminal justice, indeed its sole standard, is convicting the guilty. This attitude makes rights of the accused subject to experimentation, dependent upon the will of a popular majority. But rights are fundamental. They are essential to our conception of personal liberty. They exist, as Madison recognized two centuries ago, to protect individuals against arbitrary government and oppressive majorities. The Bill of Rights will never prevent all injustices, nor does the original expression of them contain all the rights found necessary to due process. But neither are they subject to diminishment without the loss of liberty. This should be the lesson from our past: we are most faithful to the framers—and to our own freedom—when we strive to advance their legacy of protecting each citizen from the power of overzealous government and from ourselves.

NOTES

1. Daniel T. Rodgers, "Rights Consciousness in American History," in David J. Bodenhamer and James W. Ely Jr., eds., *The Bill of Rights in Modern America: After 200 Years* (Bloomington: Indiana University Press, 1993), 3.

2. The intervening Seventh Amendment guarantees the right to a jury trial in most civil cases.

3. *Frazier v. United States*, 419 F. 2d 1161, 1176 (1969).

4. Stephen J. Markham, "Foreword: The 'Truth in Criminal Justice' Series," *Journal of Law Reform* 22 (1989): 425, 428.

5. An opposite view is expressed in Akhil Reed Amar, *The Constitution and Criminal Procedure: First Principles* (New Haven, Conn.: Yale University Press, 1997), 90: "The deep principles underlying the Sixth Amendment's three clusters and many clauses (and, I submit, underlying constitutional criminal procedure generally) are the protection of the innocent and the pursuit of truth." Significantly, Amar bases his claim on a parsing of the text, not on a detailed reading of historical evidence.

6. *Shaughnessy v. United States*, 345 U.S. 206, 224 (1953).

7. Zechariah Chafee Jr., *How Human Rights Got into the Constitution* (Boston: Boston University Press, 1952), 44.

8. John Phillip Reid, *The Concept of Liberty in the Age of Revolution* (Chicago: University of Chicago Press, 1988), 11–38; Forrest McDonald, *Novus Ordo Secloram* (Lawrence: University Press of Kansas, 1985), 9–55.

9. Bradley Chapin, *Criminal Justice in Colonial America, 1606–1660* (Athens: University of Georgia Press, 1983), 61, lists over sixteen procedural rights guaranteed in the several colonial codes, including no search and seizure without warrant, right to reasonable bail, grand jury indictment in capital cases, trial by jury, and no cruel and unusual punishment, among others.

10. John Phillip Reid, *Constitutional History of the American Revolution: The Authority of Rights* (Madison: University of Wisconsin Press, 1986), 47–59.

11. David J. Bodenhamer, *Fair Trial: Rights of the Accused in American History* (New York: Oxford University Press, 1992), 40.

12. Henry Steele Commager, *The Empire of Reason: How Europe Imagined and American Realized the Enlightenment* (Garden City, N.Y.: Doubleday, 1977), 219.

13. Robert Allen Rutland, *The Birth of the Bill of Rights* (Chapel Hill: University of North Carolina Press, 1963), 126–218.

14. Kenneth R. Bowling, "'A Tub to the Whale': The Founding Fathers and Adoption of the Bill of Rights," *Journal of the Early Republic* 8 (1988): 223–52.

15. Jack N. Rakove, *Original Meanings: Politics and Ideas in the Making of the Constitution* (New York: Knopf, 1996), 333.

16. Ibid., 335. In a letter to Madison, Jefferson wrote, "In the arguments in favor of a declaration of rights, you omit one which has great weight with me, the legal check which it puts in the hands of the judiciary."

17. Ibid., 338–39.

18. Chief Justice John Fortescue of the Court of King's Bench in the mid–fifteenth century wrote, "Indeed, one would much rather that twenty guilty persons should escape the punishment of death, than one innocent person should be condemned and suffer capitally." Quoted in Chapin, *Criminal Justice in Colonial America*, 3.

19. Richard D. Younger, *People's Panel: The Grand Jury in the United States, 1634–1941* (Providence, R.I.: Brown University Press, 1963), 56–84. There was a strong democratic impulse behind the attacks on the nineteenth-century grand jury, at least during the antebellum decades. See David J. Bodenhamer, "Criminal Justice and Democratic Theory in Antebellum America: The Grand Jury Debate in Indiana," *Journal of the Early Republic* 5 (Winter 1985): 281–302.

20. Bodenhamer, *Fair Trial*, 86.

21. Albert W. Alschuler, "Plea Bargaining and Its History," *Columbia Law Review* 79 (January 1979): 1–43.

22. For a case study of how this practice developed in one American jurisdiction in the nineteenth century, see Lawrence M. Friedman and Robert V. Percival, *The Roots of Justice: Crime and Punishment in Alameda County, California, 1870–1910* (Chapel Hill: University of North Carolina Press, 1981), 237–60.

23. *Boyd v. United States*, 116 U.S. 616, 632 (1886). The characterization of Boyd's effect on the Fourth Amendment was made by Justice William Brennan in *Abel v. United States*, 362 U.S. 217, 255 (1960).

24. *Weeks v. United States*, 232 U.S. 383, 393 (1914).

25. Bradford P. Wilson, "The Fourth Amendment as More Than a Form of Words: The View from the Founding," in Eugene W. Hickok Jr., ed., *The Bill of Rights: Original Meaning and Current Understanding* (Charlottesville: University of Virginia Press, 1991), 167–68.

26. Bodenhamer, *Fair Trial*, 88–91.

27. *Powell v. Alabama*, 287 U.S. 45 (1932).

28. *Palko v. Connecticut*, 302 U.S. 319, 325–26 (1937).

29. Bodenhamer, *Fair Trial*, 92–108.

30. *Breithaupt v. Abram*, 352 U.S. 432, 442 (1957).

31. *Ohio ex rel. Eaton v. Price*, 364 U.S. 274 (1960).

32. See, in general, Richard C. Cortner, *The Supreme Court and the Second Bill of Rights: The Fourteenth Amendment and the Nationalization of Civil Liberties* (Madison: University of Wisconsin Press, 1981).

33. Earl Warren, *The Memoirs of Earl Warren* (Garden City, N.Y.: Doubleday, 1977), 332.

34. G. Edward White, *Earl Warren: A Public Life* (New York: Oxford University Press, 1982), 217–30, 358–69.

35. *Gideon v. Wainwright*, 372 U.S. 335 (1963). A classic study of the case is Anthony Lewis, *Gideon's Trumpet* (New York: Random House, 1964).

36. As quoted in Cortner, *Supreme Court and the Second Bill of Rights*, 196.

37. *Malloy v. Hogan*, 378 U.S. 1 (1964).

38. *Pointer v. Texas*, 380 U.S. 400 (1965).

39. Ibid., 405.

40. The theory of selective incorporation, accepted in *Malloy v. Hogan* (1964), held that the due process clause of the Fourteenth Amendment incorporated many of the rights of the first eight amendments, thus restraining state discretion to adopt different criminal procedures.

41. *Mapp v. Ohio*, 367 U.S. 656 (1961).

42. Bodenhamer, *Fair Trial*, 114–16, 122–24.

43. *Massiah v. United States*, 377 U.S. 201 (1964); *Escobedo v. Illinois*, 378 U.S. 478 (1964); *Miranda v. Arizona* 384 U.S. 457 (1966).

44. The rule of automatic reversal has governed coerced confession cases since *Malinski v. New York*, 324 U.S. 401 (1945).

45. *Miranda v. Arizona*, 457.

46. Ibid., 470–75.

47. Anthony Lewis, "A Talk with Warren on Crime, the Court, and the Country," *New York Times Magazine*, 19 October 1969, 126.

48. *Miranda v. Arizona*, 572.

49. See, generally, Liva Baker, *Miranda: Crime, Law, and Politics* (New York: Atheneum, 1985).

50. Ibid., 508.

51. Leonard W. Levy, "History and Judicial History," in Virginia Van der Veer

Hamilton, ed., *Hugo Black and the Bill of Rights: Proceedings of the First Hugo Black Symposium in American History on "The Bill of Rights and American Democracy"* (University: University of Alabama Press, 1978), 24.

52. *Chapman v. California*, 386 U.S. 24 (1967).

53. *Duncan v. Louisiana*, 391 U.S. 150 (1968).

54. *Benton v. Maryland*, 395 U.S. 784, 790–95 (1968).

55. *New York Times*, 4 July 1971, 1-A.

56. *United States v. Harris*, 403 U.S. 582 (1971).

57. *United States v. Calandra*, 414 U.S. 348, 354 (1974).

58. *United States v. Leon*, 468 U.S. 897 (1984).

59. Only in cases involving the death penalty did the Court move beyond the Warren Court's conception of defendants' rights. See Bodenhamer, *Fair Trial*, 132–36.

60. *Colorado v. Connelly*, 479 U.S. 157 (1986). Four years later, the Court declined six to two to weaken Miranda further by holding that once the suspect requested counsel all questioning must stop until a lawyer was present, whether or not the accused had consulted with an attorney. *Minnick v. Mississippi*, 498 U.S. 146 (1990).

61. *United States v. Salerno*, 481 U.S. 739 (1987).

62. *Arizona v. Fulminante*, 499 U.S. 279, 310 (1991).

63. Ibid., 310. Rehnquist quoted with approval from an earlier case that the harmless error doctrine is essential to preserve "the principle that the central purpose of a criminal trial is to decide the factual question of the defendant's guilt or innocence, and promotes public respect for the criminal process by focusing on the underlying fairness of the trial rather than on the virtually inevitable presence of immaterial error."

64. *Schad v. Arizona*, 501 U.S. 624, 642 (1991).

65. Ibid., 650.

66. Earl Warren, "The Law and the Future," *Fortune* (November 1955): 106, 226.

67. *Coleman v. Thompson*, 501 U.S. 722, 726, 738, 750 (1991).

68. Ibid., 758–59, 764–65.

69. *Payne v. Tennessee*, 501 U.S. 808, 813, 828 (1991).

70. Ibid., 850.

71. Ibid., 848.

72. *Malinski v. New York*, 324 U.S. 414 (1941).

73. As quoted in Rakove, *Original Meaning*, 332.

3 The Twelfth Amendment

David P. Currie

The Twelfth Amendment, ratified in 1804, was designed to remedy a simple defect in Article II's original provisions for election of the president and vice president in order to enhance effectuation of the country's will. That apparently simple task proved both more difficult and more controversial than one would be likely to expect. Moreover, the amendment soon proved to have an unfortunate side effect that was surely not intended, although it was by no means unforeseen. From the beginning opponents complained that the amendment would diminish the quality of the vice president, and it did. But perhaps the most abiding lesson of the intricate debates on the proposal is what a tricky and difficult business it is to draft amendments to the Constitution.

It looked great on paper. The electors were to vote for the two people they thought best qualified to be president. The one who came in second would take over if the president was unable to perform his duties and in the meantime would preside over the Senate. If anything happened to the president, we would be in good hands.[1]

It worked beautifully the first three times. Twice the electors chose George Washington and John Adams; then they chose Adams and Thomas Jefferson. It is hard to see how they could have done better. It went haywire in 1800. Nobody voted for two possible presidents. Republicans voted for Thomas Jefferson, whom they wanted to be president. They also voted for Aaron Burr, who they thought would make a good vice president. Federalist electors did the same thing for John Adams and one of the Pinckneys.[2]

The Republicans won. Both of them. And then, because there was no way for the electors to make clear which of their favorites was to occupy which office, it fell to the House of Representatives to choose between them.[3] The Federalists voted for Aaron Burr, who was supposed to be vice president. It took thirty-six ballots before one of them flinched, and the country almost ended up with no president at all.[4] The growth of political parties had wrecked the framers' well-laid plans.[5]

Any thinking person could see that something had to be done. The Federalists, except Hamilton, disagreed.[6]

Jefferson took office in March 1801; Congress did not meet again until December. Not long afterward the New York legislature petitioned Congress to propose a constitutional amendment requiring electors to vote separately for president and vice president so that the debacle of 1800 would not occur again.[7] In the future the president would be someone the electors had wanted to be president. We would live happily ever after.

But the Republicans in Congress were too busy dismantling the federal courts to pay attention. It was not until May 1802, as the session drew to a close, that Republican representative Philip Van Cortlandt of New York moved to consider the proposed amendment. Some of his colleagues protested that there was no time to do so, but the House voted to take up the proposal, the speaker conveniently ruling that a two-thirds majority was not required.[8]

Samuel Mitchill of New York explained that the electoral machinery designed by the framers no longer worked, and after ten weeks of inaction the House rammed the proposed amendment through in a single day, without significant debate on the merits. It was a simple matter, said Lucas Elmendorf of New York; it did not require much discussion. It did look simple, and the text of the proposal expressed it simply: "That in all future elections of President and Vice President, the persons voted for shall be particularly designated, by declaring which is voted for as President, and which as Vice President." But James Bayard of Delaware, who at this point professed to believe in designation, warned that the question might prove more difficult than it seemed, and events certainly bore out his prediction.[9] The proposal fell short by a single vote in the Senate, and it was not taken up in the following session.[10]

The Republicans got serious about their amendment when the Eighth Congress met in October 1803. On the first day of the session Congressman John Dawson of Virginia reintroduced the proposal for separate ballots in the House, and within a few days New York's new senator, DeWitt Clinton, was heard attempting to hustle it through the Senate without committee consideration while the Tennessee and Vermont legislatures were still in session.[11] The next presidential election was fast approaching; the sponsors wanted to take no chances.

More thoughtful supporters, however, perceived that to require the electors to vote separately for president and vice president would necessitate changes in other provisions of Article II as well, and it was nearly two months before the amendment was finally dispatched to the states.[12] The Federalists put up a battle royal.

Let's get it out of the way at the outset. The Federalists had selfish partisan reasons for opposing the Twelfth Amendment. Knowing they were unlikely to be able to muster a majority of the electors in the foreseeable future, they did their best to preserve the unholy possibility that they might be able to choose between their opponents in the House. But base motives often engender good arguments, and we learned a lot from the Federalists during the lengthy debate.[13] A surprising number of issues were raised and discussed. Let us take them one at a time.[14]

The Basic Objection

Under the original plan, said the Federalists, the vice president was a person the electors thought would make a good president; he was the one who came in second in the presidential race. If there were separate ballots, that would no longer be the case. Electors would choose as vice president someone they thought would be a good vice president, and since the responsibilities of that officer were trivial, they would tend to select someone of inferior talents. When the president disappeared, we would be stuck with an inferior president.[15] That sounded right enough, and events promptly confirmed the Federalists' forebodings. In the very next election the Republicans placed the mantle on George Clinton of New York.

Longtime governor of that state and president of its convention to ratify the Constitution, Clinton had been a political figure of some significance.[16] By 1805, however, he was sixty-six years old, and he could no longer cut the mustard. "Mr. Clinton," wrote John Quincy Adams in 1806, "is totally ignorant of all the most common forms of proceeding in Senate. . . . His judgment is neither quick nor strong. . . . In this respect a worse choice than Mr. Clinton could scarcely have been made."[17]

Clinton's problem was not one simply of inexperience. Senator William Plumer of New Hampshire, who from the first had feared that the "aged old gentleman" would "make a sorry figure" as vice president, was unsparing in his condemnation after Clinton had been in office for over two years.[18]

> The Vice President preserves very little order in the Senate. If he ever had, he certainly has not now, the requisite qualifications of a presiding officer. . . . [H]e has more than once declared bills at the third reading when they had been read but once—Puts questions without any motion being made—Sometimes declares it a vote before any vote has been taken. And sometimes before one bill is decided proceeds to another. From want of authority, & attention to order he has prostrated the dignity of the Senate.[19]

Buoyed by these encomiums, Clinton was reelected by an overwhelming majority in 1808 and might have continued in office indefinitely, had he not mercifully been called to his reward just before the next election in 1812.[20]

Clinton was by no means unique. Republicans of the Virginia Dynasty never squandered their star players by putting them on hold; Madison, Monroe, and the second Adams all moved to the presidency from the responsible office of secretary of state.[21] It was a risky strategy, for in the meantime the Constitution required that if anything happened to the president someone patently less competent would take his place. Fortunately the presidents of the period were sturdy, and neither Clinton nor his less than illustrious successors were called upon to step into the president's oversized shoes until the electors made the mistake of selecting an elderly chief executive in 1840. By that time the tradition of mediocrity was well established, and the country ended up with nearly four years of John Tyler.[22]

There have been exceptions, of course: John C. Calhoun, Theodore Roosevelt, Lyndon Johnson, Hubert Humphrey.[23] But third-rate vice presidents were not just an early-nineteenth-century phenomenon.[24] Who was Taft's vice president? Woodrow Wilson's? Herbert Hoover's?[25] The Twelfth Amendment is stacked against selection of a vice president qualified to take over the presidency.[26]

The trouble with the Federalist argument was that the rise of political parties had already frustrated the framers' expectation that the second-best person would become vice president. Aaron Burr and C. C. Pinckney were a far cry from George Clinton, but few would have said either of them ought to be president in 1800. Electors voted for them in the expectation they would end up as vice president, just as they would have under the Twelfth Amendment. Clinton would probably have been elected even if the amendment had never been adopted.

There was an alternative to separate ballots that would have both avoided a repetition of the 1800 deadlock and restored the integrity of the vice presidency, and it is instructive that no one seriously suggested it. The amendment had only to provide that each elector cast one vote for president instead of two. For it was the requirement that electors cast two votes that had caused all the trouble. Let each elector pick only the best candidate, and there would no longer be conscious votes for individuals of lesser stature. Never again would there be a tie between a party's presidential and vice presidential candidates. The best aspirant would be president, the second his understudy, just as the framers had originally intended.

But it wouldn't do anymore, would it? The rise of political parties had ruined this part of the framers' plans too. Once people began to vote for programs instead of personalities, to put the leader of the losing party in position to succeed to the presidency would frustrate the popular will.

Do We Need a Vice President?

There had been complaints about the vice presidency from the beginning. The presence of the president's surrogate at the head of the supposedly independent Senate generated uneasiness on the score of separation of powers, and it seemed a prodigious waste of talent to reduce the country's second citizen to the role of parliamentarian.[27] Presidential succession could have been assured by designating some officer of real responsibility, as was done when the vice presidency was vacant. Once the party system had made it increasingly likely that the vice president would be a cretin, the case for abolishing the office became even stronger. The prospect of separate ballots for president and vice president, by guaranteeing that the president would be succeeded by a person nobody thought should occupy that office, seemed to put the last nail in the coffin. As soon as the amendment was introduced in the Eighth Congress, New Jersey senator Jonathan Dayton moved to abolish the vice presidency.[28]

Even some Republicans expressed sympathy for this proposal, and no one attacked it on its merits. But DeWitt Clinton opposed it as an effort "to put off or get rid of the main question," and it lost. A similar fate befell a similar effort in the House.[29]

Clinton was probably right as a matter of strategy. One of the Federalist tactics was to complicate the issue and divide the supporters by ornamenting the proposed amendment with all sorts of additional suggestions, some of them attractive enough on their own but all calculated to divert attention from the object in view. Republican leaders doggedly insisted that the main issue be presented as simply as possible in order to maximize the chances of adoption and thus rejected additional proposals even when brought forward by their own members.[30] Now was not the time to limit the president to two terms, to require that electors be chosen by the people, to make persons born in Louisiana eligible for the presidency, and least of all to try to reallocate representation—and thus electoral strength—in proportion to the number of free citizens. Nor was it the time to consider Dayton's proposal to eliminate the office of vice president.[31]

Nearly two hundred years have since passed, and apparently it is still not time. Four additional amendments have dealt with the presidency, two of them with the problem of presidential succession.[32] Yet the vice presidency, with all its warts, remains. Indeed, the country's most recent pronouncement on the subject went so far as to *enhance* the vice presidency by requiring the president (with congressional approval) to fill the office when it becomes vacant, thus reducing the likelihood that the president will be replaced by a person entrusted with important governmental responsibilities to pretty near zero.[33]

Thus there is an uncanny staying power to the notion of the vice presidency as we know it. Is there something to be said for it after all? There may be.

It is obviously imperative that presidential succession be specified in advance. When the president is out of the picture, there must never be the scintilla of a doubt as to who is in charge. But that does not prove that there should be a separate office of vice president. It means only that the law—preferably the Constitution, to obstruct partisan tinkering—must make clear who is next in line, as statutes have done since 1792 for cases in which there is no vice president.[34] The great advantage of an independent vice presidency is that without it presidential duties would fall to someone who had been chosen by Congress or who had not been elected at all.[35]

One of the objections voiced when the president pro tempore was initially placed second in line after the vice president was that it undermined the framers' determined efforts to minimize the possibility that a president might be selected by and thus beholden to Congress.[36] A vice president chosen by electors independent of the legislature reinforces the separation of powers. To give precedence to a cabinet officer, as the statute once did in the case of a double vacancy, vests presidential authority in an officer chosen neither by the people nor by their representatives.[37] A vice president chosen by presidential electors reinforces the democratic principle.

The Twenty-fifth Amendment is in this respect a compromise. Once the vice presidency is vacant there is no time for a new election, and the old electors' mandate is out of date. Nomination by the president reduces the risk that the new vice president will be an instrument of Congress; congressional approval ensures that the possible future president be acceptable to the representatives of the people.

It may be that we really do live in the best of all possible worlds.

What If the Electors Can't Decide?

Article II had contemplated two situations in which the electors might prove unable to select a president: two candidates might receive the same number of votes from a majority of electors, as Jefferson and Burr did in 1800, or there might be no candidate with a majority.[38] In either case, the House of Representatives, with each state having one vote, was to make the choice.[39]

By limiting each elector to a single vote for president, the proposed amendment eliminated the possibility that there might be two candidates with a majority. Whatever the number of votes, it is impossible for two people each to have more than half of them.[40] But the possibility remained that the electors might scatter their votes with such prodigality that there was no majority at all. Maryland representative Joseph Nicholson proposed to deal with this case as it had always been dealt with: the House would choose among those five individuals who had received the greatest number of electoral votes.[41]

This simple solution proved to be highly controversial. It made sense to choose among five candidates, James Jackson of Georgia argued, when they were to fill two offices; now that the president was to be chosen separately, the same reasoning suggested a choice among no more than three for each position.[42] Moreover, as Jackson reminded the Senate, John Jay had been fifth on the list in 1800; under Clinton's similar proposal the House could have made him president, although the electors had given him only one vote.[43]

"The intention of the constitution," said Senator Samuel Maclay of Pennsylvania, was "that the people, not the House of Representatives, should choose the President."[44] "By taking the number three instead of five," said Virginia senator Wilson Cary Nicholas, "you place the choice with more certainty in the people at large, and render the choice more consonant to their wishes."[45] Senator Adams argued that reducing the number from five to three would injure the smaller states. "Filling the blank with three," he insisted, "will be excluding the candidates from the small States from the House—& may materially affect their rights."[46]

In thus attempting to divide the supporters of the amendment, Adams was opening an old wound. The great compromise of the constitutional convention, the reader will recollect, was between the large states (which obtained representation proportional to population in the House) and the small (which were awarded equal representation in the Senate). Very early in the debate Senator Pierce Butler of South Carolina, who was not even a Federalist, had argued that the amendment itself would injure the smaller states by making it possible for a few large states to select both the president and the vice president.[47] Appropriately, it was Samuel White of little Delaware who elaborated this contention. The five largest states—Massachusetts, New York, Pennsylvania, Virginia, and North Carolina—possessed a clear majority of electoral votes. If electors voted separately for president and vice president, these five states might "totally exclude" the remaining states "from any participation in the election."[48]

Plainspoken Senator Jackson pointed out the improbability of a combination between Federalist Massachusetts and Republican Virginia.[49] White was hysterical if he was honest. But there was a more fundamental objection to White's argument. Since each elector had two votes under the original constitutional provision, the large states had *always* been able to choose both president and vice president.

It was true that an attempt to do so was somewhat risky under the original provisions. In order to avoid a tie between its two candidates, the majority faction had to withhold votes from one of them. If it withheld too many (as the Federalists had done in 1796), it would lose the vice presidency.[50] If it withheld too few, opposition electors could sabotage its plans by voting for the majority's vice presidential candidate. As Albert Gallatin had observed, a single Federalist elector could have made Aaron Burr president in 1800.[51]

But that was only to say that Article II lent itself to manipulation in order to frustrate the wishes of a majority of the electors. It took a lot of gall to turn this defect into an argument *in favor* of the original provisions. It would seem more convincing to say it was too high a price to pay for whatever ephemeral boost the old system gave to the possibility of electing a candidate from one of the smaller states.

Adams's contention that the small states were injured by reducing the number of House presidential choices from five to three was more subtle. The idea seemed to be that if the House could consider more candidates, the larger states could not name all of them; someone from one of the small states was more likely to be on the list. And then, because each state had an equal voice in the House's choice, the small states might band together to select a president of their own.[52]

To attack this proposition on the grounds that it was undemocratic to allow a small fraction of the population to choose the president was to challenge the principle of the rule that the House was to vote by states in selecting a president and of the great compromise on which it was based.[53] There was something to be said for the response that any choice of the executive by members of the legislature was an uncomfortable erosion of the separation of powers that ought to be permitted only in the case of unavoidable necessity.[54] But the best argument against all the hand wringing about the rights of small states may have been that those who engaged in it were living in Never-Never-Land. The horror stories they conjured up seem altogether too Machiavellian to be convincing.

After much palaver the House opted to allow itself to choose among the top five contenders.[55] In the Senate, small-state Republicans displayed a marked lack of enthusiasm for allowing the House to choose among five candidates, and party discipline prevailed. As Maryland senator Robert Wright emphasized, the important thing was that the electors should vote separately for president and vice president; it did not much matter whether in default of their choice the House should choose among five candidates or three. The House ultimately accepted the Senate's decision that the choice should be made from the top three candidates.[56] The first president elected from a really small state was Franklin Pierce in 1852.[57]

What If the House Can't Decide?

It was not very important, said South Carolina representative Benjamin Huger, whether the House opted for Jefferson or for Burr in 1800: "I cannot persuade myself that the political salvation of the Republic depends upon the election of any man as President." The real lesson of the 1800 election was that some provision must be made for the case in which neither the electors nor the House was able to select a president.[58]

There was no provision for this case in the original Constitution. The vice president was to take over in a variety of contingencies but not if no president was elected.[59] Indeed, such a provision would have been pointless under the original Article II, since there was no vice president until the president was chosen.[60] Nor could Congress provide for such a case pursuant to its authority to secure succession when there was no vice president, for the inability to elect a president was not among the contingencies contemplated by that provision.[61]

Designed as it was with the single object of providing for separate ballots, the initial amendment proposal contained no solution for this problem either.[62] No sooner had Federalist senators lost the skirmish over how many candidates to put before the House than Thomas Pickering of Massachusetts proposed to plug the lacuna by providing that if the House made no choice within twenty-four hours, "then the President shall be chosen by law."[63] Samuel Smith of Maryland noted that the Federalists had contemplated such a course in 1800 and that anyone who had taken it "would have met the fate of an usurper, and his head would not have remained on his shoulders twenty-four hours." Pickering's motion did not prevail.[64] Pickering's suggestion that Congress might choose the president by lot was greeted with ridicule.[65] Huger's passing reference to a resolution on the basis of age was ignored.[66] Senator Adams then moved that if the House failed to make a timely choice, the vice president should assume the president's duties.[67] This expedient was now practicable, since failure to choose a president no longer frustrated selection of his successor.[68] It was also logical, since the whole point of having a vice president was to take over when the presidency was empty.[69]

Yet as Representative James Elliott of Vermont argued, it was also perverse. The purpose of the proposed amendment was to ensure that the electors' choice of a president was respected. To give presidential responsibilities to a vice president chosen by separate ballot would guarantee that they were exercised by someone whom no elector had wanted to be president. "I therefore think the amendment will make the Constitution worse than it now is," Elliott concluded, "believing as I do that it may bring a man into the Presidency, not contemplated by the people for that office."[70]

Connecticut representative Calvin Goddard said that if the House was unable to choose a president, there ought to be a new election.[71] That was all very well, but elections take time and might fail to produce more satisfactory results. As Goddard acknowledged, someone must be designated "to administer in the meantime," and arguments would begin all over as to who it should be.[72]

When the shouting was over, both Houses had agreed that if the House was unable to choose a president, the vice president should carry out his duties.[73] Pennsylvania representative John Smilie appeared to sum up the prevailing sentiment: in this marginal situation it was better to hand the reins of government to a person nobody had wanted to hold them than to risk having no amendment at all.[74]

Choosing the Vice President

Under the original Constitution the choice of a vice president was simple: the honor, such as it was, fell to the disappointed presidential hopeful who had received the most electoral votes. It was either a consolation prize or a penance in the eye of the aspiring beholder. Now the vice president was to be chosen separately. But how? As introduced, the resolution provided that "the person having the highest number of votes for Vice President, shall be Vice President." If two or more individuals tied for first place, the Senate would choose between them.[75]

The first amendment to the proposal offered in the Senate was to require a majority of electoral votes to choose a vice president.[76] That had been and remained the criterion for selecting the president, but in the case of the vice president the original Article II contained no such provision.[77] That omission, said Virginia senator John Taylor, was deliberate; to require a majority would make the election of a vice president more difficult.[78]

The institution of a separate ballot for vice president, replied Stephen Bradley of Vermont, called for a departure from the original provision. It was imperative that the individual who might step in for the president be a person of great respectability. So long as the vice president was runner-up in the presidential contest, his respectability was assured. With that security removed, an alternate guarantee must be devised; like the president, the vice president must enjoy the support of a majority of electors. Senator Wright agreed: the original provision for election by a mere plurality was not "consonant with the spirit of representative democracy." The Senate accepted Bradley's majority rule, and no one challenged it in the House.[79]

This new requirement made it necessary to provide for the possibility that no candidate would receive a majority, and Bradley looked to the presidential provisions for an analogy: as the House was to choose a president from the top three candidates, the Senate should choose a vice president from the top two.[80] And thus, as under the original Constitution, two officers would emerge from the five candidates who got the most electoral votes.[81] The Senate adopted this suggestion as well, and it was not disputed in the House.[82]

It followed from Bradley's concern for a broad basis of support that if the vice president did not have a majority of the electors behind him, he must have a majority of the Senate, and his revision so required.[83] Indeed, continuing the analogy to the formula for election of the president by the House, it required "a majority of the whole number" of senators, as Article II required "a majority of all the states." It was this last provision that had produced the ultimate deadlock in 1800, for in that election Jefferson had won a majority of the states that were able to cast their votes.[84]

The particular difficulty in 1800 had been that two states were equally divided and thus unable to vote for either candidate. There was no risk of a deadlocked state delegation in Bradley's proposal, as the senators were to vote as individuals, not as states.[85] The lean requirement that the Senate choose between two rather than three candidates also made a clear choice much more likely. Yet there were other ways in which both candidates might still fall short of a majority of all senators. Since there was normally an even number of senators, if the vice president was missing there might be a tie; since a majority of *all* senators was needed, absences might deprive even a candidate favored by more than half of those voting of the number requisite to election. Something therefore had to be done for the case in which both the electors and the Senate were unable to select a vice president.

This issue became acute once it was suggested that the vice president should assume the president's duties if no president was chosen. What happened if it proved impossible to elect either a president or a vice president? Punctilious Senator Adams had an answer for this problem too. If neither office could be filled, then presidential powers should be "discharged by such person as Congress may by law direct, until a new election may be had, in manner already prescribed by law."[86] James Hillhouse of Connecticut had an alternative solution. The Senate should choose someone to run the government "till the Electors may again meet and choose a President."[87] By this he seemed to mean the task should be assigned to the president pro tem.[88]

Hillhouse objected to Adams's solution on the grounds that "a period of agitation" was not the time to decide who should exercise presidential powers; he preferred "making provision by law before the happening of the event, for in a high state of party he could see no likelihood of an agreement." Adams said that was what he had in mind.[89] Thus the two proposals appeared to coalesce. Before a crisis arose, Congress should designate the officer who would become interim president in the event of a double electoral failure, just as, pursuant to Article II, it had done for the case of other double vacancies.[90] That officer, both Hillhouse and Adams seemed to assume, would be the president pro tempore, as in analogous cases under the existing law. The Senate would already have been called into session for 4 March, the day the outgoing president's term expired.[91] If by that time neither a president nor a vice president had been designated, the Senate would be obliged to name a president pro tem. That officer would then act as president until a special election could be held, and the crisis would be averted.[92]

It was a neat solution, though if the Senate could not choose a vice president, it was not clear why it would be able to choose a president pro tem in his place. Perhaps it was enough that, as Jackson pointed out in criticizing the proposal, on 4 March a third of the old senators would have lost their seats.[93] Like the provision for the vice president to act in default of a president, Adams's proposal meant that the post would probably be filled by a person the electors had not wanted; but this would be true only until the special election, and the Senate had already decided it was better than having no president at all.

Adams's proposal, however, was lost without a division.[94] The gap that had threatened the country in 1800 had been narrowed, but it was not closed. If neither a president nor a vice president was selected by 4 March, there was no way short of another constitutional amendment that either could be chosen until either the House or the Senate met again.

An additional minefield that could have blown the gap even wider was swept clean by the Senate, though it had been twice overlooked by the House. Article II had made no provision respecting the vice president's qualifications. It did not need to; it was pretty likely that whoever finished second in the presidential race, as the vice president then had to do, would be qualified to step in as president. Once the vice president was chosen on a separate ballot, this was no longer so certain. Under the amendment as proposed by the House, as Connecticut's Uriah Tracy archly pointed out, "we might have had a man in the Chief Magistracy from Morocco, a foreigner, who had not been in the country a month."[95] The unaltered provision that no one failing to satisfy the requirements of age, citizenship, and residence was "eligible to the office of President" might easily have been read to prevent that result, and it would be a foolish elector indeed who voted for a vice president who could not fulfill his central function.[96] But from the beginning the Senate took no chances on this one.[97] As adopted, the amendment provides flatly that "no person constitutionally ineligible to the office of president shall be eligible to that of vice president of the United States."[98]

Procedural Problems

We are not through yet. The debate over a separate ballot for the vice president also raised a host of difficult questions about the process of constitutional amendment.

The most basic question was whether the proposal could be adopted at all. The prominent role Article II gave the smaller states in electing the president, said Representative Samuel Thatcher of Massachusetts, was part of the price for other rights they had given up in accepting the new Constitution. "It follows, that although we may modify the forms of the Constitution, in such a manner as will operate equally upon all the States, we cannot, under the article providing for amendments, ingraft new principles into the Constitution which will destroy the rights of individual States, without the consent of those States."[99]

This was unvarnished invention. One with the curiosity to inspect Article V of the Constitution, which provides for amendments, will find no hint of it there. The basic provision is as broad as it can be: "The Congress, whenever two thirds of both Houses shall deem it necessary, shall propose amendments to this Constitution." Three explicit and inapplicable exceptions underscore the unqualified scope of this authority: when the framers wanted to limit the amending power, they said so.[100]

Constitutional language, of course, often means less than it appears to say. The judicial power, the tax power, and the commerce power have all been held limited by implicit considerations of state sovereignty despite the absence of supporting evidence in the text.[101] The power to admit new states is restricted by an equal-footing doctrine that is explicit only in the Northwest Ordinance, not in the Constitution.[102] And one of our most revered legal scholars has persuasively warned against interpreting the explicit authority to make "exceptions" to the appellate jurisdiction so broadly as to permit Congress "to destroy the essential role of the Supreme Court in the constitutional plan."[103]

Nevertheless, the Supreme Court has consistently declined to discover unwritten restrictions on the amending power, and for good reason.[104] The limitations that have been found implicit in other congressional powers derive from the Constitution itself: its conception of autonomous states as members of a federal union and the imperative of judicial enforcement of constitutional commands. The amending power is different not in degree but in kind. It makes no sense to argue that a measure is inconsistent with substantive constitutional principles when the question is whether to change the Constitution itself; constitutional amendments by definition are departures from the present Constitution.

Of course a constitution *could* provide that some of its provisions were so fundamental that they were not subject to the normal amendment process.[105] Article IV places an external restriction of this type on state constitutions by guaranteeing the states "a republican form of government."[106] Article V, as noted, contains three such limitations. Two of them expired by their own terms in 1808, suggesting that restrictions on the amending power were viewed as exceptions grudgingly conceded to expediency. The third, which survives in solitary splendor, preserves one of the most pernicious of all constitutional provisions, whose adoption had been central to the compromise that made the Constitution possible: "No state, without its consent, shall be deprived of its equal suffrage in the Senate."

It was on this unfortunate but inspired provision that Representative Thatcher built in fabricating his contention that the Constitution did not permit an amendment that would deprive the small states of the exaggerated importance Article II gave them in choosing a president in the House. Indeed, the underlying principle is identical. The equality of sovereign states, insofar as embodied in the Constitution, was a fundamental element of the deal struck between large and small states at Philadelphia; to alter it is to destroy the basis of the constitutional bargain.[107]

But that is not what the Constitution says. The terms of the bargain were spelled out with fitting precision in the document itself, for they were too important to be left to interpretation. The states were given an equal voice in the House selection of the president as well as in the Senate, but only the latter provision was expressly insulated from amendment. The very existence of this conspicuous exception argues against an implicit one for the role of the states in the House; the framers focused expressly on the need to protect state equality from the amending process and chose to protect only the equal power of the states in the Senate.[108] The Eighth Congress expended little energy on Thatcher's objection. Representative John Jackson of Virginia read Article V aloud and said it plainly authorized the proposed amendment; if a member who argued the contrary had "paid a proper attention to the subject, . . . he would not have hazarded the observation."[109]

In another respect, however, it was opponents of the proposed amendment who emphasized the latitude afforded by Article V to their exercise of judgment, and this time they were right. Several state legislatures had attempted to instruct or request their senators and representatives to fight for separate presidential and vice presidential ballots. Nobody argued that these expressions were binding, and Federalists insisted they were not.

Whether state legislatures could instruct senators at all had been debated from the beginning. State legislatures appointed them; in a very important sense they were meant to represent the states. In contrast to the Articles of Confederation, however, the Constitution did not provide for recall of senators by the bodies that had appointed them; the omission suggested that, once appointed, senators were expected to exercise their own judgment.[110] As had been pointed out in earlier discussions of the question, electors could not tell the president what to do after they chose him, and he could not issue instructions to judges he had placed (with Senate consent) on the federal bench.[111]

The generic issue of instructions to senators was left to one side in the debates over the Twelfth Amendment.[112] The argument that seemed to find universal acceptance was that the amending process was a special case. In this instance, said Representative Thatcher, "the Constitution has . . . made each House of Congress and the State Legislatures a check upon each other."[113] To permit one actor in this three-cornered drama to direct the actions of another would make nonsense of the explicit requirement that the Senate as well as the states agree to the proposal.[114]

As a last desperate gambit, defeated Federalists were heard to mumble that there should be a fourth actor in the play, the president of the United States. Article I, section 7 required that not only bills but "every order, resolution, or vote to which the concurrence of the Senate and House of Representatives may be necessary" (with the insignificant exception of adjournment) be submitted to the president for possible veto.[115]

This language was certainly broad enough to cover constitutional amendments. It was no objection that Article V expressly gave "Congress" the power to propose them; as Plumer noted, that was equally true of legislative powers under Article I.[116] Arguably, however, the special procedural safeguards of Article V itself—state ratification and a two-thirds vote of both Houses—were designed as a substitute for rather than a supplement to the veto provisions of Article I.[117] Congressional practice, of course, had already settled the question; none of the earlier amendments had been sent to the president for approval.[118] "As to precedents," Plumer confided to his diary, "I believe they are against the motion—but it is to be observed that they are precedents established without debate, or without a particular attention to the subject—& therefore they prove nothing."[119] This was not a bad point, and it applied in part to the Supreme Court's square holding on the subject, which nobody seems to have cited. The issue had been argued and decided in *Hollingsworth v. Virginia* in 1798, but the incomplete reports of the day fail to reveal any reasons that the Court may have given in support of its conclusion.[120]

In accord with that conclusion the Senate resolved twenty-three to seven that it was not necessary to submit the proposed amendment to the president. Each House then voted simply to ask him to transmit the proposal to the executives of the several states, that they might seek the legislative approval that Article V required.[121]

Two Thirds

One of the safeguards against improvident action that Article V imposed on the amending process was that of an extraordinary majority: "The Congress, whenever two thirds of both Houses shall deem it necessary, shall propose amendments to this Constitution." The debates laid bare two points of contention about the meaning of this requirement. On what questions was a two-thirds vote called for, and what constituted "two thirds of both Houses"?

The first of these issues arose on the first day of serious discussion in the Senate, when the president pro tempore (Kentucky senator John Brown) inquired whether an extraordinary majority was required on all votes respecting constitutional amendments. "A debate took place on this proposition," say the *Annals of Congress*, "tedious, intricate, and desultory, which it was very difficult to follow, and often to comprehend."[122]

Let us try to make it simple. Republican supporters of the proposed amendment who wanted to facilitate the process contended that the two-thirds requirement applied only to final approval of the proposal in each House. Federalist opponents, conceding that a simple majority might resolve mere procedural questions, tended to argue that a two-thirds vote was also required on preliminary votes affecting the substance of the proposal, such as on a motion to amend the resolution after it had been introduced or even to consider the subject in the first place.[123] The principal argument on each side was that the opposing position produced such absurd consequences that it could not have been intended.

Senator Plumer spelled out the Federalist approach for himself in his diary. *Not* to require a two-thirds vote on preliminary questions would permit a bare majority to "add to, or take from an amendment, such parts thereof, as will change the very *principles* of the original resolution—& thereby prevent two thirds of the senators from voting in favor of it."[124] This argument was dead on arrival. It would indeed be perverse to permit a simple majority to frustrate the desires of two thirds of the senators, but it is difficult to see how that could occur. If two thirds of the members support the original proposal, there is not likely to be a majority to change it.

Senator Wright made the opposite argument that to *require* a two-thirds vote in order to amend the proposal would permit a minority "to arrest every proposition . . . before it passed the threshold," but if there were not two thirds in favor of the change there was arguably little point in making it since it was not likely to be ultimately approved.[125] This last point may have been the strongest one available to the Federalists, but there is no record of their having made it. Israel Smith of Vermont tried to help them instead with another argument that Plumer spelled out best in his diary:

> When a bill is under consideration, every section at the second reading is passed in detail by the major[ity] vote; & no amendment whatever can obtain but by the same majority that is requisite to pass the bill itself at the third reading. And why should not the same two thirds be requisite to amend this resolution that is necessary for its final passage? The principle is the same.[126]

But it is not clear that the reason a majority is required to amend an ordinary bill is to ensure congruence between preliminary and ultimate voting requirements; to permit a minority to do so would be a startling departure from the normal democratic principle.

Senator Maclay tried to buttress the argument for a simple majority by invoking the Senate's constitutional authority to establish its own rules.[127] No Senate rule required an extraordinary majority on preliminary questions regarding constitutional amendments, he seemed to be saying, and there was no reason to adopt one. "It was fair to infer that in Legislative proceedings the simplest form was most eligible; who would apply a clumsy apparatus while one simple and sufficient was at hand?"[128]

This argument had implications far beyond the immediate issue before the Senate, and it was a little scary. Could the rules of the Senate really disfranchise its members by requiring a two-thirds majority to pass ordinary bills? Or does the constitutional vesting of authority in "Congress," reinforced by the reference to bills that pass "the House of Representatives and the Senate" and a scattering of exceptional provisions for an extraordinary majority, imply that a traditional majority vote is the constitutional norm?[129]

The Republican position prevailed in both Houses; on all preliminary questions a simple majority sufficed.[130] As Wright persuasively noted, this interpretation was in accord with past practice; though the question had never been so thoroughly discussed, neither House had ever required an extraordinary majority before the final vote.[131] Fortunately, there were enough alternate arguments on the merits of the issue that it cannot be said that the Senate embraced Maclay's unsettling proposition.[132] Indeed, the best argument was one not yet mentioned, and its author once again was Senator Wright: "Gentlemen cannot or will not keep in mind that the proposition before the House is not an alteration of the Constitution, but the formation of a proposition upon which two-thirds of the House must ultimately decide."[133] That is to say, the words of the Constitution supplied the answer: a two-thirds vote was required only to "propose" a constitutional amendment, not for preliminary skirmishing along the way. Senator Plumer rightly perceived that the purpose of the provision was "to render it difficult to attain amendments," but that purpose did not require that the rule be extended to preliminary questions, as he contended.[134] For the reason for making amendment difficult is to require a broad consensus before taking the grave step of altering the fundamental law; that purpose is fully satisfied by reading Article V according to its own terms to require a two-thirds vote only to approve the final proposal.

The second issue as to the meaning of the two-thirds requirement arose only at the end of the Senate proceedings, when the Senate voted twenty-two to ten to approve the proposed amendment. That meant that two thirds of the senators present and voting had endorsed it, but two senators were not recorded. Two thirds of thirty-four is twenty-three, and Tracy objected that Article V required two thirds of all members.[135] This objection was overruled too, but this time it was not so easy; the text of the Constitution did not resolve this question.

Senator Plumer set the parameters of the debate in a fine speech recorded in his diary but not in the *Annals*.[136] What Article V required was a two-thirds vote of "both Houses," that is, of the House and the Senate.[137] What was the Senate? Article I, section 3 said it was "composed of two Senators from each State." Two thirds of the Senate was therefore two thirds of all senators, just as Article I, section 5, which defined a quorum as a majority of "each House," was understood to require a majority of all its members.[138]

A comparison with other provisions requiring extraordinary majorities, Plumer argued, strengthened this conclusion. The impeachment and treaty provisions expressly required the concurrence of "two thirds of the members [or senators] present," but the amendment provision conspicuously did not; like the provision for overriding a presidential veto, it referred simply to two thirds of each "House."[139] Thus "the term *two thirds* as applied to either house, by the Constitution, includes two thirds of the whole number composing the House, unless the terms are particularly qualified"; when the framers meant two thirds of those present, they said so.[140]

Plumer closed his argument on this question with another powerful argument of consequences so intolerable that they could not have been intended:

> If the concurrence of *two-thirds* of all the members composing the Senate were not necessary to propose an amendment, it would follow that twelve Senators (the representatives of six States), when only a quorum is present, might propose an amendment contrary to the opinion & against the will of twenty two senators—And that the vote of these twelve who are but little more than *one* full *third* of the Senate, should be considered as constitutionally performing the act that required the concurrence of *two thirds*.[141]

It was not easy to reconcile such a result with the obvious purpose of Article V to require a broad consensus in order to amend the Constitution.

Roger Griswold of Connecticut resumed the attack when the proposed amendment reached the House of Representatives. There was nothing properly before the House, he declared, since the proposal had not legally been approved by the Senate; Article V required the votes of two thirds of all senators. Federalist representatives essentially reiterated what Plumer had said in support of this conclusion.[142] But it is in the House debates that we first read the Republican side of the story.

The most effective defense was that the Senate's action was in line with the accepted understanding regarding the passage of ordinary legislation. Though the Constitution was silent as to the number of votes needed to pass a bill, it was universally agreed that a majority was required in accordance with the immemorial practice of legislative assemblies. But it was equally understood that in this case a majority meant more than half of those who were present, not of all members who had been elected. There was no doubt that Article V was meant to raise the ante in the case of constitutional amendments, but it did so by requiring those present to approve them by more than a bare majority. The framers expressly changed the multiplier for determining the requisite majority; there was no reason to think they had also changed the multiplicand.

House Republicans flirted with this argument but never quite put it together. If a "House" meant the whole number of its members, said Virginia's John Randolph, it could not meet unless every one of them was present. But the Constitution wisely refuted this absurdity by providing that a mere majority was a quorum.[143] Thus, as Tennessee representative G. W. Campbell

added, a simple majority could keep a journal, adopt rules, and adjourn, although in each case authority was given to the "House." Thus in all these
instances "House" meant a majority of the House, and two thirds of a House
was therefore two thirds of a majority. For "House and Quorum," Caesar
Rodney of Delaware concluded, "are convertible terms."[144]

Randolph also called attention to another two-thirds requirement that
earlier speakers had apparently overlooked. Article I, section 5 authorized
"each House" not only to determine its own rules and discipline its members but also, "with the concurrence of two thirds," to expel a member. It was
obvious, said Randolph, "that two-thirds of those present could expel in such
a case."[145]

It wasn't obvious at all. Like the amendment provision, the expulsion
clause did not specify what it meant by two thirds of a "House," if that was
what it meant; Thatcher would soon cite it along with the veto provision as
another instance in which, because of its silence on the question, two thirds
of the whole House was required.[146] The juxtaposition of expulsion in a
single clause with discipline and rules, which presumably required only a
majority of a majority, does beef up the general argument that two thirds in
that context means two thirds of the same number. And the impeachment
and treaty provisions, invoked by Plumer and Thatcher to show that when
the framers meant two thirds of those present they said so, might have been
used to give firmer support to an argument suggested by Randolph's reference to expulsion. Several matters arguably just as portentous as constitutional amendment or veto were expressly entrusted to two thirds of a quorum; rather than constituting exceptions to the general rule, the explicit
impeachment and treaty provisions showed what the Constitution meant by
two thirds of the Senate or the House.

In resolving the issue in the Senate the president pro tempore had invoked
precedent, and Republicans placed great weight on precedent in the House.[147]
The 1789 journals, they maintained, showed that the Bill of Rights had been
approved by two thirds of those present, not by two thirds of all members.[148]

The record proved something less than conclusive. As Thatcher pointed
out, North Carolina and Rhode Island had not been represented in 1789.
Thus there were only twenty-two senators, not twenty-six; the sixteen reported in attendance were more than two thirds of the total body.[149] While
the House clerk had certified that the amendments were approved by two
thirds of the members present, his interpretation of Article V could not bind
the House; and since the yeas and nays were not taken, it was entirely possible that the proposal had in fact been endorsed by two thirds of all the
members.[150]

But the Republicans had the votes in the House as well as in the Senate. The apparent precedent of the Bill of Rights, coupled with the fact that a majority normally meant a majority of those present, nurtured by a fervent desire to pass the amendment, and reinforced by powerful arguments that the House had no right to look behind the Senate's certification that it had indeed approved the proposal, was enough to carry the day.[151] The House voted eighty-five to thirty-four to consider the Senate resolution.[152]

Many years afterward, largely on the basis of long-established practice, the Supreme Court held that two thirds of the members present sufficed to override a presidential veto under the substantially identical terms of Article I, section 7.[153] The question seems close, and readers may make up their own minds. Despite the force of the analogy to passage of a bill by a majority of a quorum, I still have trouble convincing myself that when the framers prescribed a two-thirds majority to ensure broad support for constitutional amendments they meant it could be provided by fewer than half the members.[154]

The End

The House approved the Twelfth Amendment on 8 December 1803 by "two thirds of the members present"; the vote was a squeaky eighty-four to forty-two.[155] Within two weeks North Carolina had ratified the amendment, and it was in place in time for the 1804 election.[156] It worked without a hitch; Jefferson was reelected by a landslide, and as we know the venerable George Clinton became vice president.[157] Aaron Burr was put out to pasture, but he was far from finished; he would soon lead a shady expedition down the Mississippi that would lead to his abortive and notorious trial for treason.

It wasn't the end, of course. Despite all the haggling and the myriad of intricate issues with which Congress had grappled, the amendment failed to plug all the holes in the leaky machinery the framers had constructed to transport a new pilot to the presidential helm. As noted, there was still no provision to deal with the possibility that neither the House nor the Senate could agree on a candidate.[158] Nor had it apparently occurred to anyone that the president-elect might die before taking office, which was a more serious risk.[159] In such a case the House was not authorized to choose a replacement, nor the vice president to assume the office, nor Congress to provide for succession. This oversight was not corrected until 1933.[160]

It would have been easy enough to fix it in 1803. All that was necessary was to direct that the vice president assume the president's duties whenever the office was vacant or its occupant disabled. But it is impossible to foresee all eventualities, which is one reason drafting is so difficult. Moreover, as already indicated, the amendment's supporters were in no mood to jeopardize their pet project by encumbering it with extraneous proposals.

Finally, the task might have proved to be more difficult than it appears. One of the central lessons of the tortuous birth of the Twelfth Amendment is that constitutional changes are seldom as simple as they seem; displace a single brick, and you may end up rebuilding the entire facade.

NOTES

1. U.S. Constitution, art. 2, sec. 1, art. 1, sec. 3.

2. This time it was Charles Cotesworth Pinckney, who had been at Philadelphia in 1787. Four years earlier it had been his brother Thomas, who had negotiated a swell treaty with Spain. Their cousin Charles was a Republican. See David P. Currie, *The Constitution in Congress: The Federalist Period, 1789–1801* (Chicago: University of Chicago Press, 1995), 281.

3. U.S. Constitution, art. 2, sec. 1.

4. This distressing story is told in hideous detail in Currie, *The Federalist Period,* 292–95. See also Tadahisa Kuroda, *The Origins of the Twelfth Amendment* (Westport, Conn.: Greenwood, 1994), chaps. 7–9.

5. See Kuroda, *Origins,* 172. Albert Gallatin perceived that Article II also created the risk that Federalist *electors* might have made Burr president in 1800 by voting for him rather than their own vice-presidential hopeful (Gallatin to Jefferson, 14 September 1801, in Henry Adams, ed., *Writings of Albert Gallatin,* 3 vols. [New York: Antiquaria Press, 1960], 1: 49, 51–52).

6. Hamilton strongly favored the proposed amendment, as he said in a letter to Bayard (4 March 1802), "because it is right that the people should know whom they are choosing & because the present mode gives all possible scope to intrigue and is dangerous as we have seen to the public tranquillity" (Harold C. Syrett, ed., *The Papers of Alexander Hamilton,* 27 vols. [New York: Columbia University Press, 1961–87], 25: 558, 559). See also his letter of 6 April 1802 to Gouverneur Morris: "Surely the scene of last session ought to teach us the intrinsic demerits of the existing plan" (25: 587, 588).

7. See *Annals of the Congress of the United States, 1789–1824,* 42 vols. (Washington, D.C., 1834–56), 11: 191, 602. (Hereafter cited as *Annals of Congress* plus volume and page numbers.) While it was up, the New York legislature also proposed that electors be elected by the voters in districts of equal population (ibid.). A similar proposal from Vermont (without specifying that districts must be equal) had been pre-

sented a few days before (11: 190). For the story of the districting proposals, which originated in part as a Republican response to unit voting in small Federalist states, see Kuroda, *Origins*, 107–14.

8. *Annals of Congress*, 11: 1285–88. See U.S. Constitution, art. 5: "The Congress, whenever two thirds of both houses shall deem it necessary, shall propose amendments to this Constitution."

9. *Annals of Congress*, 11: 1289–90, 1293–94, 1287, 603, 1287–88. Bayard may have been honest in his profession, for he had favored both designation and districting in an exchange of letters with Hamilton the month before. See Syrett, ed., *Papers*, 25: 587–89, 600–601, 605–10.

10. *Annals of Congress*, 11: 304. For the suggestion that the Republicans thought the time was not ripe, see Kuroda, *Origins*, 123–24.

11. *Annals of Congress*, 13: 372, 19. Senator Brown of Kentucky, the president pro tempore, even declared it unnecessary that the proposal be read three times on different days because a resolution to amend the Constitution was not a "bill" within the meaning of the Senate rule. Uriah Tracy of Connecticut acknowledged that the rule did not apply but argued that the gravity of the subject demanded that it be followed by analogy, as the vice president had determined in other cases in which the concurrence of both Houses was required. See also Everett S. Brown, ed., *William Plumer's Memorandum of Proceedings in the United States Senate, 1803–1807* (New York: Macmillan, 1923), 16–17.

12. See *Annals of Congress*, 13: 374 (Rep. Nicholson), 775–76. Nicholson's more detailed proposal, which Dawson accepted, appears on pages 375–76. The Senate version was soon modified to conform in most respects with this proposal (see 13: 84–85). At one point Senate Republicans had to admit that they were stalling their own urgent proposal because at the moment they did not have the votes to adopt it (see Brown, ed., *Plumer's Memorandum*, 32–33). It was the House that first passed the amendment (see *Annals of Congress*, 13: 544) ten days after it was introduced; the Senate, as Roger Griswold complained, ignored the House version and sent the House an amendment of its own (13: 646).

13. Ironically, it was Federalists who had first suggested separate ballots for president and vice president after having lost the vice presidency in 1796 by throwing away too many votes for Pinckney in order to avoid the risk of tying him with Adams. See Kuroda, *Origins*, 108–9.

14. The entire story is related in detail in ibid., chaps. 11–16.

15. See *Annals of Congress*, 13: 143–45 (Sen. White), 155 (Sen. Plumer), 169–70 (Sen. Tracy), 535 (Rep. Hastings), 733–34 (Rep. Taggart), 750–51 (Rep. Roger Griswold). See David E. Kyvig, *Explicit and Authentic Acts: Amending the United States Constitution, 1776–1995* (Lawrence: University Press of Kansas, 1996), 115–16.

16. See, generally, E. Wilder Spaulding, *His Excellency George Clinton* (New York: Macmillan, 1938).

17. Charles Francis Adams, ed., *The Memoirs of John Quincy Adams*, 12 vols. (Phil-

adelphia: J. B. Lippincott, 1874–77), 1: 385. One commentator tells us that before agreeing to accept the vice presidency Clinton had "refused a chance for an eighth term as Governor of New York on the grounds of age and disability" (Kuroda, *Origins*, 163).

18. Brown, ed., *Plumer's Memorandum*, 348–49. "Tho' he complained to me that the office was too inactive for him," Plumer added, "yet, I fear, he will find it too laborious for his advanced age" (349).

19. Ibid., 593; see also 450, 635. Plumer's biographer called Clinton "a political relic" (Lynn W. Turner, *William Plumer of New Hampshire, 1759–1850* [Chapel Hill: University of North Carolina Press, 1962], 121). Clinton's biographer acknowledged it was a pity that his "prematurely aged" subject had succeeded the skilled and vigorous Burr: "Clinton's seven years in the vice presidency did considerably less than nothing to enhance the old warrior's reputation, for by 1805 in his late sixties, he could make no claims to constructive statesmanship of a national variety or even to ordinary ability as a presiding officer" (Spaulding, *George Clinton*, 279).

20. See Louis Clinton Hatch, *A History of the Vice Presidency of the United States* (New York: American Historical Society, 1934), 139–40.

21. Seven dollars gets you twelve you don't know who was vice president during Madison's second term or under Monroe or John Quincy Adams. Answers can be found in the next note.

22. The answers are Elbridge Gerry, Daniel Tompkins, and John C. Calhoun. Gerry had been a significant political figure, a signer of the Declaration of Independence, a delegate to the constitutional convention, a member of the House of Representatives, and most recently governor of Massachusetts. Whether he had ever been presidential material may be doubted. By the time he became vice president he was nearly sixty-nine, and he perished the following year. Tompkins had served for ten years as governor of New York, and he cannot have been without talent, as Madison once offered to make him secretary of state. One observer, however, reported that he was absent during four fifths of his term (Turner, *William Plumer*, 121). Calhoun too was a person of parts, if of increasingly unacceptable views; he resigned his post in 1832 for the more meaningful post of senator from South Carolina.

23. Professor Hatch called Calhoun "the only American statesman of the first or second rank who held the vice presidency in the century between its occupancy by Jefferson and by [Theodore] Roosevelt" (Hatch, *A History*, 71).

24. "With a few notable exceptions," wrote Lynn Turner in 1962, "the vice-presidents since Aaron Burr have verified the dismal predictions of 1804" (*William Plumer*, 121).

25. Taft: James S. Sherman of New York, longtime member of the House of Representatives. "The Sherman nomination," one correspondent wrote, "is regarded as a mere filler. It is generally admitted here that he brings no element of strengh to the ticket" (Hatch, *A History*, 354). Wilson: Thomas Marshall, who had been governor of Indiana for four years but who had never held any other public office. Hoover:

Charles Curtis of Kansas, who had better credentials than most. He had served nearly thirty-five years in Congress and was Senate majority leader at the time he was selected (at age sixty-eight). And then there was Spiro Agnew . . .

26. After adoption of the Twelfth Amendment, wrote Professor Corwin, "the vice presidency was ordinarily a somewhat secondary pawn in the game of choosing a President" (Edward S. Corwin, *The President: Office and Powers* [New York: New York University, 1940], 61). See also Joseph Story, *Commentaries on the Constitution of the United States,* 3 vols. (Boston: Hilliard, Gray, 1833), 2: sec. 1463: "The amendment has certainly greatly diminished the dignity and importance of the office of vice-president."

27. George Mason argued at the convention that the vice-presidential provisions "mixed too much the Legislative & Executive" (Max Farrand, ed., *The Records of the Federal Convention of 1787,* rev. ed., 4 vols. [New Haven, Conn.: Yale University Press, 1937], 2: 537); Elbridge Gerry said, "We might as well put the President himself at the head of the Legislature" (2: 536). For the touchiness of the first Senate on this question, see Currie, *The Federalist Period,* 12 (discussing the controversy over how the vice president was to sign bills); compare the Senate's discomfort in passing upon a proposed treaty in the president's presence (24–26). Modern efforts to find meaningful duties for the vice president in the executive branch have only exacerbated this problem. "My country," wrote John Adams to his wife shortly after becoming vice president, "has in its wisdom contrived for me the most insignificant office that ever the invention of man contrived or his imagination conceived" (John Adams to Abigail Adams, quoted in Corwin, *The President,* 60).

28. *Annals of Congress,* 13: 21; see also 13: 22 (Sen. Dayton): "The reasons of erecting the office are frustrated by the amendment to the Constitution now proposed; it will be preferable, therefore, to abolish the office."

29. See *Annals of Congress,* 13: 23 (Sen. Jackson), 21, 84, 671–75.

30. See ibid., 13: 20 (Sen. Samuel Smith), 23 (Sen. Breckinridge).

31. For the two-term proposal, see ibid., 13: 19 (Sen. Butler). Representative Huger proposed that electors be chosen by the people; Gaylord Griswold said it would promote democracy. Rodney said he favored the principle but opposed attaching it to the pending proposal "lest by grasping at too much they might lose all," and Huger's motion failed (13: 664–67). For the eligibility of Louisiana-born persons, see 13: 85 (Sen. Adams). Adams was otherwise quite hostile to anything respecting that new dominion; his sudden concern for the electability of its inhabitants seemed a little less than sincere. For the reallocation of representation, see 13: 536 (Rep. Hastings) and 538 (Rep. Thatcher). Hastings seemed to think the Constitution did not permit this change to be made before 1808, but the problem may have been more practical than legal; it was only the ratio for direct taxation, not for representation, that Article V expressly protected against amendment before that date (U.S. Constitution, art. 1, sec. 9, clause 4). Finally, for Dayton's proposal, see *Annals of Congress,* 13: 22 (Sen. Nicholas): "The Senate had . . . better not admit the amendment, even if convinced that it was correct, because it might jeopardize the main amendment."

32. U.S. Constitution, amends. 20, 22, 23, 25.

33. Ibid., amend. 25, sec. 2.

34. See Currie, *The Federalist Period,* 139–44.

35. Story, *Commentaries,* 2: sec. 1446.

36. See Currie, *The Federalist Period,* 140.

37. 24 Stat. 1, sec. 1 (January 19, 1886).

38. This scenario was to be realized in 1824.

39. U.S. Constitution, art. 2, sec. 1.

40. $2(n/2 + x) > n$, where n and x are positive numbers. Senator Clinton, who had unthinkingly copied Article II's default provisions into his proposal, was caught with his pants down and sheepishly agreed to drop the reference to a double majority. See *Annals of Congress,* 13: 17; Brown, ed., *Plumer's Memorandum,* 15; Kuroda, *Origins,* 133–34. This episode may be thought to suggest that there is something to be said, in amending the Constitution, for proceeding with what the Supreme Court would later refer to as all deliberate speed.

41. *Annals of Congress,* 13: 374–75. Clinton's Senate proposal, embodying the same principle, had left the number of candidates for later determination (13: 17).

42. See Brown, ed., *Plumer's Memorandum,* 42–43: "Five is the number in the constitution from which the President & Vice President are to be selected in case of no choice by the Electors. By confining the House to three from whom they must choose the President, & the senate to two candidates from whom we must choose the vice president we make the amendment conform to both the spirit & letter of the constitution." See also *Annals of Congress,* 13: 116 (Sen. Taylor), 422 (Rep. Dawson), 736–37 (Rep. Holland).

43. *Annals of Congress,* 13: 101, 40 (Sen. Nicholas), 88 (Sen. Samuel Smith); see also Brown, ed., *Plumer's Memorandum,* 39.

44. Brown, ed., *Plumer's Memorandum,* 40. This Maclay was the younger brother of Senator William Maclay of the same state to whom we are indebted for the closest approximation we have of a record of the debates in the First Congress. See Currie, *The Federalist Period,* 10. Samuel Maclay served from 1803 until 1809. Unfortunately, the habit of keeping a diary does not seem to have run in the family.

45. *Annals of Congress,* 13: 103 (adding that to require that the president have significant popular support would make him less dependent upon Congress). See also 13: 107 (Sen. Cocke), 113–14 (Sen. Jackson), 114–15 (Sen. Taylor), 120–23 (Sen. Samuel Smith) (noting that because the House voted by states House election enabled the nine smallest states, with only 20 percent of the population, to choose the president), 376–77, 424 (Rep. Clopton). On the same ground, several Representatives suggested the number should be two and not three: 13: 376 (Rep. Clopton), 420–21 (Rep. Joseph Clay), 421 (Rep. G. W. Campbell).

46. Brown, ed., *Plumer's Memorandum,* 41. Adams had prefaced this argument with the observation that it scarcely behooved him, as representative of a large state, to become the champion of the small ones. Dayton, from little New Jersey, picked up the cue: "By filling the blank with three you give power to the large States exclusively

to nominate and choose your President" (42). See also *Annals of Congress*, 13: 428 (Rep. Rodney), 692 (Rep. Purviance), 738–39 (Rep. Thatcher).

47. *Annals of Congress*, 13: 85–86.

48. Ibid., 13: 145, 155 (Sen. Plumer), 746–47 (Rep. Roger Griswold). See also Henry Adams, *History of the United States of America during the Administrations of Thomas Jefferson and James Madison*, 2 vols., ed. Earl H. Harbert (New York: Literary Classics of the United States, 1986), 390–92, arguing that the amendment "swept away one of the checks on which the framers had counted to resist majority rule by the great States" and "stripp[ed] the small States of an advantage which had made part of their bargain."

49. *Annals of Congress*, 13: 157.

50. Under the original provision, said Roger Griswold, the large states could hope to secure both offices only by giving "each of their candidates nearly an equal number of votes; in which case it will be left in the power of a small State to decide the election" (ibid., 13: 747).

51. See note 5. See also *Annals of Congress*, 13: 171 (Sen. Tracy); Kuroda, *Origins*, 141.

52. See also *Annals of Congress*, 13: 97 (Sen. Adams): "Certainly it is a much higher power to elect from five than from three." It might also have been argued that the more people had a chance of being selected by the House, the more would be likely to run for president, thus increasing the likelihood that no one would attain a majority and that the House would actually make the choice. In a House election, as already noted, the small states have more influence because each state has a single vote. This scenario was actually depicted by an *opponent* of the small-state position in arguing against permitting the House to choose among five pretenders, on the grounds that election by the House was an evil to be averted whenever possible. See 13: 100 (Sen. Taylor).

53. For more on this idea, see note 52.

54. See note 45.

55. See *Annals of Congress*, 13: 496–97, 544.

56. Ibid., 13: 124, 102–3, 683, 775.

57. "In the years since 1804, very few candidates for either executive office have actually come from a small state" (Turner, *William Plumer*, 121). In addition to the jousting that took place over the number of candidates among whom the House was to choose, there was pesky technical sniping over how the requirement should be phrased. Senator Jackson complained that if there were votes for fewer candidates than the prescribed number there could be no choice at all (Brown, ed., *Plumer's Memorandum*, 39–40), but that was foolish; the language was taken directly from Article II, and its obvious intention was that five candidates be considered if that many had received votes. Adams's objection was more troublesome. How was the House to decide among "the three highest on the list," as the draft then provided, "when the third and fourth candidates were equally high in votes" (*Annals of Congress*, 13: 91, 92–93)? Taylor lamely suggested that the House might comply by

choosing either of the top two or maybe even by making a choice "out of any three of the four" (13: 93). Possibly to obviate this embarrassment, the draft was altered to require a choice not from "the three highest on the list" but from "the persons having the highest numbers, not exceeding three, on the list" (13: 125, 127). This awkward locution engendered considerable lamentation when the Senate's proposal arrived in the House. Moaning that it was unclear whether the new terminology limited the House's choice to three persons or to three classes defined by the numbers of votes they had received, Roger Griswold gleefully professed to believe that it permitted selection only of candidates who had received precisely three votes, which was patently absurd (13: 677). Thatcher thought it meant "not the three or five highest on the list, but the three highest numbers, containing an indefinite number of persons" (13: 671), an interpretation suggested by the history of the change in phrasing but producing a result that ran counter to the Senate's clear goal of restricting the number to three in order to ensure that the House's choice reflected the popular will. Several Republican speakers endorsed this interpretation; see 13: 678 (Rep. John Randolph), 680 (Rep. Rodney), 725 (Rep. G. W. Campbell). Griswold, Elliott, and Dana continued to protest that the language was ambiguous, but the motion to clarify it lost badly (13: 678, 679, 681); as adopted, the amendment infelicitously requires a choice among "the persons having the highest numbers, not exceeding three, on the list."

58. *Annals of Congress*, 13: 533.

59. U.S. Constitution, art. 2, sec. 1: "In case of the removal of the president from office, or of his death, resignation, or inability to discharge the powers and duties of the said office, the same shall devolve upon the vice president."

60. Ibid.: "In every case, after the choice of the president, the person having the greatest number of votes of the electors shall be the vice president." That is how Aaron Burr was chosen. See Currie, *The Federalist Period*, 293 and note 471.

61. U.S. Constitution, art. 2, sec. 1: "The Congress may by law provide for the case of removal, death, resignation or inability, both of the President and Vice-President." See Currie, *The Federalist Period*, 294.

62. The amendment as it appeared when the debate on this question began is printed in *Annals of Congress*, 13: 126–27.

63. Ibid., 13: 128.

64. Ibid., 13: 130, 132.

65. Ibid., 13: 129. Hillhouse defended Pickering's suggestion, noting that decision by lot "was very common at Athens" and preferable in any case "to the choice at the point of the bayonet" (13: 129). Senator Wright commented, "The rights of freemen are not to be gambled away, or committed to chance, or sorcery, or witchcraft; we look to reason and experience for our guides" (13: 131). Adams too was "totally adverse to any decision by lot" (13: 131).

66. Ibid., 13: 533.

67. Ibid., 13: 132; see also 13: 136 (Sen. Taylor).

68. Of course, it was still possible that the separate process for choosing a vice

president would also fail, and for that more remote eventuality Adams proposed, in accord with Pickering's more immediate suggestion, that presidential duties "be discharged by such person as Congress may by law direct, until a new election shall be had, in manner already prescribed by law" (ibid., 13: 132).

69. See ibid., 13: 703–4 (Rep. Gregg).

70. Ibid., 13: 668–69, 693, 734 (Rep. Taggart), 753 (Rep. Dennis), 710 (Rep. Lowndes): "We alter our Constitution to prevent, among others [sic] reasons, the person from being President who was not intended by the electors; and in the same resolution we prescribe, under circumstances much more likely to happen, that the Vice President shall act as President." Indeed, Representative Chittenden added, the proposed provision would enable the House to reverse the electors' priorities by simply refusing to select a president (13: 670). Representative Thatcher even suggested it would be better to make no provision for the House's failure to choose a president: "A dread of the evils of anarchy and of an interregnum" would be a salutary "inducement" to the House to do its duty (13: 671). See also Brown, ed., *Plumer's Memorandum*, 45 (Sen. Wright), 72 (Sen. Plumer).

71. *Annals of Congress*, 13: 718, 754 (Rep. Dennis). Having already given the House too few candidates to choose from, Goddard complained, the Senate, by providing for the vice president to take over in case of default, was attempting "to take the choice from us, the immediate representatives of the people" (13: 716–17).

72. Ibid., 13: 718. Representative Hoge's motion to provide that the vice president should act for a year pending the outcome of a special election was defeated sixty-three to forty (13: 727).

73. See ibid., 13: 210 (Senate), 775 (House).

74. Ibid., 13: 670, 703 (Rep. Gregg, arguing that it was better to make the wrong man president than to end up without one).

75. Ibid., 13: 667. One of the early versions of the proposed amendment neglected to omit the superseded provision for the defeated presidential candidate to become vice president, with which it was inconsistent; see 13: 375 (Rep. Nicholson). This was another of the little embarrassments brought about by the unseemly haste of the amendment's sponsors, and it was quickly corrected.

76. Ibid., 13: 19 (Sen. Bradley).

77. See ibid., 13: 93 (Sen. Taylor), 95 (Sen. Wright).

78. Ibid., 13: 93. Before the rise of political parties, a majority vote for second place might have been thought too much to expect, and in fact it was achieved neither in 1788 nor in 1796.

79. Ibid., 13: 91, 94, 95, 97.

80. Ibid., 13: 91.

81. See note 42.

82. *Annals of Congress*, 13: 106.

83. Ibid.

84. See Currie, *The Federalist Period*, 293.

85. In response to Wright's objection, Bradley said it was unnecessary to treat each state as a unit in the Senate, since there was already an equal number of senators from each state (*Annals of Congress*, 13: 96).

86. Ibid., 13: 132, 136–37.

87. Ibid., 13: 133. Although this formulation seemed to indicate that Hillhouse thought the electors previously chosen should meet a second time, he soon suggested otherwise by saying he saw "no reason why the Government should not go on until an election should take place."

88. Ibid., 13: 133: "Mr. Hillhouse thought there would be no danger of the Senate omitting to elect their President, who is, on a vacancy, the Vice President in fact."

89. Ibid., 13: 137, 138.

90. See Currie, *The Federalist Period*, 139–44.

91. See *Annals of Congress*, 13: 138 (Sen. Adams).

92. Before Adams clarified that he was not suggesting that the statute itself be passed after 4 March, Jackson had objected that on that date one third of the senators would lose their mandates, Wright that there would be no way to summon the House because there would be no president to proclaim a special session (ibid., 13: 137–38). The clarification eliminated the latter objection, and as Adams noted, two thirds of the Senate was sufficent to elect a president pro tem; a bare majority constituted a quorum, and no extraordinary majority was required (13: 138; see also U.S. Constitution, art. 1, secs. 3, 5). Besides, as Adams added, the states might already have chosen new senators to replace those whose terms had expired.

93. See note 92.

94. *Annals of Congress*, 13: 139. A similar proposal by Senator Hillhouse that did not depend upon selection by the Senate after 4 March also failed without a division.

95. Ibid., 13: 178.

96. U.S. Constitution, art. 2, sec. 1. Against such an interpretation it could be urged that when the presidency was vacant the vice president did not *become* president; the "powers and duties of the said office" merely "devolve[d]" on him. Compare the further provision of the same paragraph that Congress might designate an officer to "act as President" in case of a double vacancy.

97. See *Annals of Congress*, 13: 91.

98. U.S. Constitution, amend. 12.

99. *Annals of Congress*, 13: 738; see also 13: 746 (Rep. Roger Griswold). Plumer expanded upon this theme in a rare departure from his general policy against burdening the Senate with long speeches. "The forms & *modes of proceeding* established by the Constitution may be amended," he argued, "but its *principles* cannot." Even the extraordinary majority prescribed by Article V could not establish a monarchy in Virginia or divide New Hampshire and Massachusetts into ten independent states. The Constitution was "a compact formed by each state with the whole," and a departure from its basic principles would release dissenting states from their obligations; "the principles of the confederacy being changed without the previous consent

of the *partners* to that confederacy, is in fact a virtual dissolution of the Union" (Brown, ed., *Plumer's Memorandum*, 54–55; see also *Annals of Congress*, 13: 154).

100. See U.S. Constitution, art. 5: "Provided that no amendment which may be made prior to the year one thousand eight hundred and eight shall in any manner affect the first and fourth clauses in the ninth section of the first Article; and that no state, without its consent, shall be deprived of its equal suffrage in the Senate." Plumer's "compact" theory (see note 99), however difficult to square with the deliberate decisions of the constitutional convention, did not help his argument; contracts often provide for their own modification, and Article V did not say that "principles" were excepted. Compare Articles of Confederation, arts. 2, 3 ("league" of "sovereign" states), with U.S. Constitution, art. 6 ("supreme law of the land"); see also Farrand, ed., *The Records*, 1: 122–23 (Madison); David P. Currie, *The Constitution in the Supreme Court: The First Hundred Years* (Chicago: University of Chicago Press, 1985), 312–13.

101. *Hans v. Louisiana*, 134 U.S. 1 (1890); *Collector v. Day*, 78 U.S. 113 (1871); *New York v. United States*, 505 U.S. 144 (1992).

102. *Coyle v. Smith*, 221 U.S. 559 (1911).

103. Henry M. Hart Jr., "The Power of Congress to Limit the Jurisdiction of Federal Courts: An Exercise in Dialectic," *Harvard Law Review* 66 (1953): 1362, 1365.

104. *The National Prohibition Cases*, 253 U.S. 350, 386–87 (1920) (Eighteenth Amendment); *Leser v. Garnett*, 258 U.S. 130, 136 (1922) (Nineteenth); David P. Currie, *The Constitution in the Supreme Court: The Second Century* (Chicago: University of Chicago Press, 1990), 177–78, n. 47.

105. The German constitution contains important restrictions of this nature. See art. 79(3) GG; David P. Currie, *The Constitution of the Federal Republic of Germany* (Chicago: University of Chicago Press, 1994), 18, 26, 33.

106. U.S. Constitution, art. 4, sec. 4.

107. See also *Annals of Congress*, 13: 746 (Rep. Roger Griswold): "The basis of this compromise ought to be considered as sacred—never to be shaken whilst the Constitution endures."

108. Moreover, even if one could extrapolate from the provision for equal Senate votes to a general principle protecting the essence of the Philadelphia compromise, it would be far from obvious that a mere reduction in the number of candidates among whom the House could choose would fall within it; the small states retained their equal say whenever the election was thrown into the House.

109. *Annals of Congress*, 13: 759. Short of the contention that the amending power was implicitly limited, numerous members argued that it should be sparingly exercised. It was essential that the Constitution be "stable & permanent," said Plumer, lest frequent changes "infuse a spirit of fickleness & love of novelty into the public mind." "A constitution perpetually changing, can never long command the veneration or esteem of any people"; amendments should be adopted only when "imperious necessity" so required (Brown, ed., *Plumer's Memorandum*, 56–57). New York representative Gaylord Griswold put it concisely: "By altering the articles of the Con-

stitution for every trivial pretext, you destroy that sacred regard which every citizen ought to have for the Constitution" (*Annals of Congress*, 13: 518; see also 13: 140–41 [Sen. White], 692–93 [Rep. Purviance], 728–29 [Rep. Taggart]). As a general principle, this was sound advice that speaks urgently to an age in which amendments are seriously put forward with respect to such ephemera as flag burning and "victims' rights," not to mention term limits and balanced budgets. The need for the Twelfth Amendment, however, was acute, and as its supporters argued, the amending process was invented to be used (ibid., 13: 700–701 [Rep. Gregg]).

110. See Articles of Confederation, art. 5, 1 Stat. 4, 5.

111. See Currie, *The Federalist Period*, 15–16.

112. See Brown, ed., *Plumer's Memorandum*, 50 (Sen. Plumer); *Annals of Congress*, 13: 177 (Sen. Tracy). In the House the argument for instructions was nonexistent to begin with; representatives were chosen not by state legislatures but by the people. Broader objections were accordingly raised. Hastings protested that he had "no idea that, when a person was chosen to represent the people, he was under any obligation to pursue a line of conduct contrary to the dictates of his own mind," Dana that the state legislatures were "not our constituents." Representative Eustis, who had brought up the deferentially worded request of the Massachusetts legislature, hastened to add that he had no "intention to oppose the sentiments of [that body] to the will of [this] House" (13: 542; see also asterisked footnote on same page).

113. *Annals of Congress*, 13: 741; see also Brown, ed., *Plumer's Memorandum*, 50 (Sen. Plumer).

114. See *Annals of Congress*, 13: 154 (Sen. Plumer), 177 (Sen. Tracy). "As well might a petite jury [*sic*] instruct a grand jury," said Senator Plumer, "to indict a particular man for a particular offence, & then decide definitely on the bill" (Brown, ed., *Plumer's Memorandum*, 51).

115. See Brown, ed., *Plumer's Memorandum*, 79–80. It was immaterial, proponents of presidential authority rightly added, that both Houses had already approved the amendment by a majority sufficient to override a possible veto; the Constitution required an opportunity for second thought even "if a bill or resolve is passed by both houses unanimously."

116. U.S. Constitution, art. 1, sec. 1: "All legislative powers herein granted shall be vested in a Congress of the United States." See Brown, ed., *Plumer's Memorandum*, 80: "Upon the same principle therefore that you exclude the president from an agency in this amendment to the constitution; you may with equal propriety exclude him from either approving or disapproving of every bill or resolve that is passed by the two Houses."

117. Representative Dana, in another context, conceded that the veto provision did not apply to proposed amendments and said that was "because the measure does not partake of Legislative character; it is in virtue of a special grant of power" (*Annals of Congress*, 13: 654). But not only is it arguable that constitutional amendment is a "legislative" act; the presentation clause says nothing of either legislative powers or special grants but speaks comprehensively of all orders, resolutions, and votes. The

argument that a veto would be "unavailing" because a two-thirds vote is already required (St. George Tucker, ed., *Blackstone's Commentaries on the Laws of England* [London: Birch and Small, 1803], 1: 325) is no more convincing: a veto may persuade members who voted for the measure to change their minds. Compare *Powell v. McCormack*, 395 U.S. 486, 508–12 (1969) (refusing to treat a two-thirds vote not to seat a member of Congress as an expulsion for which a two-thirds vote was required).

118. See Currie, *The Federalist Period*, 196, n. 181.

119. Brown, ed., *Plumer's Memorandum*, 80.

120. *Hollingworth v. Virginia*, 3 U.S. 378, 381 n.(a); see Currie, *The First Hundred Years*, 21–22.

121. Brown, ed., *Plumer's Memorandum*, 80–81.

122. *Annals of Congress*, 13: 81.

123. See ibid. (Republican sens. Franklin and Wright; Federalist sens. Adams and Dayton), 82 (Federalist sen. Hillhouse), 83 (Federalist sen. Pickering). Republican senators Butler and Israel Smith endorsed the Federalist position (13: 82, 83). See also Senator Plumer's remarks to his diary (Brown, ed., *Plumer's Memorandum*, 35–36). The example of amending a resolution after it had been introduced was mentioned by both Butler and Plumer, the idea of considering such an idea in the first place by Butler alone (*Annals of Congress*, 13: 82; Brown, ed., *Plumer's Memorandum*, 36).

124. *Annals of Congress*, 13: 36; see also 13: 82 (Sen. Hillhouse).

125. Ibid., 13: 81.

126. Brown, ed., *Plumer's Memorandum*, 36. See also *Annals of Congress*, 13: 83 (Rep. Smith).

127. U.S. Constitution, art. 1, sec. 5.

128. *Annals of Congress*, 13: 81.

129. See U.S. Constitution, art. 1, secs. 3, 7, 8, art. 2, sec. 2, and art. 5.

130. *Annals of Congress*, 13: 84 (Senate), 381, 744 (House). The Senate vote on this procedural question was eighteen to thirteen; there is a certain bootstrap quality about Senator Brown's ruling that a simple majority sufficed to decide whether two thirds was required.

131. Ibid., 13: 81. See also 1: 71–72, where the Senate acceded to a House amendment to the proposed text of the Bill of Rights. The vote was ten to ten, and Vice President Adams broke the tie.

132. Both sides essayed comparisons to the arguably analogous cases of treaties and bills vetoed by the president, but neither had anything very useful to say about them. See ibid., 13: 81–83 (Sens. Dayton, Hillhouse, Wright, Pickering, and Taylor).

133. Ibid., 13: 82.

134. Brown, ed., *Plumer's Memorandum*, 36.

135. *Annals of Congress*, 13: 209.

136. Brown, ed., *Plumer's Memorandum*, 48–50.

137. Nobody suggested that "both Houses" was different from "each House," that is, that Article V required the votes of two thirds of the members of Congress in

joint session. Such a rule would have diminished the influence of the Senate and therefore of the states, since the Senate was the smaller body. More decisively, it would have departed without apparent reason from the normal bicameral principle in a case in which such a departure would have seemed especially inappropriate. The structure of Article V strongly suggests, as Representative Thatcher argued in another context, that because of the seriousness of amending the Constitution, "the Constitution has . . . made each House of Congress and the State Legislatures a check upon each other" (*Annals of Congress*, 13: 741; see text at n. 113).

138. Brown, ed., *Plumer's Memorandum*, 48.

139. Ibid., 49. See U.S. Constitution, art. 1, sec. 3 (impeachment), art. 1, sec. 7 (veto), art. 2, sec. 2 (treaties).

140. Brown, ed., *Plumer's Memorandum*, 48–49. Plumer drew additional support from Article II, section 1, which specifies that when the House sits to elect a president a quorum must include "a member or members from two thirds of the States" and that at the last election had been understood to require "a full *two thirds* of *all* the States in the Union" (49). He might have made more of the fact that by the same reasoning Article V itself, in requiring two thirds and three fourths "of the several states" to demand a constitutional convention and to ratify amendments, pretty clearly referred to all of them (46–47). His effort to suggest that the pattern was to require two thirds of the whole body for decisions that were unusually important (see page 49, which discusses the veto provision) was less successful; it fails to explain why a less exacting standard was set for removing the president from office.

141. Ibid., 49–50. There were thirty-four senators. A quorum was therefore eighteen. Twelve was two thirds of a quorum and therefore potentially of those present and voting. See *Annals of Congress*, 13: 649–50 (Rep. Lowndes).

142. *Annals of Congress*, 13: 646, 647–48 (Rep. Roger Griswold), 649–50 (Rep. Lowndes), 651–52 (Rep. Thatcher), 654 (Rep. Dana), 658–59 (Rep. Dennis), 661–62 (Rep. Roger Griswold).

143. U.S. Constitution, art. 1, sec. 5. See also *Annals of Congress*, 13: 648.

144. *Annals of Congress*, 13: 653–54 (Rep. Campbell), 656–57 (Rep. Rodney), 656. Representative Eustis's further contention that if "House" meant all the members they must all be present before an amendment could be proposed (or a veto overridden) was a loser; as Representative Dennis explained, Article V required only that two thirds of all members vote for the proposal (13: 650, 658).

145. Ibid., 13: 648.

146. Ibid., 13: 651.

147. Ibid., 13: 209.

148. See ibid., 650 (Rep. Thomas), 652 (Rep. John Randolph), 656 (Rep. Rodney). Randolph and Rodney added that the House had twice passed proposals for separate presidential and vice-presidential ballots by a majority of present members (13: 648, 662).

149. Ibid., 13: 652.

150. See ibid., 13: 654 (Rep. Thatcher), 659 (Rep. Dennis).

151. See ibid., 13: 653 (Rep. G. W. Campbell), 655 (Rep. Rodney, both insisting that each House was sole judge of its own proceedings), 654 (Rep. Dana, arguing that the House could take notice of the *Senate Journal*, which revealed there had not been the requisite majority), 657–58 (Rep. Dennis, conceding there was a presumption that the Senate's certification of the amendment was correct but arguing it had been rebutted in this case), 660–61 (Rep. Roger Griswold, arguing that the House could examine the whole record for itself to determine whether the constitutional requirement had been met). Even judges, it should be noted, tend to be reluctant to resolve constitutional questions of this nature. Compare *Leser v. Garnett*, 258 U.S. 130, 137 (1922) (refusing to look behind state legislature's certification that it had satisfied procedural requirements for ratifying the Nineteenth Amendment); *Geja's Cafe v. Metropolitan Pier & Exposition Auth.*, 153 Ill. 2d 239, 258–60, 606, NE 2d 1212, 1221 (1992).

152. *Annals of Congress*, 13: 663. For those who are still counting, this was less than two thirds of the entire House; under the 1802 apportionment the House had 141 members. See 2 Stat. 128 (January 14, 1802).

153. *Missouri Pacific Ry v. Kansas*, 248 U.S. 276 (1919). Legislative precedents involving constitutional amendments played a prominent role in this opinion.

154. As if it were not enough that there was uncertainty over what "two thirds" meant, there was also a minor dustup over Article V's further requirement that the proposed amendment be approved by "the legislatures of three fourths of the several States." For once nobody could detect ambiguity in the constitutional language (though later events would expose questions about what "legislature" meant in this context). What aroused sharp-eyed observers was the provision in the resolution itself that the ballot amendment would become law "when ratified by three-fourths of the Legislatures of the several States." The drafting of this clause was negligent in the extreme; the discrepancy between this phrasing and that of Article V made it possible for Representative Thatcher to argue that Congress appeared to be attempting to require "ratification by three-fourths of each Legislature, and not, as expressed in the Constitution, of the Legislatures of three-fourths of the States" (*Annals of Congress*, 13: 681). Acknowledging that the choice of words was unfortunate, Representative Thomas explained that it had been borrowed from the resolution accompanying the Bill of Rights, that it meant the same thing as the Constitution, and that it didn't matter anyway because nothing the resolution said could alter the constitutional requirement (13: 742–43). Besides, to send the amendment back to the Senate with a trivial change in wording would have delayed if not endangered the project itself, as Thatcher no doubt intended; his motion to amend the proposal to conform to Article V was mown down on the spot without a division (13: 681). For an earlier dispute over application of the three-fourths requirement of Article V, see Currie, *The Federalist Period*, 208.

155. *Annals of Congress*, 13: 775. In anticipation of ratification, Congress promptly passed an act designed to bring the election machinery into conformity with the new

constitutional provisions whenever they were approved. Among other things, Congress had the foresight to provide that in case the electors did not receive timely notice that the amendment had become law they should cast alternative ballots under both the old and new systems in order to ensure the validity of the election. See 2 Stat. 295, 295–96, sec. 2 (March 26, 1804); see also Currie, *The Federalist Period*, 136–39 (discussing the earlier statutory provisions).

156. See Kuroda, *Origins*, 156–61. The Federalist bastions of Connecticut, Delaware, and Massachusetts rejected the amendment. The New Hampshire legislature approved it, but the governor vetoed its action, raising the question of what Article V meant by its deceptively straightforward requirement of ratification by the "legislatures" of three fourths of the states. Fortunately it didn't matter, as the thirteen states that unambiguously ratified were a paper-thin three fourths of the seventeen states. The Supreme Court has still not decided whether the governor has any part in the ratification process.

157. Jefferson and Clinton received 162 electoral votes apiece to 14 for C. C. Pinckney and Rufus King. The Federalists won only Connecticut, Delaware, and two votes from Maryland; even Massachusetts went Republican. See *Annals of Congress*, 14: 56.

158. See text at note 94.

159. See Story, *Commentaries*, 3: sec. 1476.

160. See U.S. Constitution, amend. 20.

4 Unintended Consequences of the Fourteenth Amendment

Richard L. Aynes

The Fourteenth Amendment has been compared to a "second American Constitution."[1] Indeed, it is said that more litigation is based upon the Fourteenth Amendment or its implementing statutes than any other provision of the Constitution. As one would imagine for such an important charter of government, there is a substantial—and some might say overwhelming—body of scholarship on the "intent," "meaning," and "understanding" of the Fourteenth Amendment.[2]

Much of the literature, understandably, seeks to find out what the framers of the amendment or the ratifiers of the amendment "intended." What did they want to accomplish by adopting this amendment? This essay treats a different question: did the amendment have consequences that were unintended by the framers? Over one and a quarter centuries ago Justice Joseph Bradley answered that question in the affirmative: "It is possible that those who framed the article were not themselves aware of the far ranging character of its terms."[3]

I suggest that those unintended consequences include the effect of the citizenship clause on the force of the Fourteenth Amendment; the unintended impotency of the privileges and immunities clause; the unintended neglect, for almost a century, of the equal protection clause to offer protection to African Americans; the unintended effect upon the rights of corporations; and, finally, in what is more than a turn of the phrase, the possibility that the framers "intended" some of the unintended consequences of the amendment.

The Citizenship Clause: An Unintended Weakening of the Amendment

The question of who can be a citizen is fundamental to any society. As one might expect of a society of immigrants, this question has replayed itself throughout American history. The question of whether one could renounce foreign citizenship to become an American citizen was one of the principal controversies between the United States and Great Britain during the period leading up to and following the War of 1812. These controversies lingered in a variety of contexts in the United States, including questions about naturalization, loyalty, the exercise of voting rights, and similar matters.[4]

As liberal attitudes of the Revolutionary War era began to harden and more repressive trends emerged, the question of citizenship began to loom large in the American drama over slavery. Some scholars, such as New York's Chancellor James Kent, articulated a theory of citizenship highly congenial to recognizing the rights of African Americans. According to Chancellor Kent, "If a slave, born in the United States, be manumitted or otherwise lawfully discharged from bondage, or if a black man be born within the United States and born free, he becomes thence forward a citizen."[5] Kent's position was shared by other important legal writers.[6] On the other hand, as southern states began increasing racial restrictions and depriving even free blacks of existing rights, proslavery scholars articulated theories suggesting that African Americans could not be citizens.[7] These legal scholars advocated a view that African Americans lacked the possibility of ever becoming citizens of the United States no matter what the place of their birth. The resolution of this issue had particular importance for at least two questions. First, could African Americans use diversity of citizenship to escape less friendly state courts and litigate their claims in the federal courts? Second, were African Americans "citizens" within the meaning of Article IV, section 2, which provided that "the Citizens of each state shall be entitled to all Privileges and Immunities of Citizens in the several states"?

In the political arena, the architects of the national antislavery strategy considered Article IV, section 2 as a recognition of national citizenship. The first time the word citizen was used in the clause ("Citizens of each state") the words clearly referred to state citizenship. The second use in "Privileges and Immunities of Citizens in the several states" employed no words limiting the terms to state citizenship. Antislavery Republicans believed that the general references to "Citizens in the several states" referred to national citizenship.

This national citizenship theory was a key part of Republican ideology. In the well-known debate between Fourteenth Amendment author John Bingham and House Judiciary chairman James Wilson over the constitutionality of the 1866 Civil Rights Act, both Bingham and Wilson agreed that national citizenship with national rights was created by Article IV, section 2. What they disagreed upon was whether those rights could be enforced by the federal government without a constitutional amendment.[8] As early as 1859 Bingham argued that there was an ellipsis in the language, and the properly interpreted Article IV, section 2 should read: "The citizens of each State shall be entitled to all privileges and immunities of citizens [of the United States] in the several states."

Bingham had served as the chairman of the House Judiciary Committee before Wilson came to Congress but lost the chairmanship when he was defeated for reelection in 1863. He returned to Congress in 1865 and later resumed the chairmanship of the Judiciary Committee. He was a nationally prominent spokesman for the Republican party who gave the kick-off campaign speech for President Ulysses Grant in 1872. Nor were his views on national citizenship idiosyncratic.

Similar sentiments can be found in the speeches of Michigan senator Jacob Howard, Ohio congressman William Lawrence, Ohio senator John Sherman, Indiana senator Henry S. Lane, and Justice Bradley in his dissent in *The Slaughter-House Cases*.[9] Adherence to the national citizenship theory is implicit in the views about national enforcement of the Bill of Rights articulated by Congressmen James Wilson of Iowa, John Kasson of Iowa, John F. Farnsworth of Illinois, Sidney Clarke of Kansas, and others.[10]

These issues played themselves out in the political arena, in Congress, and in the courts. The *Dred Scott* decision provided the most dramatic forum for discussion of the citizenship issue.[11] In that case Chief Justice Roger Taney purported to hold that African Americans could not become citizens. In an often quoted line, Taney indicated that African Americans "had no rights which the white man was bound to respect." The *Dred Scott* decision became a political issue in and of itself. The attack upon the majority opinion was not simply one of legal correctness. Many popular and professional authorities argued that the language involving the citizenship of all African Americans was dicta and had no binding precedential value. Further, to the extent that the *Dred Scott* decision may have decided Dred Scott's fate, legal and political critics attempted to limit that decision to its own facts, arguing that it affected Dred Scott and Harriet Scott but no one else.

The classic statement of the position limiting the precedential effect of *Dred Scott* was made by leading Illinois political figure and soon-to-be president Abraham Lincoln. Through the use of rhetorical questions he conceded the decision was binding upon Dred and Harriet Scott: "But who resists it? Who has, in spite of the decision, declared Dred Scott free and resisted the authority of his master over him?"[12]

Finding the decision lacked the indicia for predicting how similar cases should be decided, Lincoln argued that it was improper to treat the case as "having yet quite established a settled doctrine for the country."[13] This was not simply campaign rhetoric. For example, the Ohio legislature passed a resolution concluding that "every free person, born within the limits of any state of this union, is a citizen thereof."[14] Republicans, like Fourteenth Amendment author John Bingham, continued to believe that Chancellor Kent's definition of citizenship, and not that of Chief Justice Taney, was correct. Indeed, during the Lincoln administration Republican authorities not only ignored Chief Justice Taney but also demonstrated their lack of respect for Taney's decision in *Dred Scott*.[15]

After *Dred Scott* an advisory opinion by Maine Supreme Court chief justice John Appleton held that Taney was wrong and that "no language can be found in the constitution which rests citizenship upon color or race."[16] At the instigation of Secretary of the Treasury Salmon P. Chase, a question was raised concerning African American citizenship. Even Lincoln's conservative attorney general, Edwin Bates, felt comfortable in ignoring the conclusion of Taney's *Dred Scott* decision and holding that African Americans could be citizens. In Bates's official published opinion, he concluded: "And now, upon the whole matter, I give it as my opinion that the *free man of color*, mentioned in your letter, if born in the United States, is a citizen of the United States; and, if otherwise qualified, is competent, according to the acts of Congress, to be master of a vessel engaged in the coasting trade."[17]

This attitude continued well through Reconstruction. While the Fourteenth Amendment itself was pending, Congress defined citizenship in the Civil Rights Act of 1866: "That all persons born in the United States and not subject to any foreign power, excluding Indians not taxed, are hereby declared to be citizens of the United States."[18] This definition was substantially the same as articulated by Chancellor Kent, Attorney General Bates, and the Lincoln administration but contrary to Chief Justice Taney's *Dred Scott* opinion.

President Andrew Johnson vetoed the Civil Rights Act. Among his objections Johnson thought Congress lacked the power to confer citizenship. He also doubted that former slaves "possesse[d] the requisite qualifications" to entitle them to the rights of U.S. citizens and complained that the 1866 act's recognition of citizenship for African Americans discriminated against a "large number of intelligent, worthy, and patriotic foreigners" who must wait for citizenship for five years and prove good moral character.[19] Congress, however, overrode the veto.

By this time, other courts had spoken on the subject as well.[20] Indeed, members of Congress had expressed the sentiment that the Thirteenth Amendment, having abolished slavery, made former slaves citizens.[21] This sentiment was echoed judicially by Chief Justice Chase in his circuit decision in *In re Turner* in 1867. In striking down Maryland apprenticeship laws as a form of involuntary servitude, Chase upheld the constitutionality of the Civil Rights Act of 1866 and concluded, "Colored persons equally with White persons are citizens of the United States."

It is fair to say that by February 1866, when discussion of the Fourteenth Amendment began, the predominant sentiment in the Congress was that African Americans were citizens and that *Dred Scott* had no effect. Indeed, during the debates on the amendment in the House, its primary author, John Bingham, concluded that "every slave[,] the minute he is emancipated becomes a 'free person,' which embraces all citizens, in the words of our Constitution, becomes equal before the law with every *other citizen* of the United States."[22]

The citizenship clause was part of neither Bingham's draft of section 1 nor the amendment as initially proposed by the House. In the view of many Republicans, and apparently the majority of the House of Representatives, there was no need for a citizenship clause. After all, *Dred Scott* was wrong, and the citizenship views of Chancellor Kent were reinforced by the national citizenship theory of Article IV, section 2 and confirmed by an attorney general's opinion and the Civil Rights Act of 1866. But there must have been doubts in the Senate. The citizenship clause arose in an obscure way from proceedings in the Senate. After initial debate, the Senate adjourned for a three-day closed caucus of its Republican members.[23] Though the exact transactions of that caucus are not known, the proposal to add the current citizenship clause to the Fourteenth Amendment emerged from it.[24]

Bingham's fellow Ohioan, Senator Ben Wade, first moved adoption of a clause defining citizenship. Wade treated the matter as declaratory, indicating that both the Civil Rights Act of 1866 and prior law required that "every person, of whatever race or color, who was born within the United States was a citizen of the United States." [25] Other Republican senators articulated similar sentiments. For example, conservative Republican senator John B. Henderson of Missouri indicated that the citizenship clause "will leave citizenship where it now is." [26]

But Wade recognized that "the courts" had thrown a "doubt" over his views and proposed "to solve that doubt and put the question beyond all cavil for the present and for the future" by adopting a citizenship clause. [27] Senator Jacob Howard, the floor manager of the Fourteenth Amendment in the Senate, offered a substitute to Wade's original proposal, which defined the citizenship clause as it was ultimately adopted: "All persons born or naturalized in the United States and subject to the jurisdiction thereof, are citizens of the United States and of the state wherein they reside." Howard reiterated that the citizenship clause was "simply declaratory of the law already." [28]

The citizenship clause, along with a proposal from the caucus to amend section 3 on the ability of former Confederates to hold office, was adopted by the Senate by a vote of thirty-three to eleven. [29] At the very least, the citizenship clause put into the Constitution what before was only written in the Civil Rights Act of 1866. Those who thought that citizenship carried with it a bundle of rights may have been referring to the citizenship clause when they indicated that the Fourteenth Amendment "constitutionalized" the Civil Rights Act. [30] What commentary exists about the citizenship clause reveals that it was thought to add no new law but simply to be a "declaratory" of existing law. [31] At the most it was intended to restate what the Republicans believed the law of the land to be; but if it meant more, it was designed to strengthen, not weaken, the amendment.

However, just five years later the United States Supreme Court in *The Slaughter-House Cases* read the privileges and immunities clause out of the Fourteenth Amendment. [32] Justice Samuel Miller used the citizenship clause and the contrasts between state citizenship and national citizenship to create an argument that severely limited the effect of the Fourteenth Amendment. [33] The way in which Justice Miller accomplished this ironic, unintended use of the citizenship clause is a tale in and of itself. [34] It may be worth noting that Miller did not embrace the Fourteenth Amendment but rather supported President Johnson's conservative counteramendment. [35] Unlike President Lincoln, Attorney General Bates, and the Republican Congress, Justice Miller also accepted *Dred Scott* as binding precedent on the issue of citizenship. [36] One puzzling aspect of Miller's opinion in *Slaughter-House* is that even though he was a keen observer of the political situation and the actions of the Congress, Miller acted as if he were unaware of the citizenship clause of the Civil Rights Act of 1866, writing that no definition of citizenship was in the Constitution, "nor had any attempt been made to define it by act of Congress."[37]

Thus, while key Republican leaders such as Wade, Howard, and Bingham may have seen the Fourteenth Amendment citizenship clause as declaratory because it stated explicitly the ellipsis in Article IV, Miller ignored such a possibility. With his contrarian views, Miller saw the limited purpose of the citizenship clause to overruling *Dred Scott*.[38] But he also saw the ability to use the clause for a "limiting" purpose. By contrasting the rights of state citizens with those of federal citizenship, Miller created an opportunity to keep alive his view of federalism. To do so he became a textualist, contrasting the language of the Article IV, section 2 citizenship clause with that of section 1 of the Fourteenth Amendment. But, as previously noted, moderate Republicans such as John Bingham and James Wilson, supported by a majority of the Congress, had already publicly read that clause to create national citizenship. Comparing two clauses that both talked about national citizenship would not support Miller's textual argument.

In the end Miller resolved the dilemma by misquoting Article IV, section 2. By reading Article IV, section 2 as a reference to state citizenship, he was able to contrast state and federal citizenship and suggest that the Constitution implied different rights under each.[39] He began by contrasting the "citizens of the United States" language of section 1 with a paraphrase of the "citizens in the several states" language of Article IV, section 2. In this paraphrase, Miller changed "citizens in the several states" to read "citizens of the several states."[40] He then proceeded to purport to quote the text of Article IV, section 2 itself but again changed the quoted material to read "citizens of the several states" instead of "citizens in the several states."

The misquotation continued throughout the opinion. Miller quoted at length the opinion of Justice Bushrod Washington, which he referred to as "the first and the leading case" on the interpretation of Article IV, section 2.[41] While Justice Washington correctly quoted the language of Article IV, section 2 in his opinion, when Miller copied the quotation into his own opinion he changed Washington's "of" to an "in."[42] A similar change in paraphrase appears in reference to the Court's holding in *Ward v. Maryland*.[43] Finally, Miller wrote the headnotes that appear before the opinion.[44] Even though Justice Bradley's dissent brought Miller's misquotation to his attention, Miller's headnote 3 continues to misparaphrase Article IV, section 2.[45]

With these misquotations, Miller was able to present a strong textual contrast between Article IV, section 2 (protection of the rights that came about because of state citizenship) and section 1 of the Fourteenth Amendment (protection of rights that came about because of federal citizenship). Though that was a distinction he could have made without resorting to textual argument, Miller claimed the contrast between his version of Article IV, section 2 and the citizenship clause of the Fourteenth Amendment provided "explicit recognition in this amendment" of the distinction.[46]

Having made the distinction, Justice Miller assigned most of the "rights" that Americans claim into the category protected by state citizenship. Miller's only illustrations of rights protected by national citizenship were those that preexisted and could be maintained without the Fourteenth Amendment. In the hands of Justice Miller the citizenship clause, rather than strengthening the amendment, as the Senate framers supposed, had the perverse and unintended effect of weakening the force and effect of the amendment.[47]

The Due Process Clause: An Unintended Potency

The framers of the Fourteenth Amendment were undoubtedly aware of the doctrine of "substantive" due process, or at least its twin "reasonableness," which can be traced to English and American common law.[48] While Chief Judge Taney sought to use substantive due process to protect slavery, Republicans sought to use it to prohibit slavery in the territories. In its Philadelphia platform of 1856 the Republican party indicated that the Fifth Amendment due process clause made it

> our duty to maintain this provision of the Constitution against all attempts to violate it for the purpose of establishing slavery in the territories of the United States by positive legislation, prohibiting its existence or extension therein. That we deny the authority of Congress, of a Territorial legislature, of any individual, or association of individuals, to give legal existence to slavery in any Territory of the United States, while the present Constitution shall be maintained.[49]

Consequently, the framers of the amendment would not be surprised to discover that the due process clause was not strictly procedural. Having acknowledged this much, it is clear that the framers of the Fourteenth Amendment did not envision the type of substantive role for the due process clause developed through the doctrine of "substantive due process" and through the doctrine of selective incorporation. Indeed, when questioned on the floor of Congress about the meaning of the due process clause, John Bingham replied that the "courts have settled that long ago, and the gentlemen can go and read their decisions."[50]

Bingham could treat the due process clause as one deserving little discussion for two separate reasons. First, while the framers undoubtedly anticipated adding additional substantive protections, they envisioned doing so through the privileges and immunities clause. This is evident from an examination of congressional debates. As summarized by Professor Charles Fairman in a lecture at Boston University: "Congress, no doubt, meant . . . to establish some substantial rights even though the state might not itself have established them for its own citizens. These were the 'privileges and immunities of citizens of the United States.'"[51]

Further, at the time the Fourteenth Amendment was proposed, every state in the Union had some sort of due process or due course of law clause.[52] The framers of the Fourteenth Amendment did not believe that they were creating a "new" provision because they acknowledged the existence of that provision in state constitutions. What the framers thought they were doing new was creating the enforceability of that provision by the federal government.

Enforceability was a two-part process. First, the framers wanted to provide a federal guarantee of due process of law as they did in section 1. Second, they wanted to provide explicit authority for enforcement. These goals were a direct response to the antislavery debate. The national antislavery theory articulated by Chase and refined by people such as Ohio attorney general Christopher P. Wolcott and John A. Bingham began with the proposition that the fugitive slave clause was only a "compact" between the states that the federal government could not enforce without an enforcement clause.[53] Support for this view came from Chief Justice Taney, whose opinion in *Kentucky v. Dennison* held that the federal government could not enforce the fugitive from justice clause of Article IV.[54]

The debate between Bingham and Wilson was one of theory and consistency against pragmatism. Bingham upheld the nonenforceability theory even if it meant that the Bill of Rights could not be enforced against the state through section 2 of Article IV. Wilson was willing to throw the theory overboard, rely upon the proslavery precedent of *Prigg v. Pennsylvania*, and legislate to enforce section 2.[55] This issue was explicitly resolved by section 5 of the Fourteenth Amendment, which allowed Congress to enforce the Fourteenth Amendment.[56] Thus, while the framers certainly would not have been surprised if the due process clause had a certain substantive component, they never intended for it to play the significant role it did in the late nineteenth and early twentieth centuries.

Like his friend Justice Robert Jackson, Fairman concluded that the privileges and immunities clause would either mean "too much" or "almost nothing" and thought the Court made an appropriate decision when it concluded the clause would mean "too little."[57] In spite of all of Felix Frankfurter's claim to rely upon historical records, his position was essentially the same. Frankfurter opposed the privileges and immunities clause of the Fourteenth Amendment and wished that it had never been adopted.[58]

It has been suggested that the demise of the substantive reading of the privileges and immunities clause in *The Slaughter-House Cases* "obligated" the justices to expand the due process clause.[59] The argument continues that the Supreme Court "compensated" for the loss of the privileges and immunities clause through an expanded reading of the due process and equal protection clause.[60] If Felix Frankfurter had provided the fifth and majority vote to Justice Hugo Black's dissent in *Adamson v. California*, then the Bill of Rights would have been enforced against the states through the privileges and immunities clause of the Fourteenth Amendment.[61] This could have negated any attempt to stretch the due process clause protections and forestall later attempts to expand its substantive protections. Ironically, it was the triumph of the Miller/Frankfurter view that the privileges and immunities clause ought to be read as a "nullity" that led to the transformation of the due process clause into a far wider substantive role than its framers had intended.

Equal Protection for African Americans: A Goal Not Met

It is very clear that the equal protection clause was designed to protect "all persons." Debates in Congress reflect familiarity with provisions and debates over the Articles of Confederation and in the early Congresses, making distinctions between terms such as "inhabitants," "white inhabitants," "citizens," and "persons." The Fourteenth Amendment framers made frequent references to the term "persons," including noncitizens such as aliens, often as the "stranger at the gate." In a highly religious era, the biblical support for protecting aliens was strong. Exodus 22:21 states: "Thou shalt neither vex a stranger, nor oppress him: for ye were strangers in the land of Egypt," and Exodus 23:9 reads: "Also thou shalt not oppress a stranger; for ye know the heart of a stranger, seeing ye were strangers in the land of Egypt."

Fourteenth Amendment author John Bingham argued that equality was the foundation of the original Constitution.[62] Even before proposing the amendment Bingham frequently made it clear that he thought due process and equal protection applied to all people. Essentially, he believed these were "inborn" or natural rights that our Constitution had chosen to protect for all people. In his eloquent words:

> No matter upon what spot of the earth's surface they were born; no matter whether an Asiatic or African, a European or an American sun first burned upon them; no matter whether citizens or strangers; no matter whether rich or poor; no matter whether wise or simple; no matter whether strong or weak, this new Magna Charta [the Fifth Amendment] to mankind declares the rights of all to life and liberty and property are equal before the law; that no person, by virtue of the American Constitution, . . . shall be deprived of life or liberty or property without due process of law.[63]

There are also frequent references during the debates to the equality provisions of the Fourteenth Amendment as ones that would protect white abolitionists, white unionists, and others.[64]

At the same time, it would be inappropriate to ignore the fact that the Reconstruction Congress anticipated that African Americans would be the major beneficiaries of the equality provisions of the Fourteenth Amendment. Indeed, even Justice Samuel Miller, in his narrow view of the Fourteenth Amendment, conceded that African Americans would benefit from the equal protection clause. According to Miller, "the one prevailing purpose" of these amendments was "the freedom of the slave race, the security and firm establishment of that freedom, and the protection of the newly-made Freeman and citizens." [65]

It is therefore ironic that the equal protection clause offered little or no benefit to African Americans. A leading scholar has noted that from the time of the *Slaughter-House* decision in 1873 to *Plessy v. Ferguson* in 1896, 150 Fourteenth Amendment cases came before the Supreme Court, of which only fifteen involved African Americans.[66]

The major examples are well known. In *Bylew v. United States*, the court held that a federal prosecutor could not use the 1866 Civil Rights Act as a basis to present a murder indictment in federal court even when Kentucky law prohibited black victims and witnesses from testifying in state court.[67] This case undermined the efforts of U.S. district attorney Benjamin H. Bristow and his ally, John Marshall Harlan, to enforce the rights of African Americans and Republicans against white terrorism. It was also contrary to the efforts of Circuit Justice Noah Swayne in *United States v. Rhodes.*[68]

In *United States v. Cruikshank* the court held that an armed, paramilitary force of whites could not be prosecuted by the federal government when they killed more than a hundred black Republicans during the Colfax Massacre.[69]

The Reconstruction Congress had passed the Enforcement Act of 1870, which, among other provisions, outlawed conspiracies of private individuals to deny constitutional rights of citizens. The Court rejected, either outright or through hypertechnical pleading requirements, claims that the citizenship clause, the First and Second Amendments, the due process clause, the equal protection clause, or the Fifteenth Amendment would support the enforcement of the statute against three convicted individuals.

The equal protection clause was not strong enough to prevent a punishment for fornication that was more severe for interracial couples than for couples of the same race.[70] Attempts to use the equal protection clause to enforce the "equal" provisions of separate but equal failed in the context of education and transportation.[71]

There was a glimmer of hope that the Fourteenth Amendment would provide protection for African Americans in jury selection cases, beginning with *Struader v. West Virginia*.[72] By a vote of seven to two the Court struck down a Virginia statute that explicitly excluded African American jurors from jury service. In two other cases, *Ex parte Virginia* and *Neal v. Delaware*, the Court held that the equal protection clause was violated even when there was no statute if uniform exclusion of African Americans from juries was the practice.[73] These seeming gains, however, were largely nullified by *Virginia v. Rives*, which held that the absence of African Americans from a jury, even if systematic, did not in and of itself create a violation of the equal protection clause that a criminal defendant could challenge.[74]

Any hope from the jury cases was quickly brought to an end by *The Civil Rights Cases*. In 1883 Justice Bradley, the son-in-law of abolitionist New Jersey justice Joseph C. Hornblower, who declared slavery unconstitutional in New Jersey, ruled the Civil Rights Act of 1875 unconstitutional, rejecting claims that it was authorized by the Thirteenth and Fourteenth Amendments.[75] Only Justice John Marshall Harlan's ringing dissent left any ray of hope for the future.

While the Court was refusing to give meaning to the national citizenship clause, refusing to enforce the Bill of Rights against the states through the privileges and immunities clause, refusing to apply the equal protection clause to enforce equal treatment before the law, and refusing to fashion due process remedies for African Americans, it was using liberal construction in other contexts. In order to protect the right of employers to insist that new employees sign a "yellow dog contract" agreeing never to join a union as a condition of employment and the "right" of employees to sign such a contract, the court struck down both state and federal bans on such contracts.[76] Justice Miller, whose crabbed construction resulted in the demise of the

Fourteenth Amendment's privileges and immunities clause, nevertheless used a very liberal construction to find a right to interstate travel from the "structure" of the government in *Crandall v. Nevada* and used the "limitations on the power which grow out of the essential nature of all free governments" to limit the power of the state to tax.[77]

In *Allgeyer v. Louisiana* the due process clause, powerless to protect the rights of African Americans, was found to prevent the state of Louisiana from requiring all corporations doing business with Louisiana residents to pay a tax.[78] The Court gave railroad regulators warning that the due process clause would restrict the state regulatory power over railroads and notice to all state governments that the due process clause would limit their regulations.[79]

While African Americans received almost no protection under the equal protection clause, white males and corporations appeared its primary beneficiaries. This produced an unintentional result of the Fourteenth Amendment: the orphaning of African Americans. While it is true that many of the initial aspirations of the amendment were recovered in the 1960s, this neglect over a period of almost a hundred years was not only an unintended result of the amendment but a result contrary to its purpose.

Protection for Corporations: An Issue Not Contemplated

In the 1920s the view prevailed that a group of railroad lawyers had conspired to hide protection for corporations within the amendment.[80] That view has long since been discredited.[81] It is no doubt true that some members of Congress who represented railroads tried to use the Fourteenth Amendment to their advantage.[82] Yet Fourteenth Amendment author John Bingham was not counsel for any railroad. In the only recorded case involving a railroad in which he was counsel he represented a farmer who opposed the railroad's interests.[83]

John Bingham continued in Congress until 1872, six years after the amendment had been proposed and four years after its ratification. In his service as chair of the Judiciary Committee, he had occasion to point out his views on the meaning of the Fourteenth Amendment. For example, he authored a majority report rejecting the argument that the Fourteenth Amendment gave women the right to vote.[84] He also articulated, in what is perhaps the clearest statement for modern ears, his view that the Fourteenth Amendment made the full Bill of Rights enforceable against the states.[85] There does not seem to be any trace of a statement by Bingham that would suggest that he contemplated the Fourteenth Amendment applying to corporations. Still, there also is no evidence indicating that the framers or the ratifiers intended to exclude artificial persons from the definition of "person." [86]

In his massive study of the Fourteenth Amendment, Charles Fairman quoted a lecture of former justice Benjamin R. Curtis as follows: "I suppose . . . that neither the framers of the Constitution nor the framers of the Judiciary Act had corporations in view." [87] Fairman added, "With equal truth one may add that the framers of the Fourteenth Amendment did not have corporations in view. . . . How far corporations would be entitled to protection under the Amendment was one of those questions left 'to the gradual process of judicial inclusion and exclusion.'" [88] Nevertheless, people have argued reasonably that at the time the amendment was adopted, the corporations were commonly understood to be "artificial persons."

We know that when we draft rules and regulations they often have unintended consequences. It would seem that Bingham and his colleagues had simply overlooked the question of whether or not corporations would be protected within the meaning of the word "persons." In this sense, the judicial conclusion that corporations were "persons" was an unintended consequence of the Amendment.

The Paradox: Did Congress Intend the Unintended Consequences of the Fourteenth Amendment?

At this point, I want to consider the somewhat paradoxical question of whether Congress intended the unintended consequences of the Fourteenth Amendment. This discussion necessarily begins with the question of the global concerns that Congress treated. Section 1 author John Bingham indicated that his purpose was to "perfect" the existing Constitution.[89] The Fourteenth Amendment itself was referred to as a new Magna Carta. In a general sense, the framers intended to improve society.

The structure of the amendment borrowed from the format used in legislation, but it was sui generis in the constitutional amendment process. To understand this one must first look at the structure of the amendment itself. The amendment contains five sections. Section 1 contains a citizenship clause, a clause providing privileges and immunities for U.S. citizens, and clauses providing for equal protection and due process for all "persons." [90] This provision, in and of itself, is an intriguing bundle of rights, but they are arguably linked together in much the same way as the various rights enumerated in the Fifth Amendment of the original Constitution.

The same connection for the topics within section 1 cannot be made between the topics covered by sections 1 and 2 or sections 3 and 4. Section 2 treats the apportionment of members of the House of Representatives and provides a sanction for prohibiting males from voting.[91] Equally dissimilar is the disqualification provision for certain former Confederates in section 3.[92] Also, standing on a seemingly independent basis are the provisions of section 4 that guarantee the public debt of the United States and prohibit compensation for lost slaves and the payment of debt of those in rebellion.[93]

The only link between these various clauses—besides the fact that they are designed to deal with post–Civil War Reconstruction—is section 5, which provides Congress with the power of enforcing them.[94] Some states have constitutional provisions requiring that disparate legislation on different subjects not be linked together.[95] If this principle were applied to the federal government, the Congress would not have presented the Fourteenth Amendment as one unified package. Indeed, in attempting to rescind Ohio's ratification of the amendment, the Democratic legislature noted that "several distinct propositions are combined in the said proposed amendment."[96]

Precedent would seem to suggest the same result. The First Congress faced a similar situation when it proposed wide-reaching changes that resulted in the Bill of Rights. That Congress proposed twelve amendments. Only ten were contemporaneously ratified, while two suffered apparent rejection. Had the Fourteenth Amendment framers imitated the action of the proponents of the Bill of Rights, they would have submitted four separate amendments, presenting to the legislators the Fourteenth, Fifteenth, Sixteenth, and Seventeenth Amendments, each having its own enforcement clause. This would have allowed the ratifiers to pick and choose among the various proposals.[97]

The Fourteenth Amendment framers could have found numerous political examples that illustrated processes that allowed ratification choices. Most important, of course, was the action of the First Congress, but other examples stood out as well. Congressmen commonly added "riders" to pending legislation so that legislation they wanted to pass could go through on the "coattails" of stronger legislation. They also had experience with so-called omnibus provisions, although many of them remembered the omnibus Compromise of 1850, which was rejected but then passed in its individual parts.

The framers of the Fourteenth Amendment obviously made a reasoned choice to link these disparate amendments together. It has been suggested that it was the submission of an omnibus provision by Robert Dale Owen to Thaddeus Stevens that was the impetus to combine several proposed amendments into one.[98] But there is other evidence suggesting that Owen was not alone in trying to link disparate provisions into one omnibus amendment. On 25 January 1866 John Bingham advocated adding to his original proposal a "provision that no State in this Union shall ever lay one cent of tax upon the property or head of any loyal man for the purpose of paying tribute or pensions to those who rendered service in the . . . atrocious rebellion."[99] Similarly, an earlier resolution in the Senate linked several different proposals together.[100] We can only surmise that the congressmen did this for the usual legislative reason: they thought they had a greater chance of having these provisions all passed if they were proposed collectively than if they were submitted individually. Stated in other language, they feared that if all of these provisions were presented separately, states might ratify some and not ratify others.

Thus understood, the framers undoubtedly intended to use the popular provisions of the amendment to secure passage of its more controversial provisions. This means that some of the consequences anticipated by the framers may not have been intended by the ratifiers. In order to appreciate this strategy, one must appreciate what the people of 1868 thought was at stake.

CONTEXT

The modern reader may have trouble appreciating the dilemma faced by those proposing the Fourteenth Amendment and those called upon to ratify it. As has often been noted, the Congress and the ratifying legislatures were focusing upon their problems, not ours.[101] One lingering controversy— whether the Bill of Rights was incorporated by the Fourteenth Amendment—can help illuminate their dilemma.

Two of the leading opponents of what has been called the "incorporation doctrine" (enforcing the Bill of Rights against the states through the Fourteenth Amendment) were Justice Felix Frankfurter and his former pupil, Harvard law professor Charles Fairman. Both held in disdain the Fifth Amendment requirement that a grand jury indictment was necessary to commence criminal proceedings, the Fifth Amendment right against self-incrimination, and the Seventh Amendment requirement for jury trials in civil cases.[102]

In his landmark concurring opinion in *Adamson v. California*, Justice Frankfurter indicated that if the ratifiers of the Fourteenth Amendment had known that it would require them to use the grand jury provisions of the Fifth Amendment, they would not have ratified the amendment.[103] Two years later, in a 1950 private letter to Fairman, Frankfurter reached the same conclusion, adding his aversion to common-law civil jury trials as an added reason.[104]

The Fairman/Frankfurter view has been hotly disputed.[105] This section tests the Fairman/Frankfurter view by considering the choices a state legislator in 1866 would face in determining whether to ratify the amendment or to preserve his state's right to avoid grand juries and civil jury trials. In effect, the important question is whether the evils of providing grand juries and civil jury trials are greater than the evils that the Fourteenth Amendment was designed to cure. The choices facing legislators or voters for state legislators in 1866 can best be understood by considering the evils sections 2, 3, and 4 of the Fourteenth Amendment were designed to overcome.

SECTION 2: APPORTIONMENT

The apportionment of representatives for the House of Representatives is of tremendous importance. It not only determines the fate of one House of the national legislature but also, through its direct influence on the electoral college, determines who becomes president. The question of whether to count for apportionment purposes slaves who could not vote was an issue that loomed large at the constitutional convention in Philadelphia. The question was compromised by calling for people held in slavery to be counted as three fifths of a person for both apportionment and taxation purposes.[106] One of the grievances of those opposed to the oligarchy they termed the "Slave Power" was that this made the votes of the slaveholding South more important than the same number of voters in the North.

After the war slavery was abolished. An African American who had previously counted as only three fifths of a person for apportionment purposes would now be counted as a full person. In spite of the initial steps Lincoln had taken toward very limited black suffrage in the South, the state governments established under Andrew Johnson all limited suffrage to white males.

The readmission of southern states counting African Americans as complete persons produced a striking anomaly: even though it had lost the war, the white South would return to Congress with even more political power in the House of Representatives and the electoral college. African Americans would have no more right to vote after slavery than before slavery, but the white elite that had caused such a costly war would increase its political power by the addition of two fifths of the African American population in the apportionment process. This added strength, combined with disloyal elements of the Democratic party in the North, could undo the results of the Civil War, in which so many lives had been lost and so much treasure had been spent.

The prospect of the loser in a civil war gaining increased political power "was unique in history."[107] This issue could have been solved by a provision that required southern states to allow African Americans to vote. But the nation was not yet prepared for such an amendment. Instead, after much debate, section 2 proposed to count the entire population of the state, but to reduce that number by the proportion of males over age twenty-one excluded from the apportionment to the entire number of males of that age. If all African Americans were excluded from voting, section 2 could actually reduce the voting power of a southern state that limited votes to whites. This would force the states to choose between increased representation with black voters or reduced representation and the ability to exclude black voters.

The problem with the apportionment provision was that it did too much and it did not do enough. Anyone who wanted a guarantee of voting rights was disappointed by its weakness. Anyone who disapproved of African American voting would be disappointed by its potential penalty if African Americans were excluded. Moral people who supported race-neutral voting would be disappointed by the penalty provision's implication: it authorized the exclusion of black voters as long as one was willing to pay the penalty. Those who believed voting was a state matter would be offended by the federal attempt to "coerce" the states into allowing African Americans to vote.

There were many reasons people could be disturbed by section 2. But if forced to choose between the objective section 2 sought to achieve (prohibiting increased power for former rebels) and returning to the common law and federal rules for civil juries and grand juries, it is unlikely that voters would reject the amendment in order to preserve jury innovations.

SECTION 3: CONFEDERATE OFFICERS

Some of the concerns over the apportionment issue addressed by section 2 were highlighted by the actions of the white South when voters elected former leaders of the Confederate States to positions in the Johnson government. Perhaps the most notorious example of this came from the state of Georgia, where Alexander Stephens, former vice president of the Confederate States, was elected in 1865 by the legislature to be a U.S. senator.[108] Similarly, Herschel V. Johnson, who had served two terms as a Confederate senator, was also elected by Georgia as a U.S. senator that same year.[109]

It is easy to explain these actions now as voters turning to the (alleged) only men of ability available, the (alleged) "natural" leaders of the community. But to the majority of northerners these men were traitors who had caused the greatest war in the history of the North American continent.

These men had been part of the "Slave Power Conspiracy" to destroy democracy. They were also thought to have been involved in war crimes that included the starvation and execution of war prisoners at Andersonville, the assassination of President Lincoln, and the execution of black Union soldiers. With over 350,000 Union soldiers killed and hundreds of thousands wounded, the North viewed the men who had led the southern Confederacy as traitors who would again harm the Union if given a chance to return to the national Congress.

Section 3 made it impossible for "traitors" with blood on their hands to enter national positions of leadership. For Thaddeus Stevens section 3 contained the most important provisions of the amendment. He claimed that without section 3 the Fourteenth Amendment "amounts to nothing."[110] This was one of the most widely debated provisions of the amendment.[111]

Northerners disagreed about the degree to which former Confederates should be disqualified from holding office. Their fear of the originators of the rebellion returning to power should not be viewed as unnatural, however. One has only to consider American reactions to the defeated in its foreign wars. After World War I, the Allies had no intention of allowing the German kaiser to remain in power. The Allies of World War II tried to structure the governments of Germany and Japan in such a way that the leadership of the Nazi party and the Japanese military would not return to power. Even after the Gulf War, the people of the United States were distressed that Saddam Hussein would remain the ruler of Iraq, because they perceived him to be the aggressor and the cause of the war. With all the loss of life in the Civil War, one can imagine northerners acting upon the same concerns.

The question remains, which was the lesser evil facing the ratifiers? It is extremely unlikely that the ratifiers would view freedom from common rules for civil juries and grand juries as being more important than keeping leaders of the rebellion from participating in the national government.

SECTION 4: SECURING THE PUBLIC DEBT

Section 4 of the amendment provided that the U.S. public debt, including payment of pensions and bounties to soldiers and their families, "shall not be questioned." Even during the war, northern Democrats talked openly of repudiating the war debt. While the amendment was pending the Democrats formulated proposals to tax the bonds of those to whom the federal debt was owed and/or to pay off the debt in depreciated currency.[112] These efforts were challenged as endangering pensions and other claims of widows and orphans of Union soldiers.[113]

Joseph James thought that the provision guaranteeing the national debt "had more influence [in assuring the amendment's passage] than many have assumed." [114] Indeed, James quoted the 18 September 1866 issue of the *New York Herald* as calling it "the great secret strength of this constitutional amendment." [115] Weighed in the balance, protection for the integrity of the war debt from repudiation by alliances of antiwar Democrats and former Confederates and insurance of the integrity of the pledged pensions to war veterans and the widows of war veterans were far more important to the voters of 1866–68 than questions of innovative grand jury and civil jury procedures.

SECTION 4: REPUDIATING THE SO-CALLED CONFEDERATE DEBT

The question of the Confederate debt was also a large one. A contemporary account estimated that the Confederate debt exceeded $2 billion, while individual states and local governments had incurred another billion dollars of debt.[116] In his testimony before the joint committee on Reconstruction former Confederate general Robert E. Lee indicated that he thought Virginians were in favor of paying the Confederate debt and that he had "never heard any one in the State with whom I have conversed speak of repudiating any debt." [117] The North Carolina Convention of 1865 at first refused to repudiate the state's Confederate debt until President Johnson intervened.[118] Even then, W. E. B. Du Bois reported that "the leading newspapers . . . called the action 'humiliating.'" [119]

One key concern was that if the Confederate debts were not treated as void, future rebellions could use the precedent to establish credit.[120] Further, it was felt that creditors who had aided the rebellion should be punished by the loss of the amount of the debt. An added fear was that loyal men of the southern states, white and black, would be taxed to pay the debts of rebels.[121] Republicans were also concerned that the leaders of the rebellion would regain political power by promising to pay the Confederate debt and supporting pensions to Confederate soldiers.[122]

A further issue was whether the southern states would use taxpayers' money in a discriminatory fashion. Georgia had appropriated $200,000 for assistance to widows and children of Confederate veterans but had made no provision for its Union veterans.[123] When North Carolina, which had contributed six regiments of Union troops to the war effort, passed legislation to provide artificial limbs to its citizens, the law made it clear that they would be supplied only to its Confederate and not to its Union veterans.[124] Again, any reluctance to follow common-law grand and petit jury procedures seems to pale in significance when contrasted with the seeming importance of protecting the Union debt and repudiating the debts that supported the rebellion.

SECTION 4: DENYING COMPENSATION FOR FORMER SLAVES

One provision of section 4 of the Fourteenth Amendment that receives little attention provides that "neither the United States nor any State shall assume or pay . . . any claim for the loss or emancipation of any slave." The slaveholders claimed slaves as property, and they were counted as such in state census records and state tax appraisals and for similar purposes. In 1868 George W. Paschal, a Unionist and former slaveholder, estimated that the value of emancipated slaves was more than $2 billion.[125] A committee of the Forty-second Congress placed the loss at $1.6 billion.[126] To place this amount in context, one needs to note that the South's entire property, including slaves, was assessed in 1860 at $4.4 billion and in 1870 at $2.1 billion.[127]

There were many claims for reimbursement of former slaveowners from the "taking" of their "property" by the federal government, whether through the Thirteenth Amendment or some other action during the war. These claims had a legal and political basis under the Fifth Amendment, which provides that no person shall "be deprived of . . . property without due process of law" and that "private property" shall not be "taken for public use without just compensation." Support for such a claim can be found in the unreversed decision of *Dred Scott* in which the Supreme Court recognized slaves as property and used the Fifth Amendment due process clause to protect them. Further, throughout the war President Lincoln had tried to coax the border states into emancipating slaves *with compensation.*[128] These attempts, even though rejected, may have further conditioned slaveowners to think that if their slaves were emancipated, they were entitled to government compensation.

Examples of these views appeared in state governmental proceedings immediately after the war. For example, the Georgia Convention, elected in October 1865 to frame a new constitution, abolished slavery but added: "This acquiescence in the action of the Government of the United States, is not intended to operate as a relinquishment, waiver or estoppel of such claim for compensation or loss sustained by reason of the emancipation of his slaves, as any citizen of Georgia may hereafter make upon the justice and magnanimity of that government."[129]

Even with Salmon P. Chase, a leading antislavery lawyer and the national architect of the antislavery movement's legal strategy, as its chief justice, the memory of *Dred Scott* was too vivid in the mind of the public to erase the possibility that a suit by even a single former slaveholder might result in a judgment against the United States for taking property without just compensation. Moreover, the perpetual fear of an alliance between former slaveholders and their former allies, northern Democrats, provided a strong incentive to lay this question to rest by a constitutional amendment. The prospect of risking between $1.5 and $2 billion in debt, when weighed against complying with common-law jury provisions, would make the latter seem petty. Faced with such a choice, even a ratifier who disdained common-law jury provisions would see ratification as a "greater good."

When viewed from this standpoint, it is possible to conclude that the framers knew, or at least feared, that one or more of the separate sections of the Fourteenth Amendment would not command the necessary support from state legislatures. This knowledge led them to link the provisions together to gain a result that the legislatures themselves may not have intended.

This unique approach had another significant consequence. As David Kyvig has written, "To combine a number of proposals into a single measure subtly but perceptibly shifted critical decision making from the ratifiers to the initial adopters of an amendment resolution. Unlike the 1790s experience, states would confront a take-it-or-leave-it, all-or-nothing choice."[130] Thus, unlike other constitutional amendments, in which the concerns of the ratifiers may be paramount, in the Fourteenth Amendment our primary focus is upon the framers. This insight may help unravel why states would vote to ratify the Fourteenth Amendment and then not conform their state constitution to comply with its provisions.[131] To be sure, they may have focused upon the bigger issues like disfranchisement and public debt and ignored less pressing matters like enforcement of the Bill of Rights. But an equally plausible explanation is that in some cases states did not want to ratify the whole package but did so as the lesser of two evils. The greater evil was not ratifying at all. This hypothesis may well help explain some of the convoluted postamendment actions by courts and state legislators upon which Fairman relied so heavily. But it may also mean that the *framers* of the amendment intended to produce consequences that the *ratifiers* did not intend.

This analysis may provide insight into the academic and judicial controversies over incorporations of the late 1940s and 1950s. The arguments that Justice Hugo Black and Chicago's William W. Crosskey made in favor of incorporation were based largely upon the intent of the framers. The rejection of those arguments by Justice Felix Frankfurter and Charles Fairman were based largely upon the intent of the ratifiers of the amendment.[132] While the full picture should include the view of both the framers and the ratifiers, as David Kyvig's insight suggests, in this instance it is the work of the framers that should trump any contrary views held by individual ratifiers.

Conclusion

This examination of the unintended consequences of the Fourteenth Amendment suggests that the framers of that amendment were as human as current legislators. In some cases, such as during the adoption of the citizenship clause, they simply did not anticipate the use to which their work could be put. The clause they hoped would strengthen the amendment was actually used to weaken it.

In other cases, such as their intention that the due process clause be a supplementary clause and not a major new protection of the amendment, they could not foresee the ways in which the judiciary would interpret first the privileges and immunities clause and then the due process clause. In other instances, such as their linking of the parts of the amendment together in one omnibus amendment, they may have had paramount political motives in mind. They may have intended to force the state legislatures to adopt a broader package of protections than would have been possible if each had been submitted separately.

The lessons we learn from this are worth remembering. We know that people in the legislative process engage in politics. We know that those creating legislation, whether of a statutory or fundamental nature, cannot predict all the results, and we know that we can only dimly see the future. While these considerations may enlighten our understanding of the Fourteenth Amendment, it should not dim our appreciation for the efforts of the Thirty-ninth Congress.

NOTES

1. James E. Bond, "The Original Understanding of the Fourteenth Amendment in Illinois, Ohio, and Pennsylvania," *Akron Law Review* 18 (1985): 435.

2. Among the classics are Charles Fairman, *Reconstruction and Reunion* (New York: Macmillan, 1971) and "Does the Fourteenth Amendment Incorporate the Bill of Rights?" *Stanford Law Review* 2 (1949): 5; William W. Crosskey, "Charles Fairman, 'Legislative History' and the Constitutional Limitations on State Authority," *University of Chicago Law Review* 22 (1954): 1; Raoul Berger, *Government by Judiciary*

(Cambridge, Mass.: Harvard University Press, 1977); Michael Kent Curtis, *No State Shall Abridge: The Fourteenth Amendment and the Bill of Rights* (Durham, N.C.: Duke University Press, 1986); Alfred Avins, "Incorporation of the Bill of Rights: The Crosskey-Fairman Debates Revisited," *Harvard Journal on Legislation* 6 (1968): 1; Akhil Amar, "The Bill of Rights and the Fourteenth Amendment," *Yale Law Journal* 101 (1992): 1193; Jacobus tenBroek, *Equal under Law* (Berkeley: University of California Press, 1951); and J. Howard Graham, "Our 'Declaratory' Fourteenth Amendment," *Stanford Law Review* 7 (1954): 2.

My own work includes "On Misreading John Bingham and the Fourteenth Amendment," *Yale Law Journal* 103 (1993): 57; "Constricting the Law of Freedom: Justice Miller, the Fourteenth Amendment, and the Slaughter-House Cases," *Chicago-Kent Law Review* 70 (1995): 627; and "Felix Frankfurter, Charles Fairman, and the Fourteenth Amendment," *Chicago-Kent Law Review* 70 (1995): 1197.

No listing would be complete, of course, without reference to Justice Black's pathbreaking dissent in *Adamson v. California*, 332 U.S. 46, 68 (1949).

3. *Live-Stock Dealers and Butchers' Ass'n. v. Crescent City Landing and Slaughter-House Co.*, 15 F. Case. 649 (CCD 1870), no. 8, 408.

4. See, generally, James H. Kettner, *The Development of American Citizenship, 1608–1870* (Chapel Hill: University of North Carolina Press, 1978).

5. John A. Bingham, *Congressional Globe*, 35th Cong., 2d sess., 1859, 892, quoting and citing James Kent, *Commentaries*, 4th ed. (New York: E. B. Clayton, 1840), 2: 257.

6. For example, Timothy Walker, *Introduction to Law*, 2d ed. (Cincinnati: Derby, Bradley and Co., 1844): "*Native Citizens*, include . . . all persons born within the jurisdiction of the United States since our independence" (131).

7. For example, *State v. Claiborne*, 19 Tenn. 331, 337 (1838) (free blacks are not citizens of the United States under Article IV, section 2 of the U.S. Constitution) and Thomas R. R. Cobb, *The Law of Slavery in America* (Philadelphia: T. and J. W. Johnson, 1858). See also *Amy (a woman of colour) v. Smith*, 1 Litt. 326 (Ky. 1822), in which the majority found that after the adoption of the Constitution only white people can become citizens (344). But in his dissent, Justice Benjamin Mills concluded that because Amy had been a citizen of Pennsylvania she was a citizen under the Article IV, section 2 privileges and immunities clause (344).

8. Aynes, "On Misreading John Bingham," 57, 71, 78, n. 124.

9. Ibid., 78–79, summaries and citations.

10. Ibid., 79–80.

11. *Dred Scott v. Sandford*, 60 U.S. (19 How.) 393 (1856). See Don E. Fehrenbacher's landmark book on the *Dred Scott* decision, *The Dred Scott Case: Its Significance in American Law and Politics* (New York: Oxford University Press, 1978); Paul Finkelman, "The Dred Scott Case: Slavery and the Politics of Law," *Hamline Law Review* 20 (1996): 1.

12. Don E. Fehrenbacher, ed., *Abraham Lincoln: Speeches and Writings, 1832–1858* (New York: Library of America, 1989), 392, speech on the *Dred Scott* decision at Springfield, Illinois, on 26 June 1857.

13. Lincoln identified them as (1) unanimous decision; (2) no apparent partisan bias; (3) consistent with past decisions and government practices; and (4) based on accurate historical data (ibid., 393).

14. Herman V. Ames, ed., *State Documents on Federal Relations: The States and the United States* (Philadelphia: University of Pennsylvania Press, 1906), 296.

15. *Ex parte Merryman,* 17 F. Case. 144 (CCD Md. 1861), no. 9, 487 (C. J. Taney in his capacity as circuit justice).

16. Opinion of the Justices, 44 Me. 505, 545 (1857).

17. Opinions of the Attorneys General, 10, 382, 413 (1862). Bates acknowledged the existence of the *Dred Scott* decision but construed it so narrowly as to have no adverse effect upon the rights of African Americans to be citizens.

18. 14 Stat. 27 (9 April 1866).

19. Veto Message, *Congressional Globe,* 39th Cong., 1st sess., 1866, 1679.

20. Robert J. Kaczorowski, "The Chase Court and Fundamental Rights: A Watershed in American Constitutionalism," *Northern Kentucky Law Review* 21 (1993): 161.

21. But see *Bryan v. Walton,* 14 Ga. 185, 198 (1853) (indicating that manumission of a slave signified nothing "but exemption from involuntary service" and did not give former slaves the right of freeborn white inhabitants).

22. *Congressional Globe,* 39th Cong., 1st sess., 1866, 430.

23. See W. E. B. Du Bois, *Black Reconstruction in America* (New York: Torchstone, 1995), 306; Fairman, "Does the Fourteenth Amendment," 2, 59–60, 67–68 and *Reconstruction and Reunion,* pt. 1: 1295–98.

24. Fairman, *Reconstruction and Reunion,* pt. 1: 1295–98.

25. *Congressional Globe,* 39th Cong., 1st sess., 1866, 2768.

26. Ibid., 3031.

27. Ibid., 2768.

28. Ibid., 2890.

29. Ibid., 3149.

30. See examples cited in Berger, *Government by Judiciary,* 22–36. But see Michael Kent Curtis, "Resurrecting the Privileges or Immunities Clause and Revising the Slaughter-House Cases without Exhuming Lochner: Individual Rights and the Fourteenth Amendment," *Boston College Law Review* 38 (1996): 1, which reaches a widely different and, I think, more accurate conclusion about the significance of this result.

31. For example, in treating similar language in the Civil Rights Act of 1866 House Judiciary chairman James Wilson of Iowa argued that it was only declaratory. Similarly, Ohio's William Lawrence, a former judge, made this comment about the statutory citizenship clause: "This clause is unnecessary, but nevertheless proper, since it is only declaratory of what is the law without it" (*Congressional Globe,* 39th Cong., 1st sess., 1866, 1832).

32. *The Slaughter-House Cases,* 83 U.S. (16 Wall.) 36 (1873).

33. Aynes, "Constricting the Law of Freedom," 627. Even Raoul Berger, who

reads the Fourteenth Amendment narrowly, rejects Miller's use of the citizenship clause to limit the reach of the amendment (*Government by Judiciary*, 45). An important new look at *Slaughter-House* is found in Curtis, "Resurrecting." An interesting and novel way to read Justice Miller's opinion as protecting a broader scope of Fourteenth Amendment protection is articulated in Robert Palmer, "The Parameters of Constitutional Reconstruction: Slaughter-House, Cruikshank, and the Fourteenth Amendment," *University of Illinois Law Review* (1984): 739. My reasons for rejecting that interpretation are set forth in Aynes, "Constricting the Law of Freedom," 653–55.

34. See, generally, Curtis, "Resurrecting," and Aynes, "Constricting the Law of Freedom."

35. Aynes, "Constricting the Law of Freedom," 660.

36. *The Slaughter-House Cases*, 83 U.S. 73.

37. Aynes, "Constricting the Law of Freedom," 660–61; *The Slaughter-House Cases*, 83 U.S. 72.

38. *The Slaughter-House Cases*, 83 U.S. 73. In *Saenz v. Roe*, 119 Sup. Ct. 1518 (1999) the Supreme Court held that the Fourteenth Amendment privileges and immunities clause protects the right to travel between different states. It is too early to tell whether this is only an aberration or whether the Court has breathed new life into this long-dormant provision of the Fourteenth Amendment.

39. *The Slaughter-House Cases*, 83 U.S. 74–76.

40. Ibid., 74.

41. Ibid., 75.

42. Ibid., 76.

43. *Ward v. Maryland*, 79 U.S. (12 Wall.) 418 (1870).

44. *The Slaughter-House Cases*, 21 L. Ed. 394, 395 (1873).

45. *The Slaughter-House Cases*, 83 U.S. 37.

46. Ibid., 74.

47. I do not mean to suggest that the majority in *The Slaughter-House Cases* could not have reached the same result if the citizenship clause had never been adopted. On the contrary, Justice Miller could have fashioned the same distinctions between state and federal citizenship out of nontextual sources and utilized that distinction to reach that same result. Indeed, *Dred Scott* itself is based upon a "novel concept of dual citizenship" (Finkelman, "The Dred Scott Case," 28). Whether Miller would have done that or not is, of course, unknown. My point here is the irony of a clause that was designed to strengthen the amendment being used to weaken it.

48. For English common law, see *Bonham's Case*, 77 Eng. Rep. 647, 652 (CP 1610) (Sir Edward Coke: "When an Act of Parliament is against common right and reason . . . the common law will . . . adjudge such an act to be void"). For American, see *Roberts v. City of Boston*, 59 Mass. (5 Cush.) 198 (1849). Even in this early school desegregation case, Chief Justice Shaw and the Supreme Court of Massachusetts indicated that this board of education's rule-making power was limited by its "reasonableness."

49. C. W. Johnson, ed., *Proceedings of the First Three Republican National Conventions — 1856, 1860, 1864* (Minneapolis: C. W. Johnson, 1893), 43.

50. *Congressional Globe*, 39th Cong., 1st sess., 1866, 1089.

51. Charles Fairman, "What Makes a Great Justice?" *Boston University Law Review* 30 (1950): 40, 77.

52. Representative Martin F. Thayer of Pennsylvania suggested that the provisions of the Fourteenth Amendment were "found in the bill of rights of every state of the Union" (*Congressional Globe*, 39th Cong., 1st sess., 1866, 2465).

53. See Aynes, "On Misreading John Bingham," 71–72, 76–78.

54. *Kentucky v. Dennison*, 65 U.S. (24 How.) 66, 90–93, overruled by *Puerto Rico v. Brandstad*, 483 U.S. 219 (1987).

55. See Aynes, "On Misreading John Bingham," 76–78.

56. Antislavery and abolitionist lawyers had long argued that the provisions of section 4 were unenforceable, except for the full faith and credit clause, because they did not have an enforcement clause. Consistency and planning for future contingencies required them to have the concern that their Fourteenth Amendment provisions would not be enforceable unless there was such a clause.

57. Aynes, "Constricting the Law of Freedom," 1240.

58. See, generally, Aynes, "Felix Frankfurter," 1197–1273.

59. Edwin Borchard, "The Supreme Court and Private Rights," *Yale Law Journal* 47 (1938): 1051, 1063.

60. Patricia Alan Luice, "White Rights As a Model for Black: Or—Who's Afraid of the Privileges or Immunities Clause?" *Syracuse Law Review* 38 (1987): 859, 861–62.

61. Black indicated that the rights were protected by both due process and privileges and immunities. But virtually all of his historical proof stemmed from the debates referencing the privileges and immunities clause.

62. For example, on 9 January 1866, Bingham articulated the view that "the true intent and meaning of the Constitution of the United States [was] '[e]qual and exact justice to all men'" (*Congressional Globe*, 39th Cong., 1st sess., 1866, 157). Later in that same speech Bingham indicated that "the divinest feature of your Constitution is the recognition of the absolute equality before the law of all persons" (158). Bingham's purpose in proposing the amendment was "to provide for the efficient enforcement by law, of, these 'equal rights of every man'" (158). The Ohio Constitution, applicable to the state in which Bingham spent almost all of his adult life, provided "that all men are born equally free and independent" (Ohio Constitution of 1802, art. 8, sec. 1) and "government is instituted for [the people's] equal protection and benefit" (Ohio Constitution of 1855, art. 1, sec. 2).

63. To John Bingham, persons included "all persons, whether citizens or stranger, within this land" (*Congressional Globe*, 39th Cong., 1st sess., 1866, 1090, 1292). Indeed, during the debate on the civil rights bill, Bingham unsuccessfully tried to substitute the word "inhabitants" for "citizens" (1292).

64. For example, ibid., 1065 (John Bingham: need to protect "thousands of loyal white citizens" in the South).

65. *The Slaughter-House Cases*, 83 U.S. 71.

66. Charles A. Lofgren, *The Plessy Case* (New York: Oxford University Press, 1987), 70, citing Charles W. Collins, *The Fourteenth Amendment and the States* (Boston: Little, Brown and Co., 1912), 48–55, 183, and adding two more cases Collins overlooked.

67. *Bylew v. United States*, 80 U.S. (13 Wall.) 481 (1871). For an excellent analysis of this case and the facts behind it, see Robert D. Goldstein, "Bylew: Variations on a Jurisdictional Theme," *Stanford Law Review* 41 (1989): 469.

68. *United States v. Rhodes*, 27 F. Case. 785 (CCD Ky. 1866), no. 16, 151.

69. *United States v. Cruikshank*, 92 U.S. 542 (1876).

70. *Pace v. Alabama*, 102 U.S. (16 Otto) 583 (1883).

71. For education, see *Cumming v. Board of Education*, 175 U.S. 528 (1899), and *Berea College v. Kentucky*, 211 U.S. 45 (1908). For transportation, see *McCazbe v. Atchinson, T. & S.F. Ry. Co.*, 235 U.S. 151 (1914).

72. *Struader v. West Virginia*, 100 U.S. 303 (1880).

73. *Ex parte Virginia*, 100 U.S. 339 (1879); *Neal v. Delaware*, 103 U.S. 370 (1880).

74. *Virginia v. Rives*, 100 U.S. 313 (1879).

75. *The Civil Rights Cases*, 109 U.S. 3 (1883).

76. *Adair v. United States*, 208 U.S. 161 (1908); *Coppage v. Kansas*, 236 U.S. 1 (1915).

77. *Loan Association v. Topeka*, 87 U.S. (20 Wall.) 655 (1874).

78. *Allgeyer v. Louisiana*, 165 U.S. 578 (1897).

79. *Railroad Commission Cases*, 116 U.S. 307 (1886); *Mugler v. Kansas*, 123 U.S. 623 (1887).

80. Charles Beard and Mary Beard, *The Rise of American Civilization: 1877–1913* (New York: Macmillan, 1927), 2: 112.

81. Howard Jay Graham, "The 'Conspiracy Theory' of the Fourteenth Amendment," *Yale Law Journal* 47 (1938): 371; Louis B. Boudin, "Truth and Fiction about the Fourteenth Amendment," *New York University Law Review* 16 (1938): 19.

82. The story of Senator Roscoe Conkling and his selective use of excerpts from the *Journal of the Joint Committee* is a familiar one. See Fairman, *Reconstruction and Reunion*, pt. 2: 725–28; Howard Jay Graham, *Everyman's Constitution* (Madison: State Historical Society of Wisconsin, 1962). As Fairman concluded, Conkling's "performance was contrived and misleading" (*Reconstruction and Reunion*, pt. 2: 726). The Court did not rule upon this issue in the *San Mateo v. Southern Pacific R.R. Case*, 116 U.S. 138 (1885). But in the argument of *County of Santa Clara v. Southern Pacific R.R.*, 118 U.S. 394 (1886), the chief justice made this announcement at the beginning of the oral argument: "The court does not wish to hear argument on the question whether the provision in the Fourteenth Amendment, which forbids a state to deny any person within its jurisdiction the equal protection of the laws, applies to these corporations. We are all of [the] opinion that it does" (396).

83. *Steubenville & Indiana R.R. v. Patrick*, 7 Ohio St. 170 (1857).

84. Report no. 22 (Victoria C. Woodhull), *Congressional Globe*, 41st Cong., 3d

sess., 1871, 1–4, reprinted in Alfred Avins, *The Reconstruction Amendments' Debates*, 2d ed. (Wilmington: Delaware Law School, 1974), 466–72.

85. *Congressional Globe*, 42d Cong., 1st sess., 1871, 84.

86. In *Connecticut General Life Ins. Co. v. Johnson*, 303 U.S. 78 (1938) (Black, dissenting), Justice Black made a textual argument that the word "person" meant "human beings" and therefore did not include artificial persons such as corporations. In 1871 Bingham introduced into the Congress legislation that would have protected the "privileges and immunities" of insurance companies (*Congressional Globe*, 41st Cong., 3d sess., 1871, 1288). But since the privileges and immunities clause applies only to citizens, it is possible to believe an insurance company is a person for due process purposes but not a citizen for privileges or immunities purposes.

87. Fairman, *Reconstruction and Reunion*, pt. 2: 724.

88. Ibid., quoting Justice Miller in *Davidson v. New Orleans*, 96 U.S. 97, 104 (1878).

89. *Congressional Globe*, 39th Cong., 1st sess., 1866, 156 ("to introduce into the Constitution . . . that which will perfect it"). See also "Eloquent Speech of Hon. John A. Bingham, Cadiz Republican," 15 August 1866, p. 2, col. 3 (object of the amendment to "restore this Republic and perfect your Constitution").

90. "Section 1. All persons born or naturalized in the United States, and subject to the jurisdiction thereof, are citizens of the United States and of the State wherein they reside. No State shall make or enforce any law which shall abridge the privileges or immunities of citizens of the United States; nor shall any State deprive any person of life, liberty, or property, without due process of law; nor deny to any person within its jurisdiction the equal protection of the laws."

91. "Section 2. Representatives shall be apportioned among the several States according to their respective numbers, counting the whole number of persons in each State, excluding Indians not taxed. But when the right to vote at any election for the choice of electors for President and Vice-President of the United States, Representatives in Congress, the Executive and Judicial officers of a State, or the members of the Legislature thereof, is denied to any of the male inhabitants of such State, being twenty-one years of age, and citizens of the United States, or in any way abridged, except for participation in rebellion, or other crime, the basis of representation therein shall be reduced in the proportion which the number of such male citizens shall bear to the whole number of male citizens twenty-one years of age in such State."

92. "Section 3. No person shall be a Senator or Representative in Congress, or elector of President and Vice-President, or hold any office, civil or military, under the United States, or under any State, who, having previously taken an oath, as a member of Congress, or as an officer of the United States, or as a member of any State legislature, or as an executive or judicial officer of any State, to support the Constitution of the United States, shall have engaged in insurrection or rebellion against the same, or given aid or comfort to the enemies thereof. But Congress may by a vote of two-thirds of each House, remove such disability."

93. "Section 4. The validity of the public debt of the United States, authorized by law, including debts incurred for payment of pensions and bounties for services in suppressing insurrection or rebellion, shall not be questioned. But neither the United States nor any State shall assume or pay any debt or obligation incurred in aid of insurrection or rebellion against the United States, or any claim for the loss or emancipation of any slave; but all such debts, obligations and claims shall be held illegal and void."

94. "Section 5. The Congress shall have power to enforce, by appropriate legislation, the provisions of this article."

95. For example, Ohio Constitution, art. 2, sec. 15(D): "No bill shall contain more than one subject, which shall be clearly expressed in its title."

96. Joint Resolution of the Ohio Legislature, 15 January 1868.

97. Of course, the framers of the original gave the ratifiers the same "binary" choice as the Fourteenth Amendment framers: accept or reject the entire proposal. Jack N. Rakore, *Original Meanings: Politics and Ideas in the Making of the Constitution* (New York: Knopf, 1996), 11.

98. Du Bois, *Black Reconstruction*, 301. See also David E. Kyvig, *Explicit and Authentic Acts, 1776–1995* (Lawrence: University Press of Kansas, 1996), 166–67. For Owen's account, see Robert Dale Owen, "The Political Results from the Varioloid," *Atlantic Monthly* 35 (June 1875): 660.

99. *Congressional Globe*, 39th Cong., 1st sess., 1866, 429, quoted in Graham, *Everyman's Constitution*, 482, n. 197.

100. See *Congressional Globe*, 39th Cong., 1st sess., 1866, 566.

101. William Nelson, *The Fourteenth Amendment* (Cambridge, Mass.: Harvard University Press, 1988), 6; Curtis, *No State Shall Abridge*, 13–15.

102. See Aynes, "Felix Frankfurter," 1221, n. 149, 1222, n. 150.

103. *Adamson v. California*, 322 U.S. 64 (1947).

104. Aynes, "Felix Frankfurter," 1235, n. 238.

105. Crosskey, "Charles Fairman"; Curtis, *No State Shall Abridge*; and Amar, "The Bill of Rights." My own efforts on this topic appear at Aynes, "On Misreading John Bingham," 103.

106. U.S. Constitution, amend. 14, sec. 2, clause 3.

107. Harold Hyman, *A More Perfect Union* (New York: Knopf, 1973), 99.

108. Du Bois, *Black Reconstruction*, 496.

109. Stewart Sifakis, *Who Was Who in the Civil War* (New York: Facts on File Publications, 1988), 343.

110. *Congressional Globe*, 39th Cong., 1st sess., 1866, 2459. Stevens went on to say, "Give us the third section or give us nothing."

111. Kyvig, *Explicit and Authentic Acts*, 168.

112. Ibid., 224.

113. Ibid., 46.

114. Joseph B. James, *The Ratification of the Fourteenth Amendment* (Macon, Ga.: Mercer University Press, 1984), 69.

115. Ibid.

116. George W. Paschal, *Annotated Constitution of the United States* (Washington, D.C.: W. H. & O. H. Morrison, 1868), 292.

117. Reconstruction Hearings, Virginia, North Carolina, South Carolina, Washington, D.C., 17 February 1866, 129.

118. Du Bois, *Black Reconstruction*, 527.

119. Ibid.

120. See, generally, Timothy Farrar, *Manual of the Constitution of the United States*, 3d ed. (Boston: Little, Brown, 1872), 532.

121. *Congressional Globe*, 39th Cong., 1st sess., 1866, 429 (John Bingham asking for a provision in the amendment to prohibit taxing loyal citizens to pay Confederate veterans' pensions).

122. Harold Hyman and William Wiecek, *Equal Justice under Law* (New York: Harper and Row, 1982), 271, n. 59.

123. Eric Foner, *Reconstruction* (New York: Harper & Row, 1988), 207.

124. McNeill Smith, "Of the Search for Original Intent . . ." *Law and Society Inquiry* 13 (1988): 583, 601, n. 36 (book review of Michael Kent Curtis, *No State Shall Abridge*).

125. Paschal, *Annotated Constitution*, 292.

126. Du Bois, *Black Reconstruction*, 605.

127. Ibid.

128. John Niven, *Salmon P. Chase* (New York: Oxford University Press, 1995), 303.

129. Du Bois, *Black Reconstruction*, 496.

130. Kyvig, *Explicit and Authentic Acts*, 166–67.

131. See, generally, Fairman, *Reconstruction and Reunion*, pt. 2. But see also Aynes, "On Misreading John Bingham," 95–96. See also Leonard W. Levy, introduction in Charles Fairman and Stanley Morrison, *The Fourteenth Amendment and the Bill of Rights: The Incorporation Theory* (New York: Da Capo Press, 1970), xv (Fairman's proof was largely "negative").

132. I have previously suggested that the difference in outcomes between Crosskey and Fairman can be found on acceptance of the normal conventions of interpretation of legislative history. In their debate over the question of whether the original constitution was intended to apply the Bill of Rights to the states, Fairman embraces and Crosskey repudiates the normal conventions. In the debate over whether the Fourteenth Amendment enforces the Bill of Rights against the states, the opposite occurs: Crosskey embraces and Fairman repudiates the normal conventions. See Aynes, "On Misreading John Bingham," 1255, n. 385.

5 Race, Class, Gender, and the Unintended Consequences of the Fifteenth Amendment

Mary J. Farmer and Donald G. Nieman

When ratified in March 1870, the Fifteenth Amendment stood as the capstone of the Reconstruction Revolution. While the Fourteenth Amendment, adopted two years earlier, had proclaimed color-blind citizenship and provided broad guarantees for the rights of citizens, it had dodged the issue of black suffrage in deference to the concerns of many congressional Republicans who judged extending the rights to vote to African Americans politically risky. By 1869, however, both the political landscape and the needs of the Republican party had changed dramatically, opening the way for congressional passage of a suffrage amendment. Prohibiting states or the federal government from denying citizens the right to vote on the basis of race, the new amendment at long last placed the principle of full equality of civil rights without respect to race into the Constitution.

The amendment's significance did not escape contemporaries. "The adoption of the fifteenth amendment," President Ulysses Grant proclaimed in reporting ratification to Congress, "completes the greatest civil change . . . that has occurred since the nation came into life."[1] The *New York Times* concurred, calling the amendment "the final crowning of the edifice of American republicanism" that "italicizes every word of the Declaration of Independence, and harmonizes our Constitution with the highest civilization to which we may aspire." Abolitionists joined the chorus. Members of the American Anti-Slavery Society, long the vanguard of the movement, saluted the amendment as "the capstone and completion of our movement" and promptly disbanded their organization.[2] African Americans joined the celebration. In Baltimore ten thousand African Americans representing dozens of community organizations paraded through the city's streets, while African American women in Philadelphia promenaded in red, white, and blue shawls.[3]

Those who celebrated the Fifteenth Amendment believed that the consequences of ratification were clear. The new amendment would extend the right to vote to black men in the eighteen northern and border states that denied them the ballot and provide additional security for the political rights of black southerners (who already possessed the right to vote as a result of congressional Reconstruction legislation).[4] As is often the case, however, the amendment had consequences far different from those its advocates intended. While it permanently opened the polls to northern blacks, the protection it provided black southerners (intended as its principal beneficiaries) proved short-lived. By the end of the century, southern Democrats had regained power and devised a variety of subterfuges that effectively eliminated African Americans from the political process. Moreover, the amendment had far-reaching consequences for southern and national politics, the woman's rights movement, and African American women's political involvement that the framers neither intended nor anticipated.

Black suffrage was central to Reconstruction era discussions of civil rights. Abolitionists and many congressional Republicans believed that, as citizens, black men were entitled to the right to vote and that only if armed with the ballot would they possess the ability to protect their newly won rights. Moreover, Republican politicians were keenly aware that African American votes were vital to the party's success in the states of the former Confederacy, where most whites damned Republicans for prosecuting a war that brought death, destruction, and emancipation to the South.[5]

Despite the attraction of black suffrage, Republican leaders proved wary of extending the right to vote to African Americans in the years following Appomattox. Although African Americans constituted only about 2 percent of the North's population, racism was deep and widespread there, and Democrats shamelessly exploited it.[6] At the end of the war, only five northern states permitted blacks to vote on the same terms as whites, and between 1865 and 1868, voters rejected equal suffrage proposals in six of the eight states where Republicans placed them on the ballot.[7] Although most Republican voters supported these measures, their defeat reminded party leaders that advocating equal suffrage for African Americans was politically unpopular.[8] Not surprisingly, then, in 1865–66, when they confronted southern whites' efforts to render emancipation nugatory through the black codes, congressional Republicans adopted the Fourteenth Amendment and civil rights legislation that guaranteed African Americans equal rights in law but stopped short of conferring the right to vote. In 1867, frustrated by continuing southern recalcitrance, Congress finally extended the right to vote to black southerners. In adopting the Reconstruction Act, Congress ordered reorganization of state government in the unrestored states of the former Confederacy and authorized black voters to participate in this process.[9] The upshot was an outburst of political activism among former slaves, the election of Republican-dominated state conventions that drafted new constitutions providing for universal manhood suffrage, and the emergence of a powerful Republican party that controlled state and local government in most of the former Confederacy.[10]

The Reconstruction Act created a double standard that embarrassed Republicans. While African Americans in the states of the former Confederacy were entitled to vote and participated actively in politics, most black northerners were denied the ballot by state laws limiting suffrage to white men. Abolitionists and Republican radicals repeatedly chided party leaders about this inconsistency, pressing them to support a federal constitutional amendment guaranteeing universal manhood suffrage irrespective of race throughout the nation.[11] However, Democratic political triumphs in critical northern state elections in 1867, coupled with the defeat of equal suffrage amendments in Ohio, New York, Kansas, and Nebraska Territory, convinced party leaders that support for a federal suffrage amendment was dangerous, especially with a presidential election looming.[12] The party's 1868 platform was silent about a suffrage amendment and justified the party's support for black enfranchisement in the South by asserting that the "guarantee by Congress of equal suffrage to all loyal men at the South was demanded by every consideration of public safety, of gratitude, and of justice."[13]

The 1868 election convinced Republican leaders to change course and throw their support behind a federal suffrage amendment when the lameduck session of the Fortieth Congress convened in December 1868. In the

South, the Ku Klux Klan had launched a reign of terror against black voters, slashing Republican turnout in most states and carrying Georgia and Louisiana for the Democrats in the presidential contest. If white political terrorism continued unabated, southern Democrats would regain political control throughout the South, repeal state constitutional provisions guaranteeing black suffrage, and eliminate the party's electoral base. Faced with this threat, Republican leaders quickly decided to push for an equal suffrage amendment.[14]

This about-face did not mean that Republican leaders threw caution to the wind. They knew that an amendment would be controversial, especially in those northern states that had suffrage restrictions in place. These included the eighteen states that denied African Americans the right to vote, as well as three northeastern states that employed property-holding and literacy tests to restrict voting by immigrants and California and Oregon, which were determined to maintain their freedom to keep Chinese from the polls. Because the Constitution required supermajorities to pass and ratify an amendment, many Republican leaders believed any measure that swept too broadly would be defeated. Constitutional requirements thus worked to reinforce the cautious approach to suffrage that had characterized the party since the end of the war.[15]

That caution was evident when the House Judiciary Committee reported a draft of the Fifteenth Amendment in January 1869. Seeking to minimize restrictions on states' authority to regulate the qualifications of voters, it merely prohibited states and the national government from denying citizens the right to vote on the basis of race, color, or previous condition of servitude, thereby permitting states to use other criteria, such as nativity, property holding, or education, to restrict the right to vote. The draft was thus calculated to appeal to voters in states such as Massachusetts, Connecticut, and California who were concerned about limiting the political power of immigrants. As the New York Tribune noted, "It leaves the States free to make such changes in their Suffrage laws not affecting these points [i.e., race, color, or previous condition of servitude] as may be called for."[16]

The Judiciary Committee's amendment drew the fire of most southern Republicans and some of their northern colleagues, who pointed out that it did not provide southern blacks adequate security. "The animus of this amendment is a desire to protect and enfranchise the colored citizens of the country," explained Willard Warner, an Alabama Republican, "yet . . . without any violation of its letter or spirit, nine-tenths of them might be prevented from voting . . . by the requirement . . . of an intelligence or property qualification." Ohio's Samuel Shellabarger agreed, adding a dire prediction: "Let it remain possible . . . to disfranchise the body of the colored race in the late rebel states and I tell you it will be done." [17]

Critics introduced several amendments designed to prevent subterfuges aimed at disfranchising African Americans. Casting the net broadly, Ohio's Shellabarger proposed a substitute that guaranteed universal manhood suffrage. His amendment forbade states from passing "any law which shall deny or abridge to any male citizen of the United States of the age of twenty-one years or over . . . an equal vote at all elections." [18] While Shellabarger's amendment failed, Senate critics fared better. A substitute offered in that body by Henry Wilson, a Massachusetts Republican, while less far-reaching than Shellabarger's, was designed to prevent the most obvious subterfuges, prohibiting states from denying the right to vote on the basis of "race, color, nativity, property, education, or religious creed." Attracting support from radicals and southern Republicans, it was adopted by the Senate.[19]

The triumph of the Senate radicals was short-lived, however. A majority of the House, fearing that the Senate's version would not be ratified by the requisite number of states, refused to concur. After more than a week of wrangling between the two houses, a conference committee reported a narrow version of the amendment similar to the one that had originally come from the House Judiciary Committee:

> Section 1. The right of citizens of the United States to vote shall not be denied or abridged by the United States or by any State on account of race, color, or previous condition of servitude.
>
> Section 2. The Congress by appropriate legislation may enforce the provisions of this article.

Feeling betrayed, southern Republicans bitterly resisted compromise. "I do not feel bound here, to vote for an amendment . . . which accomplishes nothing and under which any State may pass a law which shall disfranchise four-fifths of the colored population without mentioning the word 'color,'" Frederick Sawyer of South Carolina explained. "I had rather have nothing than to have this." [20] With time running out on the Fortieth Congress, however, Republicans closed ranks, accepting the narrowly drawn amendment as the best that could be obtained.[21]

In the short run, at least, the advocates of compromise were vindicated. The amendment was ratified in little more than a year, and Congress quickly adopted legislation to enforce its guarantees. Three Enforcement Acts, adopted between May 1870 and April 1871, dramatically expanded federal authority to prosecute state officials and private individuals who denied qualified persons the right to register or vote and provided stiff penalties for those who were convicted. During the early 1870s, federal marshals and attorneys, often backed by troops, used the acts to wage an all-out war on the Ku Klux Klan. In upstate South Carolina, where the Klan had created a reign of terror during and after the 1870 elections, federal officials made hundreds of arrests. By late 1871, 195 York County Klansmen resided in the county jail, popularly known as the "United States Hotel"; in nearby Spartanburg County, federal officials filled the jail and rented two additional buildings to accommodate Klansmen. During 1871 and 1872, federal attorneys brought successful prosecutions in federal courts in Columbia and Charleston, winning convictions in some 150 cases. The government launched similar campaigns in other states, notably North Carolina, Mississippi, and Alabama, breaking the Klan's back. But Klan violence clearly took its toll between 1868 and 1871, driving Republicans from power in North Carolina, Tennessee, and Georgia. Nevertheless, the Enforcement Acts, adopted under the authority of the Fifteenth Amendment, and the government's energetic application of them brought a temporary peace to the South, afforded black voters protection, and helped Republicans in other states retain power.[22]

The enforcement effort of the early 1870s proved but an interlude in southern Democrats' campaign to redeem the South from Republican rule and smash black political power. Democrats renewed their campaign of political violence against African Americans in the mid-1870s, developing less blatant but no less effective techniques of intimidation designed to reduce black turnout. With northern Republicans reeling from devastating losses in the wake of the depression of 1873, the Grant administration feared that massive intervention in the South would further alienate northern voters. While federal officials investigated acts of violence and intimidation, made arrests, and initiated prosecutions, they failed to respond with the level of force they had employed against the Klan and that was essential to stop the new Democratic offensive. The tools were available, but Republicans lacked the will to use them. Consequently, by 1877, Democrats had driven Republicans from power at the state level throughout the South.[23]

Restoration of Democratic control did not end black voting in the South. Although Democrats routinely employed intimidation, outright violence, and fraud to carry elections, black southerners continued to vote in large numbers in most southern states throughout the 1880s and well into the 1890s. Nor was African American voting without effect. Republicans retained control in many heavily black counties, winning elections for local officials, state legislators, and even members of Congress. They also periodically mounted serious challenges to Democrats at the state level, notably in Tennessee and North Carolina. Even in states where Republicans were too weak to threaten Democratic hegemony, continued black voting posed a very real threat. The 1880s and 1890s witnessed deep political splits among white southerners. Many poor white farmers, disaffected by the Democrats' economic conservatism and political elitism, turned to third parties such as the Greenbackers, Readjusters, and Populists. Republican leaders and black voters frequently joined forces with white dissidents, mounting serious challenges to Democratic control in Alabama, Texas, Florida, and Arkansas and briefly ending Democratic rule in Virginia and North Carolina.[24]

Threatened by continued black political activism, Democratic leaders sought to disfranchise African Americans. However, they found the Fifteenth Amendment a far more effective barrier than Republican radicals had predicted when the amendment had been debated in 1869. The amendment permitted literacy tests, poll taxes, and property requirements for voting that, even if fairly enforced, would dramatically reduce the black electorate. Adoption of such measures met sharp opposition, however. Because many white sharecroppers and tenants were poor and illiterate, poll taxes and literacy tests threatened to strip them of the vote, deprive them of an important symbol of independence, citizenship, and manhood, and drive them down to the status occupied by blacks. Poor whites, therefore, bitterly resisted racially neutral disfranchising measures, blocking their adoption in most states in the 1870s and 1880s. Only Georgia and Virginia, which experimented with poll taxes in the 1870s, and South Carolina, which in 1882 adopted a complicated system of balloting that effectively disfranchised illiterates, adopted disfranchising laws during these years. In other states, most notably Texas, where a proposed Constitution was rejected by voters in 1874 because it included a poll tax, white opposition prevented adoption of disfranchising laws prior to the late 1880s.[25]

Between 1889 and 1908, proponents of disfranchisement gained the upper hand and pushed through legislation and constitutional revision that effectively disfranchised African Americans in every southern state. Most Populists and representatives of white-majority counties continued to resist disfranchisement, as did African Americans. However, black belt Democrats, hoping to undercut the alliances between African Americans and white dissidents that had threatened their political dominance, pushed ahead with a renewed sense of urgency. Recalling the alleged horrors of "Negro rule" during Reconstruction and appealing to the need to protect white women from black men emboldened by notions of equality, they insisted that whites must close ranks behind disfranchisement. The disfranchisers also made strategic concessions to poor whites, offering loopholes that ostensibly protected poor whites from losing the right to vote.

By 1908, when Georgia adopted its new constitution, the disfranchisers had triumphed throughout the South. Each of the eleven states of the old Confederacy made payment of a poll tax a requirement for voting. Most states required payment well in advance of elections, and five heightened the effect of the tax by making it cumulative (i.e., requiring voters to pay poll taxes for previous years as well as the year of election). Seven states coupled poll taxes with literacy tests, and seven adopted the Australian (or secret) ballot, which served as a de facto literacy test because illiterates were unable to read it. Except for Florida, each of the Confederate states supplemented the poll tax with a literacy test or a secret ballot or both. In five states, Democratic leaders established loopholes for whites in an effort to reduce white opposition. Several exempted from literacy tests (but not payment of poll taxes) persons who owned a certain amount of property (usually $300) or enfranchised those who could explain a passage of the state constitution when it was read to them by a registrar. (Presumably, registrars would be white Democrats sympathetic to white but not black illiterates.) Several states supplemented these with grandfather clauses that waived literacy tests for men whose ancestors had been entitled to vote prior to 1867 (the year southern blacks had gained the right to vote) or had fought for the Union or Confederacy.[26]

Ultimately, then, the critics of the Fifteenth Amendment's narrow prohibition on interfering with the right to vote were vindicated. The disfranchising devices that Democrats adopted at the end of the century effectively eliminated black southerners from the political process. By 1910, only 15 percent of adult black men in Virginia were registered to vote; in Mississippi and Alabama the figure stood at less than 2 percent.[27]

Because of the way in which the Fifteenth Amendment was formulated, however, disfranchisement had consequences that were neither intended nor anticipated by those who adopted it. The amendment required disfranchisers to adopt measures that were, at least on their face, race neutral and therefore applied to whites as well as blacks. Despite assurances that only blacks would be affected and loopholes designed to protect whites, the new measures disfranchised a significant number of whites. Many were too proud to admit that they could not read and declined to exploit the loopholes, while many white sharecroppers (like their black neighbors) were too poor to pay their poll taxes. While approximately 80 percent of white men in Virginia and Alabama remained registered, the figure declined to 60 percent in Mississippi and 50 percent in Louisiana.[28]

Despite their protestations to the contrary, elimination of many poor whites from the electorate pleased Democratic leaders. As the *Charlotte Observer* explained, the movement was intended to end "the dangers of rule of negroes and lower class whites." John B. Knox, the president of the Alabama disfranchising convention, agreed: "The true philosophy of the movement was to establish restricted suffrage, and to place the power of government in the hands of the intelligent and virtuous."[29] In the eyes of many Democratic leaders, those who were disfranchised certainly lacked virtue. After all, they were the very men who had been most likely to bolt the party and join the third parties that had threatened Democratic hegemony during the 1880s and 1890s. With poor whites' electoral participation reduced, dissidents found it difficult to mount effective challenges to the Democratic party. The result was a half-century of one-party rule in the South. Ironically, then, Republican caution in framing the amendment played an important role in the creation of the "Solid South," a political system that preserved an oppressive racial caste system in the name of white supremacy, relentlessly ignored the needs of poor whites, and remained impervious to Republican inroads until the 1960s. How different the history of southern politics would have been had Congress adopted the version of the Fifteenth Amendment offered by Ohio's Samuel Shellabarger, guaranteeing the vote to all males who had reached the age of twenty-one.[30]

The Fifteenth Amendment also had far-reaching consequences for the alliance between abolitionists and woman's rights advocates that its framers neither intended nor anticipated. This alliance dated back to the 1830s and had long advocated universal suffrage and equal rights for all Americans irrespective of race or sex. But the Fifteenth Amendment, with its extension of the franchise to black men but not to women, forced the Equal Rights Association (the organizational union of the two groups formed in 1866) to come to grips with the question: "Is it more important that Negroes should vote than that women should vote?"[31] Doing so would, however, prove fatal to the alliance of abolitionists and feminists.

The demise of this abolitionist-feminist coalition came in May 1869 as the Equal Rights Association considered whether to endorse the Fifteenth Amendment, which had recently been adopted by Congress.[32] Outraged with the amendment's failure to prohibit denial of the right to vote on the basis of sex as well as race, Elizabeth Cady Stanton and Susan B. Anthony opposed the amendment, arguing that equality was indivisible.[33] Insistent that the Fifteenth Amendment represented "the culmination of one half of our demands," however, Frederick Douglass urged the amendment's prompt ratification.[34] Underscoring the urgency of securing the ballot for black men, Douglass explained:

> When women because they are women, are hunted down through the cities of New York and New Orleans, when they are dragged from their homes and hung upon lamp-posts; when their children are torn from their arms and their brains dashed out upon the pavement; when they are objects of insult and outrage at every turn; when they are in danger of having their homes burnt down over their heads; when their children are not allowed to enter schools; then they will have an urgency to obtain the ballot.[35]

Many black women also understood this urgency. Frances Ellen Watkins Harper, an African American woman who participated in the abolitionist, temperance, suffrage, and woman's rights movements between 1854 and 1890, agreed with Douglass. Although she supported universal suffrage first, she understood that "black males must have the vote and that the plight of black women was more related to their race than their gender."[36] Moreover, a majority of the Equal Rights Association understood the pragmatic political realities of Reconstruction politics and the priorities of the Republican party. Political expediency, then, as well as the recognition that acquiring the vote for black men was "an urgent necessity" led a majority of its members to suspend commitment to universal suffrage, at least for the time being, and support the Fifteenth Amendment.[37]

In the end, arguments that it was the "Negro's hour" prevailed, but not without consequence. More concerned with the "woman question" than the "Negro question," ardent feminists like Stanton and Anthony resigned their membership in the Equal Rights Association rather than endorse the Fifteenth Amendment. Indeed, Anthony insisted she would "cut off this right arm of mine before I will ever work for or demand the ballot for the Negro and not the woman."[38] Likewise, Stanton's response to endorsing the Fifteenth Amendment was to proclaim that she "did not believe in allowing ignorant negroes and foreigners to make laws for her to obey."[39] Rather than accepting black suffrage without woman suffrage, then, these women formed the National Woman Suffrage Association (NWSA), opposed the ratification of the Fifteenth Amendment as well as the Republican party, and divorced themselves from African American causes.[40]

Not all feminists severed their ties with the abolitionists or turned their backs on African American issues. With the Equal Rights Association shattered, a group of woman's rights advocates led by Lucy Stone, Henry Blackwell, William Lloyd Garrison, and Julia Ward Howe formed the American Woman Suffrage Association (AWSA) in November 1869. Insistent that "suffrage for women is the great key that will unlock to her the doors of social and political equality," this more conservative organization endorsed the Fifteenth Amendment and the Republican party alongside its efforts to secure the ballot for women.[41]

Despite the continued ties between abolitionists and woman's rights advocates in the AWSA, the debate over the Fifteenth Amendment and the formation of the NWSA marked the emergence of an independent woman's rights movement. The feminism of women like Stanton, Anthony, and their allies, who were now free to explore other aspects of women's oppression and emancipation, became much more radical. The break with abolitionism in 1869 also drove the NWSA to launch a campaign of grass-roots organizing that became at once more gender-based, elitist, and racist.[42] Indeed, white women who participated in this new, independent woman's rights movement often resorted to racist arguments to support the enfranchisement of white women. "While the dominant party with one hand lifted up TWO MILLION BLACK MEN and crowned them with the honor and dignity of citizenship," Anthony wrote in the feminist newspaper the *Revolution*, "with the other they dethroned FIFTEEN MILLION WHITE WOMEN—their own mothers and sisters, their own wives and daughters—and cast them under the heel of the lowest orders of manhood."[43] This racism divided black and white women and continued to characterize the woman's rights movement long after the two feuding camps of feminists reconciled their differences and formed the National American Woman Suffrage Association (NAWSA) in 1890. By the end of the century, then, the crisis precipitated by the Fifteenth Amendment had fostered an independent woman's rights movement fixed on the suffrage issue, but it had also sown the seeds of distrust that would long divide black and white women.[44]

The creation of this independent woman's rights movement left African American women in a difficult position. Were they black or were they women? Oppressed by both race and sex, they divided over the issue. Despite the racist and class-bound nature of the woman's rights movement, many African American women remained active in the cause.[45] Some black women like Sojourner Truth sided with the NWSA and supported enfranchising women, including black women, over black men. Truth believed that "if colored men get their rights, and not colored women theirs, you see the colored men will be masters over the women, and it will be just as bad as it was before."[46] Many, however, fell into the ranks of the AWSA, remaining loyal to both African American and woman's rights. Frances Harper maintained that "when it was a question of race I let the lesser question of sex go."[47] Harper endeavored to identify herself neither as an African American nor as a woman but as an African American woman "who recognized that for most Americans race was the key definer of her existence."[48]

However African American women chose to identify themselves, the climate of Reconstruction led them to pursue different strategies of political involvement. African American women actively participated in what historian Tera W. Hunter has described as "a grass-roots political culture that valued the participation of the entire community."[49] They may not have possessed the ballot, but they took part in political rallies and parades; attended, stood guard, voiced their opinions, and voted on resolutions at political meetings; formed their own clubs and political associations such as the Rising Daughters of Liberty Society; and displayed buttons on their clothing endorsing their favorite political candidates. During the 1868 elections in Yazoo County, Mississippi, for instance, maids and cooks bravely sported buttons portraying Gen. Ulysses S. Grant while working in the homes of their former masters.[50] But perhaps even more pressing, black women recognized a political duty to make sure that their men voted Republican, even taking time from work to accompany them to the polls.[51] Somewhat dismayed and perhaps even bemused, a witness in South Carolina reported that "no mens [sic] were to go to the polls unless their wives were right alongside of them; some had hickory sticks . . . and dare their husbands vote any other than the Republican ticket."[52] Another observer in Georgia recounted in 1872 that "Negro women, if possible, were wilder than men. They were seen everywhere, talking in an excited manner, and urging the men on."[53]

Although no doubt unintentional, the Fifteenth Amendment had secured participation by African American women as well as men in the political process. By their attendance at and participation in political gatherings, African American women asserted their determination to be a part of the reconstructed American political system. Clearly they saw themselves as political beings, even if they could not cast ballots. Indeed, as Hannah Flouroy, "a cook & washer of the first character" from Georgia, once explained to a white Republican leader seeking shelter from the Klan, "I am a republican, tooth and nail."[54]

Even after African American men were removed from the political arena by disfranchisement, African American women sustained, indeed even intensified, their political activism. Building on the political culture constructed by work in the temperance and abolitionist movements, churches, benevolent societies, and the Republican party, black women championed causes that benefited all African Americans. Within this organizational framework, they rebuilt their families and communities, obtained education for themselves and their families, and struggled to overcome low-paying jobs and poverty. Moreover, African American women attacked persistent social ills within their communities from every angle. They formed clubs and organizations that obtained various social services just as a rudimentary welfare system began to emerge at the state and local levels. Clinics, schools, kindergartens, orphanages, and reformatories gradually appeared in African American communities as a result of their efforts. They also combated racism. Led by women such as Ida B. Wells-Barnett, Angelina Weld Grimke, Mary Church Terrell, and Lottie Wilson Jackson, they challenged southern disfranchisement, Jim Crow segregation, and antimiscegenation laws as well as lynching. African American women at the turn of the century were grassroots activists who initiated progressive reforms paralleling those of their white counterparts. But their efforts to "uplift the race" were accomplished often without financial resources and without the political assistance of African American men. "From the debris of disfranchisement," historian Glenda Gilmore has argued, "black women discovered fresh approaches to serving their communities and crafted new tactics designed to dull the blade of white supremacy."[55]

The unintended consequences of the Fifteenth Amendment reached well beyond the nineteenth century, casting a long shadow over mid- and late-twentieth-century American politics. Those who supported the amendment were well aware that it would confer the right to vote on blacks in some fourteen northern states that excluded them from the polls in 1869. Because so few African Americans lived in the North, however, this was not congressional Republicans' principal objective. Indeed, support for black suffrage, which was not popular among white voters, probably cost them more votes among northern whites than it gained. In adopting the Fifteenth Amendment, Republicans were principally concerned with the South, where black suffrage—the key to the success of Republican Reconstruction policy—appeared vulnerable and in need of federal support.[56]

Despite its framers' intentions, the Fifteenth Amendment had its most long-lasting consequences in the North, where the African Americans whom it enfranchised did not lose the right to vote. Like their southern counterparts, black northerners eagerly embraced the right to vote and became actively involved in politics. During the decades following ratification, black northerners used the ballot effectively, winning notable legislative victories against segregation. After the U.S. Supreme Court struck down federal legislation banning discrimination in public accommodations in *The Civil Rights Cases* (1883), African Americans worked on behalf of state laws that guaranteed equal access to public places. They achieved notable success, winning passage of public accommodations laws in seventeen northern states between 1884 and 1900. During these years black northerners also secured legislation prohibiting school segregation in seven states, bringing to fourteen the number of northern states that mandated integrated schools. These laws were too often unenforced, and de facto segregation was common throughout the North. During the 1920s, for example, Harlem's famed Cotton Club, which featured the best African American musical performers, turned away African American customers. Nevertheless, race relations remained far more fluid in the North than in the South, and black northerners were far less likely to encounter the daily humiliations that Jim Crow segregation imposed on black southerners.[57]

The Fifteenth Amendment's greatest effect on the North, however, occurred in the decades following World War II. By 1950, five decades of migration by black southerners to the cities of the North and West had dramatically increased the North's African American population. Moreover, northern blacks' political clout was magnified because it was concentrated in the urban areas of key industrial states. During the 1930s, the Democratic party's commitment to working people broke African Americans' historic ties to the party of Lincoln, drawing a large majority into FDR's New Deal coalition. After World War II, as the North's black population grew and the Republican party became competitive once again, African Americans constituted a crucial block of swing voters in the fiercely contested industrial states of the Northeast, Midwest, and West.[58]

Critical to Democratic electoral success, black northerners enjoyed a growing influence in national politics and policy during the decades after World War II, helping to force civil rights on the national agenda for the first time since the end of Reconstruction. In 1948, facing an uphill battle for reelection, President Harry Truman attempted to shore up support among black voters in the North by launching a major civil rights initiative. In February he sent Congress a long message on the subject, requesting antilynching legislation, a tough federal ban on discrimination in employment and interstate transportation, and voting rights legislation. Five months later he issued an executive order mandating "equality of treatment and opportunity" in the armed forces and establishing an interservice committee to supervise desegregation.[59] Northern Democrats' commitment to civil rights remained strong during the 1950s and 1960s, keeping the issue on the national political agenda. Of course, the rising tide of nonviolent black protest that began with the Montgomery bus boycott in 1955 and grew ever more insistent during the next ten years was critically important in forcing Democratic leaders to place civil rights at the top of their agenda. Nevertheless, the party's commitment to civil rights, which began in the 1940s, created the institutional support that was a precondition for significant civil rights reform. And that commitment owed a great deal to the increasing importance of northern blacks in the Democratic coalition, a development that would not have been possible without the adoption of the Fifteenth Amendment eight decades earlier.[60]

The Fifteenth Amendment not only shaped the political alliances critical to the passage of modern civil rights legislation, it influenced the content of that legislation as well, often in ways that the amendment's framers would have found bewildering. The Reconstruction era Republicans who drafted the Fifteenth Amendment hoped to preserve a state-centered federal system. While they increased national power over individual rights significantly, they did so in ways that left states with broad authority to define the rights of their citizens. The Fifteenth Amendment was a case in point. It did not prescribe uniform national qualifications for voting; rather, it left states free to define the qualifications of voters so long as they did not discriminate on the basis of race, color, or previous condition of servitude. Indeed, it was this formulation that opened the door to the subterfuges employed by southern Democrats in the 1890s to gut the amendment.

As Congress and the courts became more receptive to civil rights reform during the 1960s, civil rights advocates attempted to close the door. They began by seeking legislation outlawing the poll tax. A once-formidable barrier to African American political participation, the poll tax had dwindled in importance. By 1960, only five southern states—Alabama, Arkansas, Mississippi, Texas, and Virginia—required prospective voters to pay poll taxes. Sensing the tax's political vulnerability, civil rights advocates urged Congress to use its authority under the Fourteenth and Fifteen Amendments to ban poll taxes by statute. Southern legislators, however, tenaciously resisted such legislation, fearing it would set a precedent for repeal of literacy tests, which remained a potent disfranchising device. Faced with the threat of a southern filibuster, the Kennedy administration and Democratic leaders in Congress opted for a conservative constitutional amendment outlawing the poll tax in federal (but not state) elections. It sailed through Congress in 1962, becoming the Twenty-fourth Amendment upon ratification in 1964.[61]

Although the anti–poll tax amendment proved a Pyrrhic victory, advocates of federal voting rights legislation persisted, continuing to press Congress for substantive action. Their moment came in 1965. In the wake of massive demonstrations against voting discrimination in Selma, Alabama, that captured the nation's attention, President Lyndon Johnson threw his support behind tough new voting rights legislation. Rallying bipartisan support among northern senators and representatives, the administration quickly won passage of the Voting Rights Act of 1965, which closed the door to discrimination that the framers of the Fifteenth Amendment had opened almost a century earlier.

The framers of the Voting Rights Act demonstrated that they had learned much from the failure of the Fifteenth Amendment. By the 1960s, white southerners' resort to poll taxes, literacy tests, and understanding clauses to defeat the purpose of the Fifteenth Amendment and their manipulation of these requirements to screen out many literate, property-holding blacks was legendary. Reformers understood that southern politicians were quite ingenious and utterly shameless in devising ways to keep African Americans from voting; if one practice were prohibited, they would devise another to take its place.

These lessons were not lost on those who framed the Voting Rights Act of 1965. The act suspended the use of any "test or device" that was a prerequisite for voting in any state in which fewer than 50 percent of adults were registered to vote in 1964, sweeping away the literacy tests that southern officials manipulated to keep African Americans away from the polls. Not content with this broad prohibition, the bill's sponsors went further, creating flexible administrative procedures to prevent as-yet-undreamed-of ways to deny African Americans access to the ballot box. In counties where there was substantial evidence of discrimination, as documented by complaints filed by twenty residents or a voting discrimination suit instituted by the Justice Department, federally appointed examiners would be appointed to register voters. The stake to the heart of disfranchisement was the bill's preclearance provision. It required states and localities with a history of discrimination to obtain prior approval for all changes in voting requirements or procedures from the Justice Department or a three-judge federal district court in Washington, D.C. Moreover, to gain approval, jurisdictions had to demonstrate that the new requirements or procedures had neither a discriminatory purpose nor effect.[62]

While these provisions were highly effective in guaranteeing black southerners the right to vote and rested on the enforcement power conferred by Congress in section 2 of the amendment, they were far more sweeping than anything the amendment's framers could have imagined. Rather than leaving states with broad freedom to define voter qualifications, as the amendment's framers expected, they created a mechanism for close federal oversight of state voting laws and procedures.

Perhaps the final irony is the Voting Rights Act's effect on southern politics. The act broke down barriers, bringing southern blacks into the political process, most of them as loyal Democrats. This led to dramatic changes in the southern Democratic party, making it far more responsive to the needs of African Americans and opening the ranks of the party's leadership to white moderates such as Jimmy Carter, Lindy Boggs, and Dale Bumpers and to African American leaders such as Barbara Jordan, John Lewis, and Harvey Gantt. However, the party's new orientation also led to a steady erosion of white support, as white voters turned to a resurgent Republican party in the 1980s and 1990s. Enforcement of the Fifteenth Amendment helped make Republicans competitive in the South but did so in a way that would have boggled the minds of the amendment's framers.[63]

Inclusion of Article V, which allows amendment of the Constitution, left the door open for change, thereby facilitating the system's adaptation and survival. Typically, the framers of amendments have hoped to remedy specific evils—slavery, demon rum, child labor, and poll taxes. Once adopted, however, these measures have had consequences their framers neither intended nor anticipated. The Fifteenth Amendment was no exception. Its framers' intentions were clear. The Fifteenth Amendment would secure the right to vote to black men, particularly to those in the South, completing the work of emancipation and securing the Republican party's future. "Nothing in all history," abolitionist William Lloyd Garrison triumphantly proclaimed in 1870, equaled "this wonderful, quiet, sudden transformation of four millions of human beings from . . . the auction-block to the ballot-box."[64]

Despite the framers' intentions, the protections afforded to African Americans by the Fifteenth Amendment were short-lived. While it permanently opened the polls to the then relatively small number of northern blacks, by the end of the century southern black men (intended to be the amendment's principal beneficiaries) had been effectively removed from the political process. Although the amendment failed to achieve its framers' goal, it nonetheless had important and far-reaching consequences that its framers neither intended nor anticipated. It ensured that disfranchisement applied to many poor whites as well as to African Americans, helping to create the Solid Democratic South. It crystallized the rift between feminists and their abolitionist-Republican allies, leading to the emergence of an independent woman's rights movement with a decidedly radical orientation and sowing the seeds of division between black and white feminists. Finally, the Fifteenth Amendment had momentous consequences for the twentieth century, creating support for civil rights in the North and ultimately shaping legislation during

America's Second Reconstruction. Ironically, this renewed civil rights activism as well as the lessons learned from the amendment's initial failure led to the triumph of the framers' vision.

At the end of the day, then, the Constitution is what we make it. Even the best-laid plans of those who drafted and amended it have produced consequences neither intended nor anticipated. It is those who inherit the work of the framers who must give the Constitution its meaning, for better or worse. The late Supreme Court justice Thurgood Marshall recognized this when he remarked during the Constitution's Bicentennial, "slavery has been abolished and the right to vote has been granted to blacks and women, but the credit does not belong to the framers." Rather, he insisted, "It belongs to those who refused to acquiesce in outdated notions of 'liberty,' 'justice,' and 'equality' and who strived to better them." After all, he pointed out, the framers of the Constitution would have never dreamed of "a Supreme Court to which had been appointed a woman and the descendant of an African slave."[65]

NOTES

1. James D. Richardson, ed., *A Compilation of the Messages and Papers of the Presidents, 1789–1902*, 10 vols. (Washington, D.C.: National Bureau of Literature and Art, 1903), 7: 56.

2. *New York Times* quoted in William Gillette, *The Right to Vote: Politics and the Passage of the Fifteenth Amendment* (Baltimore: Johns Hopkins University Press, 1965), 161 (first quote); *National Anti-Slavery Standard*, 15 May 1869, quoted in James M. McPherson, *The Struggle for Equality: Abolitionists and the Negro in the Civil War Era* (Princeton, N.J.: Princeton University Press, 1964), 427.

3. Gillette, *The Right to Vote*, 162.

4. For black suffrage in the North, see Xi Wang, *The Trial of Democracy: Black Suffrage and Northern Republicans, 1860–1910* (Athens: University of Georgia Press, 1997), 5–6, 21–23, 40–43; Eric Foner, *Reconstruction: America's Unfinished Revolution, 1863–1877* (New York: Harper and Row, 1988), 223–24.

5. McPherson, *The Struggle for Equality*, 239–43, 294–99, 301–29, 333–34, 336–39, 342–46, 350–58, 360–63, 410–24; Michael Les Benedict, *A Compromise of Principle: Congressional Republicans and Reconstruction, 1863–1869* (New York: W. W. Norton, 1974); Wang, *Trial of Democracy*, 7–39.

6. Foner, *Reconstruction*, 25–26, 31–32.

7. The five that permitted blacks to vote on the same terms as whites were Massachusetts, Maine, New Hampshire, Rhode Island, and Vermont (Donald G. Nieman, *Promises to Keep: African Americans and the Constitutional Order, 1776 to the Present*

[New York: Oxford University Press, 1991], 28). Referenda were held in Connecticut, Kansas, Iowa, Minnesota, New York, Nebraska, Ohio, and Wisconsin. Only voters in Iowa and Minnesota approved measures extending the right to vote to black men (Foner, *Reconstruction*, 222–23).

8. Wang, *Trial of Democracy*, 5–6, 21–23, 40–43; Foner, *Reconstruction*, 223–23; Gillette, *The Right to Vote*, 21–45.

9. For congressional Reconstruction policy, see LaWanda Cox and John H. Cox, *Politics, Principle, Prejudice, 1865–1866: Dilemma of Reconstruction America* (New York: Free Press, 1963); Benedict, *A Compromise of Principle*; Foner, *Reconstruction*.

10. Foner, *Reconstruction*, 281–345; Donald G. Nieman, "African Americans and the Meaning of Freedom: Washington County, Texas as a Case Study, 1865–1886," *Chicago-Kent Law Review* 70 (1994): 541–82; Leon Litwack, *Been in the Storm So Long: The Aftermath of Slavery* (New York: Alfred A. Knopf, 1979), 545–56.

11. McPherson, *Struggle for Equality*, 382–83, 420–23; Wang, *The Trial of Democracy*, 42.

12. Michael Les Benedict, "The Rout of Radicalism: Republicans and the Elections of 1867," *Civil War History* 18 (November 1972): 334–44; Wang, *The Trial of Democracy*, 41; Gillette, *The Right to Vote*, 32–38.

13. Kirk H. Porter and Donald B. Johnson, eds., *National Party Platforms, 1840–1956* (Urbana: University of Illinois Press, 1956), 38.

14. Benedict, *A Compromise of Principle*, 327–31; Wang, *The Trial of Democracy*, 41–42.

15. Foner, *Reconstruction*, 446–47; Wang, *The Trial of Democracy*, 43.

16. *New York Tribune*, 1 December 1868, quoted in Benedict, *A Compromise of Principle*, 331.

17. *Congressional Globe*, 40th Cong., 3d sess., 1869, 862 (4 February, remarks of Willard Warner); appendix, 97 (29 January, remarks of Samuel Shellabarger).

18. Ibid., 743 (29 January).

19. Ibid., 1034, 1041 (9 February).

20. Ibid., 1623 (25 February), 1299 (17 February, remarks of Frederick Sawyer).

21. McPherson, *Struggle for Equality*, 424–26; Wang, *The Trial of Democracy*, 43–46.

22. Allen Trelease, *White Terror: The Ku Klux Klan Conspiracy and Southern Reconstruction* (New York: Harper & Row, 1971), 383–418; Lou Falkner Williams, *The Great South Carolina Ku Klux Klan Trials* (Athens: University of Georgia Press, 1996); Everett Swinney, "Enforcing the Fifteenth Amendment, 1870–1877," *Journal of Southern History* 28 (May 1962): 202–18.

23. Nieman, *Promises to Keep*, 89–92; William Gillette, *Retreat from Reconstruction, 1869–1879* (Baton Rouge: Louisiana State University Press, 1979), 211–334.

24. J. Morgan Kousser, *The Shaping of Southern Politics: Suffrage Restriction and the Establishment of the One-Party South, 1880–1910* (New Haven, Conn.: Yale University Press, 1974), 11–44; Nieman, *Promises to Keep*, 101–3; Foner, *Reconstruction*, 590–92; Eric Anderson, *Race and Politics in North Carolina, 1872–1901: The Black*

Second (Baton Rouge: Louisiana State University Press, 1980); Nieman, "African Americans and the Meaning of Freedom."

25. Kousser, *The Shaping of Southern Politics*, 17, 82–91.

26. Ibid., 83–265.

27. Ibid., 61.

28. Ibid.

29. Quoted in C. Vann Woodward, *Origins of the New South, 1877–1913* (Baton Rouge: Louisiana State University Press, 1951), 331.

30. Kousser, *The Shaping of Southern Politics*, 224–65.

31. Ellen Carol DuBois, *Feminism and Suffrage: The Emergence of an Independent Women's Movement in America, 1848–1869* (Ithaca, N.Y.: Cornell University Press, 1978), 63–66; Bettina Aptheker, *Woman's Legacy: Essays on Race, Sex, and Class in American History* (Amherst: University of Massachusetts Press, 1982), 42–46; and Benjamin Quarles, "Frederick Douglass and the Woman's Rights Movement," *Journal of Negro History* 25 (January 1940): 38 (quote).

32. Rosalyn Terborg-Penn, "Discrimination against Afro-American Women in the Woman's Movement, 1830–1920," in Sharon Harley and Rosalyn Terborg-Penn, eds., *The Afro-American Woman: Struggles and Images* (Port Washington, N.Y.: Kennikat Press, 1978), 17–27; Aptheker, *Woman's Legacy*, 46–50; DuBois, *Feminism and Suffrage*, 163–89; Paula Giddings, *When and Where I Enter: The Impact of Black Women on Race and Sex in America* (New York: William Morrow and Company, 1984), 64–68; and for a full account of the convention proceedings, see also Elizabeth Cady Stanton, Susan B. Anthony, and Matilda Joslyn Gage, eds., *History of Woman Suffrage*, vol. 2, *1861–1876* (New York: Fowler and Wells, 1882), 378–400.

33. Philip S. Foner, ed., *The Life and Writings of Frederick Douglass*, 4 vols. (New York: International Publishers, 1955), 4: 44; Aptheker, *Woman's Legacy*, 47.

34. Quarles, "Frederick Douglass and the Woman's Rights Movement," 41; Foner, *The Life and Writings of Frederick Douglass*, 4: 43; Aptheker, *Woman's Legacy*, 47.

35. *Revolution*, 20 May 1869, quoted in Stanton, Anthony, and Gage, eds., *History of Woman Suffrage*, 2: 382.

36. Bettye Collier-Thomas, "Frances Ellen Watkins Harper: Abolitionist and Feminist Reformer, 1825–1911," in Ann D. Gordon, Bettye Collier-Thomas, John H. Bracey, Arlene Voski Avakian, and Joyce Avrech Berkman, eds., *African American Women and the Vote, 1837–1965* (Amherst: University of Massachusetts Press, 1997), 50; see also Giddings, *When and Where I Enter*, 65–68.

37. *Revolution*, 21 May 1868, quoted in Quarles, "Frederick Douglass and the Woman's Rights Movement," 40; Adele Logan Alexander, "Adella Hunt Logan and the Tuskegee Woman's Club: Building a Foundation for Suffrage," in Mary Martha Thomas, ed., *Stepping Out of the Shadows: Alabama Women, 1819–1990* (Tuscaloosa: University of Alabama Press, 1995), 97; and DuBois, *Feminism and Suffrage*, 162–63, 187–89.

38. Quoted in Aptheker, *Woman's Legacy*, 47.

39. *Revolution*, 27 May 1869, quoted in Marjorie Spruill Wheeler, ed., *One Woman, One Vote: Rediscovering the Woman Suffrage Movement* (Troutdale, Oreg.: New Sage Press, 1995), 70.

40. For a complete discussion of the split in the Equal Rights Association and the formation of the National Woman Suffrage Association, see DuBois, *Feminism and Suffrage*, 163–97; see also Foner, *Reconstruction*, 447–48; Alexander, "Adella Hunt Logan," 97–98; Giddings, *When and Where I Enter*, 67–68.

41. AWSA Convention in Stanton, Anthony, and Gage, eds., *History of Woman Suffrage*, 2: 763–64, quoted in Wheeler, ed., *One Woman, One Vote*, 71; for a discussion of the formation of the AWSA, see also DuBois, *Feminism and Suffrage*, 163–64, 195–200; Foner, *Reconstruction*, 448; Alexander, "Adella Hunt Logan," 97–99; Giddings, *When and Where I Enter*, 67–68.

42. Ellen Carol DuBois, *The Elizabeth Cady Stanton–Susan B. Anthony Reader: Correspondence, Writings, Speeches* (Boston: Northeastern University Press, 1992), xvi; see also DuBois, *Feminism and Suffrage*, 162–202.

43. Quoted in Rosalyn Terborg-Penn, "Afro-Americans in the Struggle for Woman Suffrage" (Ph.D. Diss., Howard University, 1977), 82; see also *We Are Your Sisters: Black Women in the Nineteenth Century*, ed. Dorothy Sterling (New York: W. W. Norton, 1984), 414.

44. Giddings, *When and Where I Enter*, 65–68, 80–83, 89, 123–31; Ann D. Gordon, "Introduction," in Gordon et al., eds., *African American Women and the Vote*, 4–6; DuBois, *Feminism and Suffrage*, 95–96, 100, 110, 174–78; Aptheker, *Woman's Legacy*, 50; Terborg-Penn, "Discrimination," 17–27; and Rosalyn Terborg-Penn, "African American Women and the Vote: An Overview," in Gordon et al., eds., *African American Women and the Vote*, 11.

45. Rosalyn Terborg-Penn's dissertation, "Afro-Americans in the Struggle for Woman Suffrage," remains the best work on African American women's involvement in the movement for woman suffrage; other prominent works on their involvement in the suffrage movement include DuBois, *Feminism and Suffrage*, Aptheker, *Woman's Legacy*, and Elisabeth Griffith, *In Her Own Right: The Life of Elizabeth Cady Stanton* (New York: Oxford University Press, 1984). Griffith's biography of Stanton is obviously focused on Stanton and admittedly pro-Stanton but nonetheless delves into her role as an abolitionist and suffragist as well as her relationships with other reformers, both black and white, male and female.

46. Sojourner Truth, "I Suppose I Am about the Only Colored Woman That Goes about to Speak for the Rights of Colored Women," in Gerda Lerner, ed., *Black Women in White America* (New York: Vintage Books, 1973), 569; see also Giddings, *When and Where I Enter*, 65.

47. Quoted in Collier-Thomas, "Frances Ellen Watkins Harper," 50; see also Sterling, *We Are Your Sisters*, 415; Foner, *Reconstruction*, 448; Giddings, *When and Where I Enter*, 65–66, 68.

48. Collier-Thomas, "Frances Ellen Watkins Harper," 49; see also Alexander,

"Adella Hunt Logan," 97–99; Cynthia Neverdon-Morton, *Afro-American Women of the South and the Advancement of the Race, 1895–1925* (Knoxville: University of Tennessee Press, 1989), 176–77.

49. Tera W. Hunter, *To 'Joy My Freedom: Southern Black Women's Lives and Labors after the Civil War* (Cambridge, Mass.: Harvard University Press, 1997), 32.

50. Elsa Barkley Brown, "Negotiating and Transforming the Public Sphere: African American Political Life in the Transformation from Slavery to Freedom," *Public Culture* 7 (Fall 1997): 107–26; Hunter, *To 'Joy My Freedom*, 32–33; Elsa Barkley Brown, "To Catch the Vision of Freedom: Reconstructing Southern Black Women's Political History, 1865–1880," in Gordon et al., eds., *African American Women and the Vote*, 81–87; Foner, *Reconstruction*, 87, 290–91.

51. *Georgia Weekly Telegraph*, 8 October 1872, quoted in Edmund L. Drago, "Militancy and Black Women in Reconstruction Georgia," *Journal of American Culture* 1 (Winter 1978): 841.

52. Quoted in Sterling, *We Are Your Sisters*, 370.

53. *Georgia Weekly Telegraph*, 8 October 1872, quoted in Drago, "Militancy and Black Women in Reconstruction Georgia," 841.

54. Virginia Shelton to William Shelton, 20 August 1866, quoted in Hunter, *To 'Joy My Freedom*, 30 (first quote); testimony of Hannah Flournoy quoted in Hunter, *To 'Joy My Freedom*, 33 (second quote); see also Brown, "To Catch the Vision of Freedom," 85–86.

55. Glenda Gilmore, *Gender and Jim Crow: Women and the Politics of White Supremacy in North Carolina, 1896–1920* (Chapel Hill: University of North Carolina Press, 1996), 147 (quote), 147–75; Hunter, *To 'Joy My Freedom*, 130–44; Rosalyn Terborg-Penn, "Discontented Black Feminists: Prelude and Postscript to the Passage of the Nineteenth Amendment," in Darlene Clark Hine, Wilma King, and Linda Reed, eds., *We Specialize in the Wholly Impossible: A Reader in Black Women's History* (Brooklyn: Carlson Publishing, 1995), 487–503; Neverdon-Morton, *Afro-American Women*, passim; Wheeler, *One Woman, One Vote*, 141–45.

56. For a contrary view, see Gillette, *The Right to Vote*. Gillette argues that congressional Republicans viewed the amendment principally as a means of enfranchising northern blacks, whom they believed were critical to providing the party a margin of victory in closely contested northern states. Scholars have not been persuaded by Gillette's argument. See LaWanda Cox and John H. Cox, "Negro Suffrage and Republican Politics: The Problem of Motivation in Reconstruction Historiography," *Journal of Southern History* 33 (August 1967): 303–30; Glenn M. Linden, "A Note on Negro Suffrage and Republican Politics," *Journal of Southern History* 36 (August 1970): 411–20; Benedict, *A Compromise of Principle*, 325–36; Earl M. Maltz, *Civil Rights, the Constitution, and Congress, 1863–1869* (Lawrence: University Press of Kansas, 1990), 142–45.

57. Valeria W. Weaver, "The Failure of Civil Rights, 1875–1883 and Its Repercussions," *Journal of Negro History* 54 (1969): 368–82; Nieman, *Promises to Keep*,

103–5; David Levering Lewis, *When Harlem Was in Vogue* (New York: Oxford University Press, 1982), 209–11.

58. Nieman, *Promises to Keep*, 130–33; Harvard Sitkoff, *A New Deal for Blacks* (New York: Oxford University Press, 1978).

59. Nieman, *Promises to Keep*, 140–42; David Levering Lewis, "Origins and Causes of the Civil Rights Movement," in *The Civil Rights Movement in America*, ed. Charles W. Eagles (Jackson: University Press of Mississippi, 1986), 3–18; Alonzo Hamby, *Man of the People: A Life of Harry S. Truman* (New York: Oxford University Press, 1995), 433–35; Donald R. McCoy, *The Presidency of Harry S. Truman* (Lawrence: University Press of Kansas, 1984), 106–9, 154, 167–71.

60. Nieman, *Promises to Keep*, 161–72; Carl F. Brauer, *John F. Kennedy and the Second Reconstruction* (Cambridge, Mass.: Harvard University Press, 1977).

61. Brauer, *John F. Kennedy*, 131–32; Steven F. Lawson, *Black Ballots: Voting Rights in the South, 1944–1969* (New York: Columbia University Press, 1976), 290. Two years after ratification of the amendment, the U.S. Supreme Court delivered the death blow to the poll tax, ruling that it discriminated against the poor and thus violated the Fourteenth Amendment's equal protection clause (*Harper v. Virginia Board of Elections*, 383 U.S. 667 [1966]).

62. Lawson, *Black Ballots*, 307–22.

63. Jack Bass and Walter DeVries, *The Transformation of Southern Politics* (New York: Basic Books, 1976); Thomas B. Edsall and Mary Edsall, *Chain Reaction: The Impact of Race, Rights, and Taxes on American Politics* (New York: W. W. Norton & Co., 1993), 41–44, 259–60.

64. *National Anti-Slavery Standard*, 5 February 1870, quoted in Foner, *Reconstruction*, 448.

65. *Washington Post*, 7 May 1987, A1.

6 Short Euphorias Followed by Long Hangovers: Unintended Consequences of the Eighteenth and Twenty-first Amendments

Richard F. Hamm

The Eighteenth Amendment, which declared beverage alcohol prohibition the nation's policy, and the Twenty-first Amendment, which repealed the prohibition amendment, have cast a series of unintended shadows on American constitutionalism, American law, American social movements, and American society. Together the two amendments contributed to constitutional law and practice through the addition of new provisions to the organic law, the innovation of time limits on ratification of amendments, the use of conventions to ratify an amendment, and the realization of a latent potential of the system—a repeal amendment. The Eighteenth Amendment accelerated the already present trend toward the development of a federal police presence, which in turn eventually contributed to the expansion of federal courts' scrutiny of policing. The amendments also, directly and indirectly, led to the demise of one of the longest lasting and most significant of American reform movements, the temperance movement. In addition, the policy of prohibition and its repeal facilitated the growth of organized crime and contributed to a cultural transformation concerning Americans' attitudes toward liquor consumption and other minor vices.

To focus on unintended consequences of amendments is to begin to walk down the perilous path of originalism. In its purist form, originalism postulates that a constitution, amendment, or law is to be understood through what its authors intended and in the context of the time when it was created. The very nature of the task of exploring the unintended consequences of an amendment requires the measuring of later practices and occurrences against the yardstick of what the authors of the amendment intended it to do. The consequences that deviate from the plans of the creators, as best as we can know them, are labeled unintended consequences. But this is a difficult line of analysis, as it is often hard to discover the intentions of the framers of an amendment. For example, thanks to the paucity of records and the divided processes of construction and ratification, it is quite hard to determine the intentions of the authors of the Bill of Rights.[1]

But for some later amendments the records are far richer, and exploring unintended consequences shifts the vantage point for viewing the constitutional system. As many amendments, especially in the Progressive era, sprang from long-standing social movements that articulated their goals, it is possible to determine the purposes of their authors. And by looking at the groups that crafted these amendments, the focus of our constitutional scrutiny is shifted from the Supreme Court (the study of which has dominated our constitutional history) to other constitutional actors. Thus the prohibition and repeal amendments are ideal test cases for exploration of our complex constitutional system.[2]

The United States has evolved a constitutional system reminiscent of the so-called unwritten English constitution. The American constitutional system encompasses the founding documents (the Declaration of Independence and the Constitution of 1787); the amendments to the federal Constitution; actions of the federal judiciary, executive, and legislature (court cases, vetoes and executive orders, and laws); practices of the state governments' executive, legislative, and judicial officers; and popular notions of proper government action. In this system, the parameters of legitimate governmental activity are laid out in constitutions but elaborated and refined in constitutional doctrines (which draw upon a broad range of sources) enunciated by courts, congresses, presidents, and state officials. Received tradition (stretching sometimes as far back as Magna Carta), politics, and amorphous ideas all influence how people in these institutions go about shaping and reshaping the constitutional system. Moreover, those who seek government action, inside and outside of these institutions, often must change aspects of this constitutional system to achieve their goals. The histories of these two amendments, and their unintended consequences, highlight many aspects of the American constitutional system.[3]

In general, this essay will delineate the groups that sought governmental action, explain their constitutional ideas, explore their interactions with the formal makers of the constitutional law and with established constitutional doctrines, and show how their intended and unintended consequences shaped the living Constitution and American society. This study begins with the temperance movement. It shows how interactions with the constitutional order shaped the drys' proposals for a prohibition amendment. It details how the prohibitionists' efforts culminated in the Eighteenth Amendment and its federal enforcement law, the Volstead Act. It explores this amendment's unintended effects on society, on the temperance movement, on law, and on constitutionalism. The essay then turns to the creation of a movement to repeal prohibition. It shows how from this movement came the Twenty-first Amendment. It ends by exploring the unintended consequences of this amendment on American constitutionalism and society.

A national prohibition amendment was a late development in the temperance movement. Temperance was a reaction to the pervasiveness of alcohol in late-eighteenth- and early-nineteenth-century American society. Most of the population, from youth to old age, consumed it, often at every meal, from breakfast through supper. It was common practice to drink at every social event and even at work. Soon after the Revolution, men like Benjamin Rush advised Americans to moderate their consumption of liquor. Worried about the corrupting effect of liquor on private and public morals, the early agitators advocated that people drink the less powerful fermented and brewed beverages instead of distilled spirits. At first, their appeals to the citizenry had little effect, yet as religious revivals altered many Americans' view of alcoholic beverages, liquor lost its legitimate role in many parts of American society. In the early part of the nineteenth century, awakened Christians saw liquor as an evil influence that threatened to weaken society by destroying individuals. They abstained from spirits themselves and sought to convince others to do so. But moral suasion did not eliminate alcohol from American society, and this failure drove some reformers to advocate legal means for abolishing liquor from American life. In the 1850s, state prohibition of liquor became the goal of many anti-alcohol advocates. After early successes, their movement faltered.[4]

Yet the first temperance crusade made liquor drinking a public issue and changed Americans' drinking habits. Liquor lost its predominance as a drink for all occasions; when many had abandoned alcohol it became harder to include it in all activities. Thus, following the Civil War, liquor consumption became centered in saloons. In 1873 about 100,000 of these establishments dotted the land. In 1890 cities with a population over 50,000 had a saloon for every 250 inhabitants. Besides their chief purpose of selling liquor, saloons served many important social functions on the frontiers and in the cities. Saloons were almost exclusively male institutions, and in the gendered world of nineteenth-century values, which assumed that women had greater moral sensibilities than men, such an orientation earned saloons an unsavory reputation.[5]

Facing the challenge of the saloons, the temperance movement after the Civil War was revitalized by the development of new temperance organizations. These new groups endorsed a national prohibition amendment. In the late 1860s and early 1870s, drys formed the Prohibition party and the Woman's Christian Temperance Union (WCTU). These drys shared the ideas put forth by J. Ellen Foster that "the traffic in alcoholic beverages breeds disunion, overthrows justice, creates domestic strife, weakens the common defense, and fastens the chain of an ignoble slavery upon ourselves and our posterity." These reformers believed that drinking exacerbated certain illnesses, diverted income from subsistence, and led to violence and misery. They thought that banning the sale of liquor would alleviate, if not solve, many social problems. And as they saw the evil as a national evil, they called for a national solution.[6]

But the birth of a prohibition amendment was delayed and complicated by the intricacies of American federalism. Prohibitionists, led by the Prohibition party and the WCTU and seeing law in moral terms, advocated a total national ban on the sale of liquor. They rejected liquor regulation programs and even the policy of prohibition by local option for towns and counties. But since their political power was weak, they mostly sought statewide prohibition. So in the 1880s, working in concert with local activists, they enacted prohibitory laws in some states, most notably, Kansas and Iowa. These dry havens soon suffered from the eroding influences of the federal system.

Federal interstate commerce law and federal tax practices challenged state prohibition. The Supreme Court interpreted interstate commerce doctrines to permit liquor sellers based in wet states to introduce their products into dry territory. In *Bowman v. Chicago and Northwestern Railroad* (1888) and *Leisy v. Hardin* (1890), the Court defined the limits of state action over liquor so as to insure freedom of commerce within the nation and to protect the federal government's power to regulate commerce. It allowed the introduction of out-of-state liquor into dry areas and the sale of such liquor in its original packages. The Court's rulings made it impossible for prohibition areas to be truly dry. Also, the federal excise tax on liquor erected a barrier to the spread of prohibition. The federal tax fostered a benign view of the liquor industry as an important, tax-paying industry. And the argument that prohibition would lead to the loss of significant tax revenues impeded temperance progress. Operations of the federal agents in collecting the tax in dry states also undermined the legitimacy of prohibition.

Prohibitionists struggled to change the federal government's commerce and tax policies. At first the party and the WCTU demanded pure solutions. They unsuccessfully urged the ban of liquor in interstate commerce and the abolition of the federal liquor tax. Instead, the Congress, responding to the Court's commerce rulings, enacted the 1890 Wilson Act. This law declared imported liquors the legal equivalent of a state's domestic liquor and subject to a state's jurisdiction "upon arrival." Congress thus established a policy of concurrent state and federal action against liquor, which the prohibitionists soon adopted. Indeed, following the same general principles, drys began to shape state laws that used federal tax records as evidence of illegal liquor selling in dry states. But, in part because dry states suffered from loopholes to federal policies designed to aid prohibition states, prohibition progress again stalled.

This pause prompted a reorganization of the temperance movement. In the mid-1890s, a new organization, the Anti-Saloon League, arose and reoriented the movement's tactics, views of law, and responses to federalism. Though the League developed a good working relationship with the WCTU, its rise pushed the Prohibition party to the margins of the movement. The League was a single-issue pressure group that concentrated on compelling elected officials to enact and enforce prohibitory laws. While not abandoning the belief that laws were in essence moral commands, the League adopted a functional approach to lawmaking. Instead of embracing pure solutions, the League supported any law that curtailed liquor sales, be it regulatory, local option prohibition, or state prohibition.[7]

The League's view of law allowed it to build on previous laws to meet renewed challenges by the federal system to state prohibition. In a number of rulings interpreting the Wilson Act, delivered in the late 1890s and through the first decade of the twentieth century, the Court made it easier to import liquor into dry states. Similarly, federal tax bureaucrats resisted all attempts to turn their records into enforcement tools for state prohibition police. But, under League direction, prohibitionists spread the practice of using federal tax records as evidence of liquor violations in the states. Moreover, they won the passage of a 1906 national law that made it much easier for state officers to access federal records. Similarly, drys used the federal commerce power to craft laws designed to aid states in enforcing their liquor policies. The first, the 1909 COD Act, regulated the cash-on-delivery trade of interstate liquor; the second, the 1913 Webb-Kenyon Act, made it a violation of federal law to send liquor into a state if it was intended to be used in violation of that state's law; and the third, the 1917 Reed Amendment to the Postal Act, banned the transportation of beverage alcohol into all prohibition states.[8]

Oddly, the 1917 law began as a wet proposal designed to embarrass the League as it converted all dry states into "bone dry" states. The League, for pragmatic reasons, never advocated state bone dry prohibition laws that included bans on the personal use of liquor. For the reason that it was far easier to pass or maintain a prohibition or local option law if some liquor were available, and for the reason that laws that set personal use limits on imports could be used effectively against suppliers of illegal saloons in dry areas, the League shied away from bone dry laws. Its pragmatism paid off as more and more states passed prohibition laws. By 1912 half the people in the nation lived under prohibition. But state action, even with strong federal aid, was not enough for many prohibitionists.[9]

The drive for what became the Eighteenth Amendment began in 1913. At that year's annual convention, the Anti-Saloon League went on record in support of a national amendment. The League organized a conference of drys that drafted language for a prohibition amendment. In December of that year this proposal was presented to Congress. This proposed amendment banned the sale, the manufacture for sale, and the transportation for sale of intoxicating beverages, authorized Congress to permit the making and vending of liquor only for "sacramental, medicinal, mechanical, pharmaceutical or scientific purposes," and granted Congress the "power to enforce this article by all needful legislation." The "for sale" language of the proposal was designed to perpetuate the "personal use" policy that had long been a part of League plans. The enforcement provision either reflected the tendencies of the proposal's authors to favor national action or was mindlessly copied from the Reconstruction era amendments. The proposal died in the Senate Judiciary Committee, while the full House debated the measure in December 1914 before voting it down.

After this defeat, the drys (led by the League) threw their energies into refining their proposal and electing a Congress in 1916 that would pass their revised amendment. Capitalizing on divisions in their opponents' ranks, the war fever that gripped the nation (which also allowed them to pass wartime bans on manufacture of liquor), and their political muscle, the prohibitionists achieved a Congress willing to pass a prohibition amendment. In maneuvering their amendment through Congress, the drys accepted two changes: a time limit on ratification and a year's delay in implementation. But the bulk of the amendment was of the drys' own crafting.[10]

When the proposed amendment went to the states it read:

> Section 1. After one year from the ratification of this article, the manufacture, sale, or transportation of intoxicating liquors within, the importation thereof into, or the exportation thereof from the United States and all territory subject to the jurisdiction thereof for beverage purposes is hereby prohibited.
>
> Section 2. The Congress and the several States shall have concurrent power to enforce this article by appropriate legislation.
>
> Section 3. This article shall be inoperative unless it shall have been ratified as an amendment to the Constitution by the legislatures of the several states, as provided in the Constitution, within seven years from the date of submission hereof to the States by the Congress.[11]

The League saw the year's deferment of the implementation of national prohibition after ratification as a compromise measure offered to counter the wets' desire for a two-year grace period. Similarly, the seven-year ratification period emerged from compromise. Suggested initially by Ohio senator Warren Harding as a four-year period, it was perceived by many as a last-ditch attempt by the liquor interests, who thought they could delay ratification long enough to defeat the amendment. But Wayne Wheeler, Ernest Cherrington, and the other leaders of the League had already calculated that if they had not won ratification by 1920, reapportionment in the states would probably end their hopes. By agreeing to Harding's proposal—extending it to seven years—in return for a concession by the wets that there would only be a one-year, not a two-year, grace period before prohibition took effect, the prohibitionists gave away nothing.[12]

These compromises aside, the Eighteenth Amendment was a prohibitionist product. Congress, at the prohibitionists' insistence, wrote into the amendment exactly the extent of prohibition that drys desired and the nature of enforcement authority that drys demanded. The drys ditched their earlier "for sale" language and adopted a total ban on beverage alcohol. Drawing on the experience of their interaction with the federal system, the drys saw the amendment as the last step in incremental steps toward total aridness. Earlier state bans, backed by increasingly strict national commerce power laws and favorable interpretations of federal tax law provisions, had made great progress in drying out the nation. But the final destruction of the liquor traffic could come only through an amendment, and so that amendment had to be "bone dry."[13]

Similarly, drys embraced the idea of concurrent state and national authority for enforcement. When the Senate stripped concurrent powers language from the proposal, drys encouraged the House to reinsert it. Prohibitionists saw this joint state and federal power as a "reservation" to the states "of power to enforce their prohibition laws." Drys did not want a national amendment to make liquor control a purely national issue. Prohibitionists argued that "nobody" desired sole national enforcement or wished to see the creation of "10,000 new federal officers" with expensive salaries. They contended that more plentiful state officials, "willing" to enforce the law, would do a better job for less money.[14]

Congress passed the amendment in December 1917 and sent it to the states. In a month over a year, the Eighteenth Amendment had been ratified by thirty-six states, then the number needed to make it part of the Constitution. On the day after the ratification, Wayne Wheeler, the legislative superintendent of the Anti-Saloon League, announced the League's implementation proposals. He gave Congress notice that "it is its duty to enact a federal prohibition law." Similarly, the states should frame prohibition statutes "in harmony with the federal amendment." Finally, educational efforts and vigilance in "maintaining in office administrators and officers determined to enforce" the laws must continue. In this program, the national prohibition code was the centerpiece of the League's plan.[15]

It was the centerpiece because the League, especially Wheeler, believed that the Constitution's supremacy clause was not changed by the Eighteenth Amendment's concurrent powers clause. He asserted that when "Congress is given power over a subject matter its acts" were "supreme no matter whether the States have power over" the same subject. State laws that conflicted with federal law were null and void. For example, no state could disregard the federal definition of intoxicating liquor and "legalize what the laws of the United States prohibit." In short, the federal law was necessary to set national standards. Under them, the states were free to enforce their old laws (if they did not conflict with the new national standards) or pass and enforce even stricter alcohol prohibitions. Under League pressure states adopted such laws.[16]

The federal prohibition law, commonly called the Volstead Act after the congressman who introduced it, was an Anti-Saloon League proposal weakened by congressional changes. It had three major sections dealing with wartime prohibition, industrial alcohol regulation, and national prohibition. The national prohibitory law outlawed the manufacture, sale, transportation, and possession of any intoxicating liquor "except as authorized in this act." Congress wrote two important exceptions into it over League protests. These were the exception allowing the home fermentation of fruit juices and the exception allowing possession of liquors in "one's private dwelling . . . for use only for the personal consumption of the owner," the owner's family, and personal guests. These two exemptions stood outside the well-devised system the act constructed and proved to be major sources of enforcement problems.[17]

The Volstead Act did many things. It set out a detailed permit system for the production and distribution of alcohol and the withdrawal from bond of existing liquor stocks for sacramental and medicinal use. With the aim of keeping alcohol from being diverted to illegal beverage use, it regulated the activities of church officials, doctors, druggists, manufacturers, and common carriers who would be involved in the legal industry. To curtail the illegal sale of intoxicants the Volstead Act banned solicitation of liquor orders and prohibited liquor advertising. To further penalize liquor sellers it instituted a system of barkeeper tort, that is, the collection of damages from the sellers of liquor resulting from the actions of intoxicated persons. It also condemned as a common nuisance any building or vehicle used in any aspect of the liquor trade and granted limited search and seizure powers to government agents. The old federal tax machinery was left in place under the law, but only to be used as a penalty aimed at those who were caught breaking the national prohibition law.[18]

The most controversial section of the Volstead Act was the part that Wheeler and other League leaders saw as key: its definition of intoxicating liquors. At Anti-Saloon League prompting, the act set the level of alcohol determined to be intoxicating at one half of 1 percent by volume. This limit, of course, forbade the manufacture of beer. In the dry view there was little choice. The federal law acted as a signpost for the states, compelling the adoption of a strict limit. According to Wheeler, a more lenient standard would cause confusion by overriding stricter state laws and encouraging "law breaking of state laws." Also to restore, by federal law, some alcoholic beverages to legitimacy seemed an abomination to prohibitionists. They also feared that if the national government recognized beer, some states would follow suit, and in wet enclaves the liquor evil would survive. The low alcohol standard set by the Volstead Act was thus integral to the prohibitionists' plans to assure a dry nation.[19]

Thus, the prohibitionists wrote into the Constitution, the nation's laws, and the states' laws their antiliquor policy. Their amendment and legislative act were designed to make the nation free of the evils of liquor. Yet this great victory of the temperance forces generated a number of unintended consequences for American society, for the prohibition movement, for law, and for constitutionalism. In the larger social realm, the system of national prohibition stimulated the growth of organized crime and contributed to a relegitimization of liquor consumption in much of American society.[20]

Before national prohibition there was an established, city-centered business of crime. There were strong connections between purveyors of vice and corrupt officials who allowed gambling, prostitution, and drinking to take place regardless of bans on such activities. While thriving, this business was small-scale. But prohibition "opened up an enormously profitable field of endeavor" to the existing criminals as the market for liquor did not disappear with the legal liquor industry. The lucrative nature of this trade prompted the expansion of organized crime. Gangsters borrowed the techniques of legitimate business: "consolidation, rational organization, and the elimination of competition." The most notorious of the expanded criminal enterprises was Chicago's crime syndicate, headed first by Johnny Torrio and then Al Capone, though most American communities of any size developed similar gangs. The mass media, including newspapers, periodicals, and films, while chronicling their corruption and violence, also romanticized these criminals, virtually making them into folk heroes. The gangsters' style of dress, speech, and way of life became models for average people. And in the gangsters' world liquor pervaded public social activities.[21]

The policy of prohibition inaugurated new patterns of drinking. Without a doubt, prohibition reduced the amount of liquor being consumed in the society. And prohibition killed off the old drinking venue, the saloon. But in its place came new venues, nightclubs, cabarets, and speakeasies, and in these arenas drinking took on new forms. A study of drinking in Butte, Montana, showed that prohibition changed the drinking patterns of women. In Butte prior to prohibition strong social rules, supported by state and city laws that banned women from saloons, made saloons "male preserves." This pattern reflected the national norm, as did the perception that women who drank in saloons were assumed to be beyond respectability. But the "blatant flouting" of prohibition "created new social spaces for drinking"—clubs and speakeasies—where women as well as men drank without social stigma. Yet national prohibition was only part of the story, as the youth rebellion, the modernist revolt against Victorian values, and other changes in women's acceptable social roles all contributed to the relegitimation of drinking. But certainly, proponents of prohibition never thought that their amendment would restore the luster to liquor's reputation.[22]

Similarly, prohibitionists did not imagine that winning their national struggle would weaken the temperance organizations. Yet for prohibitionists the Eighteenth Amendment proved to be a Pyrrhic victory. The decline came in different ways for the two leading temperance organizations: the Anti-Saloon League and the WCTU. But no matter what the course of their decline, it provoked temperance organizations to become inflexible in trying to preserve their victories. Their refusal to compromise in turn fueled the growth of repeal sentiment.

With the realization of its goal of a dry nation, the Anti-Saloon League lost direction. It debated whether to concentrate on consolidating its victory in the United States or on spreading the message of prohibition across the globe. Also, differences among League leaders in their approach toward temperance that had been submerged during the struggle for the Eighteenth Amendment surfaced after its passage. Basically, the League divided into two camps distinguished by means. One group, headed until his death in 1927 by Wayne Wheeler and then by F. Scott McBride, favored law enforcement as the League's chief role, while the other group, led by Ernest Cherrington, thought that with the amendment achieved the League should focus on educating the public. At the same time, the League was under attack. As the first two decades of the century had seen a steady ascent in League power and prestige, the twenties and early thirties saw a rapid decline in the League's reputation and reach. A congressional investigation into League methods generated much negative publicity; the bad impression intensified when two League leaders, James Cannon and William Anderson, were put on trial for financial misdeeds. Indeed, money became a problem for the League, as donations began falling with the adoption of the amendment and continued to fall throughout the era of national prohibition.[23]

The creation of national prohibition also weakened the WCTU, although in a far less direct manner. The organization did not suffer a decline in membership in the twenties, nor was its leadership rocked by scandal. Rather, the drys' success prompted female opponents of prohibition to organize. In the 1920s, especially as prohibition enforcement faltered, women began to form anti–Eighteenth Amendment societies. The first efforts (the Molly Pitcher Clubs formed in 1922 and the Women's Committee for Modification of the Volstead Act formed in 1926) were halting, but by 1929 the Women's Organization for National Prohibition Reform (WONPR) had been created. By December 1931 this organization had enrolled over 400,000 women nationwide, passing in membership the number of women in the national WCTU. It was not just a numbers game; rather, the ranks of the WONPR came from "college-educated, upper middle-class women." Signs appeared "of slipping class orientation during the 1920s" for the WCTU, while the "WONPR attracted a large portion of its members from the same classes that fifty years before" had sustained the WCTU. Moreover, the WONPR turned the maternalist and separate spheres ideologies, which had been the foundations of WCTU support for the amendment, against prohibition. Thus, through the period, the WCTU weakened considerably.[24]

Racked by divisions, weakened financially, and distracted by their enemies' attacks, prohibitionists responded by trying to maintain what they had won with the Eighteenth Amendment and Volstead Act. For a decade (from the 1919 resolution of the American Federation of Labor that called for a beer exemption to prohibition through the winning essay of the 1929 Hearst Contest that proposed the "modification of the Volstead Act to allow the sale of light wines and beer"), prohibitionists were presented with programs of compromise between bone dry national prohibition and repeal of prohibition. Moreover, as public support measured by opinion polls, state referenda, and state repeal of enabling laws turned against prohibition, drys would have been prudent to accept such a modification of their program. But they publicly attacked these proposals, including a trial balloon floated by George Wickersham before the 1929 Governors Conference. And they spent much of their political capital in blocking such plans. For instance, in 1930, drys had their legislative supporters smother in committee sixty modification proposals. By their intransigence the drys pushed their opponents toward repeal. "It was all or nothing for the drys, so that they ended with nothing."[25]

While the policy of prohibition virtually died with repeal, the Eighteenth Amendment had a long-lasting consequence for American law: the growth of the national law enforcement establishment. This unintended consequence is particularly ironic, as prohibitionists thought they had created a system of concurrent enforcement of the Eighteenth Amendment that would avoid the creation of a large federal bureaucracy and keep policing in the hands of the states. The assumptions behind the concurrent enforcement clause presumed that the states would do the lion's share of the work.

Yet during national prohibition the idea that the federal government had a role in law enforcement proved an excellent excuse for states to abdicate their law enforcement responsibilities. Some states were slow to enact prohibition laws. In 1921 Wayne Wheeler counted ten such states. Eventually every state but Maryland enacted such a law. But even when enacted, officials in thirsty states did as little as they could and let federal officials bear the brunt of their constituents' hostility to the enforcement of prohibitory laws. Also, parsimonious state legislatures refused to allocate sufficient funds for the implementation of prohibition on the grounds that the national government should pay for enforcement. In 1926 the state legislatures allocated eight times more to implement fish and game laws than to enforce prohibition. This ratio reflected state legislatures' assumptions that local law enforcement officials in the course of their duties would go about enforcing prohibition. Thus, general appropriations for the police supported implementation of the policy but underscored the point that most states refused to spend extra to enforce prohibition. And concurrent enforcement, the idea that another body stood ready to uphold the law, led some states— including Massachusetts, Montana, Nevada, New York, and Wisconsin—to repeal their enforcement laws. Thus when the states failed to do their share of policing in the course of the 1920s and 1930s, the federal government stepped into a larger law enforcement role.[26]

The place of prohibition in the creation of the federal police was aptly described by Lawrence Friedman, a leading authority on U.S. legal history, when he wrote, "Probably nothing in the first half of the twentieth century matched prohibition in expanding the federal crime effort." This larger federal enforcement role was built on existing foundations. At the adoption of prohibition the structure of the federal law enforcement machinery included federal agents, scattered through various departments charged with enforcing laws that carried criminal penalties; U.S. attorneys, usually political patronage appointees under the loose authority of the Justice Department who prosecuted defendants in federal district courts; and three federal prisons for those sentenced to incarceration by federal courts. During prohibition, the histories of the police, prosecutors, and prisons all show the same pattern of growth and increasing bureaucratization.[27]

In the late nineteenth century, and especially in the Progressive era, the national government started to enact laws based on its enumerated powers that began the process of building piecemeal a national police force. The process could require existing federal agents to take on new roles. For example, Congress placed regulatory taxes on oleomargarine that to implement expanded the duties of federal collectors of internal revenue. Or the process could lead to the creation over time of a new federal agency with police powers. Thus, the Harrison Narcotics Act was initially enforced by Internal Revenue officers, then from 1919 to 1930 by a division of the prohibition unit, and subsequently by the Federal Bureau of Narcotics. Finally, the process could be used by existing federal organizations to expand both their activities and personnel. For instance, though not designated the chief enforcer of the Mann Act, the Federal Bureau of Investigation took it upon itself to enforce the act and open field offices in various cities to do so. Thus the federal government patched together a national police, with agents spread through various departments.[28]

The national policy of prohibition added to the existing duties of federal law enforcers and created a whole new category of officers. The very creation of national prohibition required customs officials, Coast Guard agents, postal inspectors, national park rangers, and others to enforce the policy of prohibition within their areas of expertise. Beyond this, the Volstead Act created a new federal police force: prohibition agents. Prohibitionists, building on their experiences in the federal system, decided that the Bureau of Internal Revenue in the Treasury Department would enforce the Volstead Act. Drys turned to Treasury officials because, according to William Anderson of the Anti-Saloon League, it would be "foolish" to construct "a new department, when there was already in existence" a bureau with the "experience, personnel, and equipment" that could be "converted" to new uses. So that drys could shape federal enforcement policy through the same tactics they had used in the states, the Volstead Act exempted these officers from the civil service laws. Since drys expected that the states would do most of the policing, they kept the prohibition enforcement force small; initially, it was only fifteen hundred officers.[29]

The federal prohibition enforcers proved to be an ineffective force because of their numbers and their nature. When state and local efforts faltered, prohibitionists in Congress, fearful of a backlash against prohibition if enforcement proved too costly, blocked any serious expansion of the numbers of officers. The numbers increased to 1,886 agents by 1929, but these numbers were never sufficient to the many tasks the agents were required to do. Also, the civil service exemption of the Volstead Act resulted in the appointment not of men susceptible to Anti-Saloon League pressure but of party hacks and patronage hunters. In a six-year period beginning in 1920, 752 prohibition officials lost their jobs for delinquency or misconduct, with drunkenness and bribery being the two largest categories for dismissal. Moreover, it took some time to design an effective structure for enforcement activities within the Treasury Department. For the first years the enforcement agents belonged to a division of the branch of Internal Revenue, then they became a unit and eventually a bureau. In 1927 civil service rules were extended to prohibition agents, and in 1930 the Bureau of Prohibition was transferred to the Department of Justice. This last move was designed to improve the efficiency of both enforcement and prosecution.[30]

While unequal to the task of fully effectuating the alcohol ban, the prohibition enforcement machinery considerably expanded the federal police presence in American life. In 1930 the complement of 1,450 front-line prohibition agents dwarfed the 350 field agents of the Federal Bureau of Investigation. Furthermore, prohibition agents engaged in activities that directly affected people. From 1921 through 1929 they averaged 59,973 arrests per year, a nine-year total of 539,759 arrests. In the same period, prohibition agents seized 45,177 cars in the course of their duties. And from January 1920 to April 1926 the agents of the prohibition unit killed eighty-nine people. While the trigger-happiness of the federal agents drew headlines, their mundane arrests for violation of prohibition burdened the federal courts.[31]

Prohibition led to a significant expansion of federal court activity. For the thirteen full fiscal years of national prohibition (1921–33), cases arising from the violation of the federal prohibition enforcement laws in the district court dockets averaged 64.6 percent of all federal cases. Equally telling were the raw numbers. In 1921 there were 29,114 prohibition cases, while by 1932 there were 65,960. At the same time, the overall number of cases handled by the federal district courts increased significantly. In 1921 there were 54,487 federal criminal cases. In 1932 the total reached 92,174.[32]

National prohibition under the Eighteenth Amendment also resulted in a reorientation of how the Justice Department prosecuted crime. For nine years, Assistant Attorney General Mabel Walker Willebrandt directed the federal prosecution of prohibition cases. Throughout her tenure she sought to make these prosecutions more efficient. At the same time she also sought to publicize federal efforts in order to spark a grass-roots campaign for prohibition enforcement. These initiatives altered the existing structures and practices of the Justice Department.

Willebrandt undertook a number of steps to rationalize federal prosecutions of the prohibition laws. She instigated a "flying squad" of special prosecutors for use when federal district attorneys "proved inept or untrustworthy." Similarly, in 1924, under the direction of Attorney General Harlan Fiske Stone, she compiled a statistical analysis of the prohibition prosecutions of each of the U.S. attorneys' offices. Stone used this information to pressure attorneys to prosecute more cases or arrange for the attorneys' resignations. Though limited by the intricacies of political patronage that dominated appointments, Willebrandt's actions represented a significant attempt to bring bureaucratic order to federal prosecutions. A mark of her success in bureaucratic terms can be seen in the growth of her staff: three assistants in 1921 and over a hundred in 1929.[33]

Willebrandt and her staff especially used their prosecutions to generate headlines. A number of times, Willebrandt supervised a prosecution or sat in the courtroom while one of her assistants pressed the case. Since women government lawyers were quite a novelty in the 1920s, her actions generated press coverage. Similarly, she focused on major corruption cases, both in the federal and local governments, again headline grabbers. This seeking of press notice was not gratuitous but part of a Justice Department campaign to display prohibition enforcement activity and make a case for cleaner government to the public. Willebrandt's extensive speaking schedule made exactly the same points. Moreover, as she was leaving office, she published, first in syndicated newspaper column form and then as a book, her vision for effective prohibition law enforcement. She called for clean government, for greater coordination between national and local officials, and especially for people to take responsibility for seeing that the law was enforced. While the public relations efforts dominated the news coverage, routine prosecutions continued. Thanks to high rates of plea bargains and dropped charges, the percentage of convictions in prohibition cases from 1922 to 1933 averaged over 82 percent. Thus many violators of national prohibition ended up in federal custody.[34]

Prohibition also contributed to the growth of federal prison populations and prompted changes in prison administration. In the era of national prohibition, the number of federal prisoners grew dramatically. In 1923 there were 4,664 federal prisoners. Seven years later there were 12,964. In 1923 5 percent of all U.S. inmates were in federal custody, but by 1930 over 10 percent were federal prisoners. The growth rate in state and federal prison populations duplicated this pattern. During the middle of the period of national prohibition (1923–30), the number of federal prisoners increased by a factor of 2.77. In the same period the prison population in the states increased by a factor of 1.39. Federal prison populations were growing twice as fast as state prison populations.[35]

Many, but never a majority, of these new federal prisoners were incarcerated for violating prohibition. The rate of imprisonment for prohibition violation, based on new commitments to federal prisons, showed upward growth through the era. For the period 1919–24 the rate was 6.9 percent, for 1924–29 it was 17.1 percent, while for 1929–34 it was 43.4 percent. The penalties of the Volstead Act in part explain the relatively low number of federal liquor law prisoners. The Volstead Act's most common mode of punishment was a fine. Thus, the increasing of federal penalties in 1929 explains the sharp spurt at the end of prohibition. Indeed, in 1930, the first year the new law was in force, almost half (49 percent) of all new federal prisoners were federal liquor laws violators.[36]

This influx of new prisoners taxed the existing system of federal prisons and prompted its expansion and reorganization. At the opening of national prohibition there were only three federal prisons for men. Generally, space in these prisons was reserved for those with long sentences; short-term male prisoners and female prisoners were boarded in various state facilities. Prisons, staffed through a patronage process, were rife with corruption and mismanagement. For the most part, federal institutions did not follow the practices prescribed by penology professionals such as segregation of young, impressionable offenders from older, seasoned prisoners and establishment of prison industries to facilitate rehabilitation. During prohibition, the federal government expanded its number of prisons to five, adding women's and young offenders' institutions. Moreover, in 1930 Congress created the Bureau of Prisons in the Justice Department. It put penal professionals in charge of the system and began instituting many of the practices used widely in the states.[37]

Thus, national prohibition prompted an expansion of the federal police establishment. An expanded federal police role became both a governmental norm and a reality in people's lives. This new norm did not disappear with the end of prohibition. Indeed, with repeal came expanded federal taxation of liquor, which required almost the same level of enforcement and regulation as used by the national government to enforce prohibition. More importantly, the nation had gotten used to expanded federal police activity. During the Depression, in response to the perception that gangsterism, kidnappings, and bank robberies were on the rise, Congress created a host of new federal policing responsibilities. Attorney General Homer Cummings, following the path pioneered by Willebrandt, orchestrated an enforcement, prosecution, and publicity campaign designed to create a grass-roots movement against crime. The chief beneficiary of this campaign was the Federal Bureau of Investigation. The FBI, under J. Edgar Hoover, hitched the publicity wave of the war against crime to scientific and professional policing and emerged as the federal government's main policing agency. The people it arrested were prosecuted by a more professional Justice Department staff and, if convicted, incarcerated in one of the growing number of federal prisons.[38]

This creation of a large federal police establishment led federal courts to lay the foundation of a significant body of new constitutional law limiting police action and regulating the conduct of federal law enforcement officials. In the years from 1920 to 1933, federal appeals courts reshaped the law of entrapment, search and seizure, double jeopardy, property forfeiture, and trial by jury. Moreover, a pattern existed in the development of these constitutional doctrines. The courts, especially the Supreme Court, first supported enforcement actions over individual rights, then drifted into ambivalence toward the policy, and by the end of the prohibition era asserted people's rights against government actions.[39]

The prohibition era's search and seizure cases indicate the range and nature of these important doctrinal developments. Before the adoption of the Eighteenth Amendment, the Supreme Court had created an exclusionary rule banning the use of evidence seized in violation of the Fourth Amendment. Moreover, the Court declared that the Fourth Amendment was to be liberally construed to protect the rights of the people. The policy of national prohibition tremendously expanded the number of search and seizure issues, generating over five hundred federal appellate cases. The Court's first Fourth Amendment prohibition decision excluded open fields around a house from areas protected by the amendment; it also declared that lawful observation by law officers was not limited by its restriction against unreasonable searches. A spate of cases in the early twenties continued this trend of narrowing the scope of the Fourth Amendment. But as individual and systematic excesses in enforcement emerged, some justices, most notably Louis Brandeis, began to worry about protecting people from government agents. By the early 1930s, the Court rediscovered its liberal preprohibition rulings. Distinguishing previous cases and creating new exceptions, the Court applied these ideals to new prohibition cases, reducing the effect of previous prohibition rulings. These liberal doctrines, which emerged by the end of the period, would be the precedents later relied on by the Warren Court when it applied the Fourth Amendment's restrictions to the states.[40]

At the same time that they remade constitutional law, federal jurists took on the role of overseer of federal police. Judges, through the case law, "exercised a supervisory role over the prohibition agency and its agents." In part, this development came because court rulings constrained the actions of the federal police. But the origins of this supervision came also from the general notion that the government itself could not become a law breaker. Judges distinguished between ends and means, arguing that the legitimate ends of prohibition could not be reached by illegitimate means. In a number of opinions judges became very critical of what they perceived as "agent misconduct," be it "invasions of the home," activities that could entice people into committing crime, or the too free use of their weapons. If federal agents displayed lawlessness the courts would refuse to sanction their activities. These supervisory statements and rulings by federal judges presaged much of the mid–twentieth century's jurisprudence of due process and rights.[41]

While the Eighteenth Amendment indirectly laid the foundation for important developments in American constitutionalism, it also directly shaped the constitutional system by introducing the idea of a time limit on ratification. While not every amendment proposal or amendment since the Eighteenth Amendment has included a time limit (the woman suffrage and proposed child labor amendments did not), the idea quickly became customary. Moreover, the time period of seven years (a process of political negotiation in the drafting of the Eighteenth Amendment) has become a standard. The Twentieth and Twenty-first Amendments include a seven-year clause in their bodies, and since the Twenty-third Amendment it has been the practice to stipulate a seven-year approval period in the resolution transmitting an amendment to the states. This habit has become so ingrained that proponents attach it almost automatically to their amendment proposals. Thus, after the ratification period and its controversial extension of the proposed equal rights amendment expired, supporters introduced a new ERA amendment in Congress with a seven-year time period for ratification.[42]

The ease with which this innovation has been accepted should not disguise its importance. A time limit on state legislative ratification was a major change incorporated into the amendment process. It significantly altered the process by which constitutional change can be achieved. It adds significantly to the already heavy burden required of amendments: approval by two thirds of the members of the Congress and three quarters of the states. The time limit allows amendment opponents to translate delay into defeat. In American constitutional law, this may be the longest-lasting unintended consequence of the Eighteenth Amendment. And this long-lasting consequence stems from the only amendment ever repealed.

While the idea of repeal of amendments had been bandied about previous to the era of national prohibition, it was an idea that had not been tested. In part, amendments were presumed to be stable because the mechanism of amending seemed so formidable. Two comments delivered in the era of national prohibition from opposites sides of the wet and dry divide point to presumed permanence of amendments. One of the cosponsors of the Eighteenth Amendment, Morris Sheppard of Texas, boasted, "There is as much chance of repealing the Eighteenth Amendment as there is for a hummingbird to fly to the planet Mars with the Washington Monument tied to its tail!" On the other hand, H. L. Mencken lamented that prohibition was in the Constitution forever because "Congress is made up eternally of petty scoundrels, pusillanimous poltroons, highly vulnerable and cowardly men: they will never risk provoking the full fire of the Anti-Saloon League." Yet within thirteen years of its implementation, thanks to the rise of new movements, changing constitutional ideas, and political transformation, the national prohibition amendment was repealed.[43]

In the field of social movements, the temperance movement's opponents shifted from liquor industry puppets to movements with significant support from groups not directly tied to the liquor interests. Learning from their opponents' success with single-issue organizations, the wets created organizations dedicated to one goal: repeal. And within a short time after repeal, these wet organizations disbanded. Three antiprohibition organizations—the Association Against the Prohibition Amendment (AAPA), the WONPR, and the Voluntary Committee of Lawyers (VCL)—reshaped the public debate over the liquor issue and reoriented the constitutional law on the topic. In the late 1920s, the AAPA (dominated by conservative businessmen) and the WONPR (a broadly based group) undertook extensive campaigns to persuade the public of the failure of prohibition and the necessity of repeal. They criticized national prohibition on many grounds, asserting that it promoted hypocrisy, encouraged law breaking, destroyed the balance of power between state and federal authority, and impaired individual rights. In short, it was so flawed that repeal—by adopting another amendment—was the only acceptable solution. By the early 1930s, the VCL overcame the idea that repeal was an impossibility and directed the impetus for change into workable channels. Through efforts at the state and national levels, the wets helped to shape both the repeal amendment and its ratification.[44]

The VCL and the AAPA were conservatives who stood squarely opposed to the expansion of the federal government's authority. They opposed woman suffrage, black suffrage, the income tax, and the proposed anti–child labor amendment, as well as the prohibition amendment. They saw these proposals as advancing social views they did not support and as invasions of the states' proper sphere of action. While their arguments against these measures began with their substance, they shifted their critique to adoption procedure. They contended that organized lobbying for the woman suffrage and prohibition amendments had resulted in the state legislatures ratifying amendments that their constituents did not support. Similar-minded people in Congress pushed proposals to make the amending process more difficult, among them a provision that amendment ratification incorporate referenda in the states. They saw the mechanism to implement such referenda in Article V of the Constitution, which stipulated that amendments could be ratified either by vote of state legislatures or through special conventions. The idea of ratification through conventions became the mainstay of the wet proposals for repeal of the Eighteenth Amendment.[45]

The leading wet organizations lobbied furiously in both major political parties for their constitutional referenda idea, and in the campaign of 1932 their work paid off. In that year, the platforms of both the Democratic and

Republican parties supported the idea of ratification referenda. The Republicans (after pledging their support for law enforcement) urged the resubmission of the prohibition amendment to popularly elected state conventions that would give "the people . . . an opportunity to pass upon" it. The Democratic party adopted a campaign plank calling for Congress to pass a repeal amendment to be submitted to state conventions. As prohibition had become more unworkable and unpopular and as dry organizations had weakened while wet ones had strengthened, both parties had embraced the idea of state conventions as referenda on the issue.[46]

The Democratic victory in the election of 1932 led to congressional passage of a repeal amendment. A proposal for a repeal amendment, based on the Democratic platform, was defeated in the first week of the lame-duck session in the House. Late in the session a Senate proposal, initially drafted by drys, was reported out of committee. It contained language giving dry states control over imported liquor and provided a federal guarantee against the return of the saloon; it also stipulated ratification by state legislatures. Vigorous wet lobbying prompted the recasting of this measure. Its final form read:

> Section 1. The eighteenth article of amendment to the Constitution of the United States is hereby repealed.
>
> Section 2. The transportation or importation into any State, Territory, or possession of the United States for delivery or use therein of intoxicating liquors, in violation of the laws thereof, is hereby prohibited.
>
> Section 3. This article shall be inoperative unless it shall have been ratified as an amendment to the Constitution by conventions in the several States, as provided in the Constitution, within seven years from the date of the submission hereof to the States by the Congress.

On 20 February it passed Congress and was sent out for ratification by state conventions.

Like the amendment proposal, the repeal process followed the wets' blueprint. The VCL fashioned the means for ratification of a repeal amendment through special conventions in the states. The proponents did not seek these conventions as deliberative bodies but rather as an analogue of the electoral college, where pledged delegates would be bound to vote the position on which they ran. Most importantly, the VCL urged at-large voting for the conventions to make the process more referendum-like and to bypass apportionment that was thought to favor the drys. Even before Congress had passed a proposal, the VCL had drafted a model bill for states to create such a special ratifying convention. They sent copies of it to every state government in the nation. When Congress delivered the Twenty-first Amendment to the states, one state had already passed a convention law, and twenty-eight states were considering such bills. States mostly followed the guidelines laid out in the bill: twelve adopted the model bill, and eight others used it with only small changes. Others borrowed parts of it; more than a majority (twenty-five states of forty-three that acted to create conventions) adopted at-large voting for the conventions. In ten months thirty-six states ratified the Twenty-first Amendment, making it part of the Constitution.[47]

It is important to note that this amendment was a thoroughly antiprohibitionist amendment. It was virtually a bald repeal, giving only a single sop to the drys. The second section of the Twenty-first Amendment emerged from the original dry repeal amendment of 1933. Its supporters believed the clause would restore control over interstate liquor commerce to the states. The language of the second clause recast that of the 1913 Webb-Kenyon Act. It guaranteed the sanctity of state liquor laws from intrusive interstate and foreign commerce liquor shipments. But even this clause was a defeat for drys. It deprived them of the ladder—the calls for cooperation between the states and federal government—that they had climbed to place prohibition in the Constitution. Thus, the Twenty-first Amendment did exactly what its framers thought it would do on the issue of prohibition, but it failed to bring about the constitutional revolution they desired.[48]

The Twenty-first Amendment made innovations in American constitutional law and created a new constitutional provision for the Supreme Court to interpret. The innovations contained in the first and third clauses of the amendment (repeal of a previous amendment and ratification through conventions), which their framers thought would limit the expansion of federal power, have proved, so far, to be constitutional dead ends. But the second clause, concerning state power over liquor in commerce, has become part of the nation's living constitutional law. Thus the nature of the constitutional law created by the Twenty-first Amendment was unintended by its creators.

Neither of the innovative aspects of the Twenty-first Amendment has become a model for revolutionary constitutional change. The repeal clause of the Twenty-first Amendment implies a breathtaking volatility in the amendment process. The very idea of amending constitutions and amendments was implied from the beginning in Article V and rests at the very center of the American design of a constitutional order. But there has been a huge discrepancy between design and implementation. Constitution and Bill of Rights worship has dominated much of the nation's history. By the nineteenth century, in much of American culture the founders were seen to have created a perfect mechanism, "a machine that would go of itself." There was little room for the alternative idea that the Constitution was what dominant political supermajorities said it was. The repeal amendment announced just that. But, uncomfortable with transgressing against the American mythology of the Constitution, repealers argued that repeal was necessary because the Eighteenth Amendment was different from all other amendments. It was, according to them, a mere sumptuary law that conflicted with rights enshrined in the Constitution and Bill of Rights and thus deserving of repeal. They constructed a veil of exceptionalism over the naked power displayed by the Twenty-first Amendment. And in the years since the Twenty-first Amendment's passage, commentators and others have embraced this supposed exceptionalism of the Eighteenth Amendment to explain the repeal and thus have overlooked the potential of repealing amendments.[49]

Ratification through conventions in the states has suffered a similar fate. The VCL and the AAPA, which created the system, saw it as a way to limit the growth of the federal government. But they soon found themselves facing a far greater expansion of the federal government in the New Deal. In response, leaders and members from both organizations flowed into the American Liberty League, an organization dedicated to opposing the New Deal. But the Liberty League ended up on the losing side of the argument as the Supreme Court, in the so-called constitutional revolution of 1937, legitimated the new role for federal authority. Convention ratification vanished with their defeat and has not resurfaced, perhaps for two other reasons. First, those inclined to seek amendments may have thought the method too complicated compared to ratification by state legislatures. Second, the argument of exceptionalism surrounding the two liquor amendments may have convinced would-be amendment makers that the method was inappropriate.[50]

While the sweeping potential of the Twenty-first Amendment was not realized, its second clause has become part of our living Constitution. This development occurred mostly after the policy of liquor prohibition had been abandoned by virtually all states and the federal government had again adopted tax policies contrary to prohibition. With repeal came federal taxation of liquor along preprohibition lines, with tax-raised revenues averaging 10.7 percent of federal income in the Depression years. True to its preprohibition form, the federal government continued to collect liquor taxes in prohibition areas. But there were few dry areas. Within four years of the amendment's adoption, forty-three of the forty-eight states had legalized the sale of all liquors. By 1940 the number of prohibition states had sunk to three, and those three allowed the sale of beer. By 1959 there were no prohibition states left, though a number of states preserved the policy in local option systems. In the same period, the states went either to a government monopoly system for liquor sales or a state-controlled license system of distribution. These lesser systems of liquor control brought about constitutional adjudication of the Twenty-first Amendment.[51]

The Supreme Court's constitutional interpretation of the second clause of the Twenty-first Amendment has followed a general pattern: at first the Court recognized broad state power under the clause and then it narrowed such power. The amendment was first held to be an exception to the federal commerce power, allowing the states to enact policies on liquor that would, without the amendment's protection, be violations of the federal commerce power. In later decisions, this broad exception to the commerce power was narrowed considerably. As the Court narrowed the amendment's reach in areas of commerce, it sustained state regulations, under the Twenty-first Amendment, of what in other contexts were First Amendment protected behaviors. But by the mid-1980s the Court had retreated from its earlier position on speech and the Twenty-first Amendment. While the early commerce rulings seemed to conform with the expectations of the framers of the Twenty-first Amendment, there is no record that they envisioned any of the later rulings on the meaning of their amendment.

Two cases in the 1930s, *State Board of Equalization v. Young's Market Co.* and *Indianapolis Brewing Co. v. Liquor Control Commission*, set the early meaning of the effect of the Twenty-first Amendment on the commerce power. In the first case, a unanimous Court, speaking through Justice Louis Brandeis, held that a state license fee for importers of beer from out of state represented, because of the Twenty-first Amendment, no interference with the federal commerce power. The Court dismissed the argument that the amendment be read as applying only to states with prohibition, declaring that "to say that, would involve not a construction of the amendment, but a rewriting of it." In so ruling, the Court denied the contention that the long history of federal commerce power legislation (the Wilson Act of 1890, the Webb-Kenyon Act of 1913, and the Reed Amendment of 1917) should be used to explain the meaning of the Twenty-first Amendment. In the second case, Justice Brandeis, again for a unanimous Court, held that a law prohibiting Michigan beer dealers from selling any beers manufactured in a state that had a law that discriminated against Michigan beer was a legitimate exercise of state power. What was obviously a retaliatory law that if applied to other commodities would have been a violation of the federal commerce power was legitimate because of the second clause of the Twenty-first Amendment. The Court held that the provisions of the Twenty-first Amendment meant that "the right of a state to prohibit or regulate the importation of intoxicating liquor is not limited by the commerce clause." Thereafter, in a 1964 opinion the Supreme Court summarized the existing state of the law on this issue by saying that because of the Twenty-first Amendment "a State is totally unconfined by traditional Commerce Clause limitations when it restricts the importation of intoxicants destined for use, distribution, or consumption within its borders."[52]

In the 1980s the Supreme Court made a number of important exceptions to this general rule. In the 1980 case of *California Liquor Dealers v. MidCal Aluminum*, the Court found that the Twenty-first Amendment did not bar the application of the Sherman Anti-Trust Act to a California system of liquor wholesaling. The law in question required all wine wholesalers and producers to file fair trade contracts with the state and prohibited the selling of wine to retailers at other than the fair trade contract price. The Court admitted that there was no clear line between federal and state power over liquor, but it found that in this case the national government's interest in enforcing a national policy of free competition overrode the state's power under the Twenty-first Amendment. In a similar 1984 case, arising from Hawaii's imposition of a 20 percent excise tax on wholesale liquor sales except for Hawaiian-made Okolehao (a hard liquor made from an indigenous shrub) and local fruit (like pineapple) wines, the Court found the state's liquor regulation violated the commerce power by discriminating against out-of-state liquors. In *Bacchus Imports, Ltd. v. Dias*, speaking for a majority of five, Justice Byron White asserted that whatever the purpose of the Twenty-first Amendment, it was "not to empower States to favor local liquor industries by erecting barriers to competition." Warning of "economic Balkanization," the Court limited the Twenty-first Amendment's reach into the commerce power.[53]

Completing the reversal of the spirit of early commerce clause doctrinal interpretations of the Twenty-first Amendment was the case of *Capital Cities Cable, Inc. v. Crisp*. The facts of the case were that Oklahoma, in its state constitution, prohibited the advertising of liquor, except for on-premise signs. While local media fell under the ban, until 1980 the provisions were not enforced for out-of-state print or television. But in 1980 cable TV operators in Oklahoma retransmitting signals from other states were required to block all wine commercials. The operators charged that this requirement violated the Federal Communications Commission's (FCC) policy that mandated federal preemption of all state regulation of cable signals. The Court ruled that the advertising ban was "only indirectly" related to the purpose of the second clause of the Twenty-first Amendment while the FCC's policy was central to the "federal objective." In brief, the Court had shortened the reach of the Twenty-first Amendment in affecting the federal commerce power; instead of a simple reservation of power, the states' action was required to be of more than the "same stature" of the conflicting federal policy to prevail.[54]

While the Court shrank the second clause of the Twenty-first Amendment's umbrella for state protection from federal commerce power, it also recognized that the amendment could be used to uphold some state laws against First Amendment challenges. The lead case, *California v. LaRue*, emerged after the liberalization of obscenity laws and the sexual revolution of the 1960s. In response to the sordid sexual atmosphere of many bars featuring "topless," "bottomless," and nude dancers, the California Alcoholic Beverage Control Board promulgated rules on such entertainment. These rules prohibited performers in licensed establishments from exposing their genitals, from performing sexual acts such as masturbation as part of their routines, and from simulating sexual acts. The regulations stood in opposition to a line of First Amendment cases that held, first, that nudity was not necessarily obscene and could be protected speech and, second, that performances must be judged in their entirety in assessing whether they were obscene and beyond the protection of the First Amendment. Even though the majority of six admitted "that at least some of the performances to which these regulations address themselves are within the limits of the constitutional protection of freedom of expression," they saw the regulations as well within the "wide latitude" of actions "accorded to the state agency that is itself the repository of the State's power under the Twenty-first Amendment."[55]

This latitude did not shrink even as the law of obscenity virtually disappeared. Thus by 1981 the Court upheld a New York law as a valid exercise of the state's power under the Twenty-first Amendment. In 1977 New York tightened its Alcoholic Beverage Control Board Law's provisions dealing with topless dancing. The previous law had allowed such dancing when the entertainer was on a platform more than a foot and a half above floor level and at least six feet from the nearest patron. The new law prohibited any display of the nipple or areola, and the penalty for violation was loss of liquor license for the establishment that sponsored such entertainment. The law was challenged on the grounds that it violated the First Amendment's right of free expression, which had been the grounds on which broader bans on topless dancing had been struck down. But the Court drew a line between an attempt to ban topless dancing in any public place and in "establishments granted a license to serve liquor." What separated the two categories was the Twenty-first Amendment. "Whatever artistic or communicative value" attached to "topless dancing" was "overcome by the State's exercise of its broad powers arising under the Twenty-first Amendment." In brief, the Twenty-first

Amendment trumps the First Amendment, an outcome not considered in the debates or public discussion surrounding its passage.[56]

In the 1980s the Court retreated from the implication that the Twenty-first Amendment could trump the First Amendment. The key ruling came in a 1996 case dealing with the issue of commercial speech, *44 Liquormart, Inc. v. Rhode Island.* In this case, the Court limited the reach of *California v. LaRue.* In striking down a 1956 Rhode Island ban on liquor price advertising, the Court disavowed LaRue's "reasoning insofar as it relied on the Twenty-first Amendment." The Court said that this disavowal did not overturn the effect of LaRue, as "the States' inherent police powers provide ample authority to restrict the kind of 'bacchanalian revelries' described in the LaRue opinion." Drawing on its commerce clause cases, the Court limited the reach of the Twenty-first Amendment. The Court declared that "we now hold that the Twenty-first Amendment does not qualify the constitutional prohibition against laws abridging the freedom of speech embodied in the First Amendment." The amendment could not "save Rhode Island's ban on liquor price advertising" because it was an impermissible limit on commercial speech, which had First Amendment protection. In effect, the Court has now denied that the second clause of the Twenty-first Amendment directly affects the First Amendment.[57]

Certainly, the framers of the Twenty-first Amendment could not have expected the shifting constitutional doctrines concerning the commerce clause and First Amendment that subsequently developed from their handiwork. Indeed, it is unlikely that the creators of the Twenty-first Amendment would recognize a society or legal order where nude dancing or the right to advertise liquor prices was considered a First Amendment right. But, in part, this society and its legal order was an unintended outcome of their success in repealing national prohibition. One of the unanticipated consequences of the Twenty-first Amendment was that the successful repeal became a fulcrum point for cultural and legal changes that transformed much of the society's view of acceptable behavior.

Scholars John Burnham and Lawrence M. Friedman, in separate works that utilize different approaches, have delineated the broad range of social and cultural transformations concerning American society's view of vice in the nineteenth and twentieth centuries. Through most of the nineteenth century, what Friedman styled a "Victorian compromise" governed social and legal attitudes toward vices such as alcohol consumption, prostitution, drug taking, and gambling. Officially, the law proscribed such behaviors, but in practice the behaviors were tolerated, provided they were discrete and "did not openly challenge official norms." Similarly, Burnham showed how what he called the minor vices (drinking liquor, smoking tobacco, taking drugs, gambling, swearing, and sexual misbehavior) were seen as improper activities in the early and mid–nineteenth century. In both law and social action, Americans condemned such behaviors, even though minor vice misbehavior was common. The behaviors could be tolerated because the core of respectability in the society remained unchallenged.[58]

But in the late nineteenth and early twentieth centuries, this compromise broke down. Urbanization spawned by industrialization undermined established values and practices. In American cities, minor vice practitioners and purveyors clustered together in the "segregated districts." These centers of the Victorian underworld, where saloons, brothels, gambling halls, and drug dens predominated, produced a subculture where drinking, smoking, drug taking, sexual license, and cursing were the norms. Furthermore, industrialism drew immigrants and many others to the cities. Poor and often stigmatized by society as disreputable, these so-called lower orders flocked to the only housing they could afford, near the geographic sin centers. Moreover, moral reformers, determined to make the official bans real bans, attempted to impose their cultural values on slum dwellers, who resisted, often by adopting the culture of the Victorian underworld as a counterculture.[59]

Similarly, others embraced the values and practices of the underworld and worked against laws establishing morality. For example, upper-class rebels, often the artistic avant garde, sought to escape the confines of respectable culture and romanticized underworld values. These cultural rebels, often using the language of individualism, attacked respectability as repressed and sought to reshape social standards. Profits to be made from supplying most of the minor vices and the emergence of new forms of media accelerated the process of inversion. To increase profits, businesses sought to make the vices respectable through various means, including advertising and sponsorship of legal change. While working separately, the forces seeking change converged on a similar goal: rejection of respectability.[60]

The repeal of the prohibition amendment marked the key transition period as repeal worked a successful inversion of values. Even though many of the repealers never sought such a wide transformation, their action brought about such change because it "signified the repeal of many implicit [social] contracts concerning behavior." While the cultural struggle ebbed and flowed for over a generation before the 1930s, after that period the moralists were in full retreat. After one legal endorsement of a moral policy was repealed, others were far more easily questioned. Thus, the second half of the century "was the period of the great counterattack," where previously unacceptable behaviors gained increasing respectability and more and more of the legal order that had proscribed them was dismantled. The inversion was, of course, never completed. For instance, drug use and prostitution have mostly remained illegal. More important, after their opponents' successes, the forces of morality have regrouped to renew their struggle to bring law into conformance with morality. But thanks in part to the Twenty-first Amendment's unplanned consequences, they are striving on a far different legal, social, and cultural terrain.[61]

The two liquor amendments cast a series of unexpected shadows on the American experience. These shadows are long but uneven. In the life of social movements, the shadows are barely discernible since the movements—temperance and repeal—that created them have virtually disappeared. In culture and society, the amendments' shadows are stronger. In particular, taken together the amendments opened the way for a partial transformation of values concerning moral behavior. And this change in social values has spawned a new round of culture wars over the meaning of respectability and the means used to obtain it. In law the Eighteenth Amendment cast an even stronger shadow as it contributed to the growth of the federal police establishment. And the deepest shadow has fallen on American constitutionalism. Not only have the amendments added new clauses for appellate judges to construe but they also expanded law enforcement activities for judges to oversee. They have also directly reshaped the amending process. From the Twenty-first Amendment came the realization of the long-latent possibilities of Article V: ratification through conventions and implementation of a repealing amendment. While never used since, the Twenty-first Amendment moved those ideas out of the realm of theory. The Eighteenth Amendment introduced the innovation of a time limit on ratification, a significant change to the constitutional order. These constitutional changes, unanticipated though they may have been, have been the most significant consequences of the two amendments.

NOTES

1. For an example of the difficulty of arriving at the original intent of the Bill of Rights, see the essays in Robert J. Cottrol, ed., *Gun Control and the Constitution: Sources and Explorations on the Second Amendment* (New York: Garland, 1994); on legal scholars' difficulties in developing and maintaining historical interpretations of constitutional provisions, see Laura Kalman, *The Strange Career of Legal Liberalism* (New Haven, Conn.: Yale University Press, 1996).

2. The Progressive era amendments are particularly suited to this analysis, even though they did not all come from social movements. For example, Robert Stanley, *Dimensions of Law in the Service of Order: Origins of the Federal Income Tax, 1861–1913* (New York: Oxford University Press, 1993) shows how policy makers within the polity directed the course of a broad, weakly organized reform in shaping the Sixteenth Amendment. And although their interpretations are far different, Sidney Ratner, *Taxation and Democracy in America* (New York: John Wiley & Sons, 1942, 1967) and David E. Kyvig, *Explicit and Authentic Acts: Amending the U.S. Constitution, 1776–1995* (Lawrence: University Press of Kansas, 1996), 194–208 also show that no organized social movement stood behind the amendment. For the other progressive amendments, see Kyvig, *Explicit*, 209–39; Stephen B. Wood, *Constitutional Politics in the Progressive Era: Child Labor and the Law* (Chicago: University of Chicago Press, 1968); Clement E. Vose, *Constitutional Change: Amendment Politics and Supreme Court Litigation since 1900* (Lexington, Mass.: Lexington Books, 1972), 47–100. For the woman's suffrage amendment, see Christine A. Lunardini, *From Equal Suffrage to Equal Rights: Alice Paul and the National Woman's Party, 1910–1928* (New York: New York University Press, 1986); Aileen S. Kraditor, *Ideas of the Woman Suffrage Movement, 1890–1920* (New York: Columbia University Press, 1965); Linda G. Ford, *Iron-Jawed Angels: The Suffrage Militancy of the National Woman's Party, 1912–1920* (Lanham: University Press of America, 1991); Suzanne M. Marilley, *Woman Suffrage and the Origins of Liberal Feminism in the United States, 1820–1920* (Cambridge, Mass.: Harvard University Press, 1996); William L. O'Neill, *Everyone Was Brave: A History of Feminism in American* (Chicago: Quadrangle Books, 1969, 1971).

3. The fullness of our constitutional system is seen in many works. See, especially, Stanley I. Kutler, *Judicial Power and Reconstruction Politics* (Chicago: University of Chicago Press, 1968); Walter F. Murphy, *Congress and the Court: A Case Study in the American Political Process* (Chicago: University of Chicago Press, 1962); Wood, *Constitutional*; Vose, *Constitutional*.

4. On the temperance movement in general, see Thomas R. Pegram, *Battling Demon Rum: The Struggle for a Dry America, 1800–1933* (Chicago: Ivan R. Dee, 1998); Jack S. Blocker Jr., *American Temperance Movements: Cycles of Reform* (Boston: Twayne Publishers, 1989); Paul Aaron and David Musto, "Temperance and Prohibition in America: A Historical Overview," in Mark H. Moore and Dean Gernstein, eds., *Alcohol and Public Policy: Beyond the Shadow of Prohibition* (Washington, D.C.: National Academy Press, 1981), 127–81; Norman H. Clark, *Deliver Us from Evil: An Interpretation of American Prohibition* (New York: W. W. Norton, 1976). For early alcohol habits and temperance movements, see W. J. Rorabaugh, *The Alcoholic Republic: An American Tradition* (New York: Oxford University Press, 1979); Mark Edward Lender and James Kirby Martin, *Drinking in America: A History*, rev. and expanded ed. (New York: Free Press, 1982, 1987). On the second temperance wave, see Ian Tyrell, *Sobering Up: From Temperance to Prohibition in Antebellum America, 1800–1860* (Westport, Conn.: Greenwood Press, 1979); Jed Dannebaum, *Drink and Disorder: Temperance Reform in Cincinnati from the Washington Revival to the WCTU* (Urbana:

University of Illinois Press, 1984); Robert L. Hampel, *Temperance and Prohibition in Massachusetts, 1813–1852* (Ann Arbor, Mich.: UMI Research Press, 1982); Frank L. Byrne, *Prophet of Prohibition: Neal Dow and His Crusade* (Madison: State Historical Society of Wisconsin, 1961).

5. Rorabaugh, *Alcoholic Republic,* 5–21; John Burnham, "New Perspectives on the Prohibition 'Experiment' of the 1920s," *Journal of Social History* 2 (1968): 51–68; Clark, *Deliver,* 14–67 (the 1873 figure is from page 50); John S. Billings, *Report of Social Statistics of Cities of the United States at 11th Census: 1890* (Washington, D.C.: Government Printing Office, 1895), 42; Norman H. Clark, *The Dry Years: Prohibition and Social Change in Washington* (Seattle: University of Washington Press, 1965), 54–63; Perry Duis, *The Saloon: Public Drinking in Chicago and Boston, 1880–1920* (Urbana: University of Illinois Press, 1983), 86–203; Elliot West, *The Saloon on the Rocky Mountain Mining Frontier* (Lincoln: University of Nebraska Press, 1979); Thomas Noel, *The City and the Saloon: Denver, 1858–1916* (Lincoln: University of Nebraska Press, 1983). By 1920 in many areas the saloon had lost its important social functions. See Madelon Powers, "Decay from Within: The Inevitable Doom of the American Saloon," in Susanna Barrows and Robin Room, eds., *Drinking: Behavior and Belief in Modern History* (Berkeley: University of California Press, 1991), 112–31.

6. J. Ellen Foster, *Constitutional Amendment Manual* (New York: National Temperance Society, 1882), 33. For the importance of religion to the temperance movement, see Joseph R. Gusfield, *Symbolic Crusade: Status Politics and the American Temperance Movement* (Urbana: University of Illinois Press, 1963); Jack Blocker Jr., "Modernity of Prohibitionists," and Charles A. Isetts, "A Social Profile of the Women's Temperance Crusade: Hillsboro, Ohio," in Jack Blocker Jr., ed., *Alcohol Reform and Society: The Liquor Issue in Social Context* (Westport, Conn.: Greenwood Press, 1979), 101–10; Robert A. Hohner, "The Prohibitionists: Who Were They?" *South Atlantic Quarterly* 68 (1969): 491–505; Richard Jensen, *The Winning of the Midwest: Social and Political Conflict, 1888–1896* (Chicago: University of Chicago Press, 1971); Paul Kleppner, *The Cross of Culture: A Social Analysis of Midwestern Politics, 1885–1900* (New York: Macmillan Free Press, 1970); Jed Dannebaum, "Immigrants and Temperance: Ethnocultural Conflict in Cincinnati, 1845–1860," *Ohio History* 87 (Autumn 1978): 125–39. On the Prohibition party and WCTU, see Jack S. Blocker Jr., *Retreat from Reform: The Prohibition Movement in the United States, 1890–1913* (Westport, Conn.: Greenwood Press, 1976); Ruth Bordin, *Woman and Temperance* (Philadelphia: Temple University Press, 1981); Jack S. Blocker Jr., *"Give to the Winds Thy Fears": The Women's Temperance Crusade, 1873–1874* (Westport, Conn.: Greenwood Press, 1985); Norton Mezvinsky, "White Ribbon Reform, 1874–1920" (Ph.D. Diss., University of Wisconsin, 1959); Mary Earhart, *Frances Willard: From Prayers to Politics* (Chicago: University of Chicago Press, 1944).

7. Richard F. Hamm, *Shaping the Eighteenth Amendment: Temperance Reform, Legal Culture, and the Polity, 1880–1920* (Chapel Hill: University of North Carolina Press, 1995), 19–226.

8. Ibid., 129–226, 235–40. On the Anti-Saloon League, see K. Austin Kerr, *Organized for Prohibition: A New History of the Anti-Saloon League* (New Haven, Conn.: Yale University Press, 1985); Peter Odegard, *Pressure Politics: The Story of the Anti-Saloon League* (New York: Columbia University Press, 1928).

9. Hamm, *Shaping*, 238–40; Kyvig, *Explicit*, 219.

10. On the drafting and nature of the amendment, see Hamm, *Shaping*, 227–35, 240–50; Odegard, *Pressure Politics*, 172–80; Kerr, *Organized*, 202–10; Vose, *Constitutional*, 69–100; Kyvig, *Explicit*, 216–26; Andrew Sinclair, *Era of Excess: A Social History of the Prohibition Movement* (New York: Harper Colophon Books, 1964), 152–70.

11. *Congressional Record*, 65th Cong., 2d sess., 1918, 423.

12. Ibid., 424, 433; Kyvig, *Explicit*, 223–24; Kerr, *Organized*, 202–3; Odegard, *Pressure*, 172–74.

13. Robert Woods, "Winning the Other Half?" *Survey*, 30 December 1916, 344–52; *Congressional Record*, 65th Cong., 2d sess., 1918, 427.

14. *Congressional Record*, 65th Cong., 2d sess., 1918, 423–25, 427.

15. *New York Times*, 17 January 1919, 1, 4.

16. Wheeler quoted in Hamm, *Shaping*, 246–50. Interestingly enough, one key congressman instrumental in shaping the language of the amendment did not share this interpretation, though the Supreme Court in *The National Prohibition Cases* defined concurrent powers along the lines laid out by Wheeler.

17. 41 Stat. 305–26 (1919).

18. Ibid., 317–18; for the constitutional history of the Volstead Act, see Arthur W. Blakemore, *National Prohibition: The Volstead Act Annotated*, 3d ed. (Albany, N.Y.: Matthew Bender and Co., 1927).

19. Wheeler, offprint of *Current History* (May 1922).

20. Kyvig, *Explicit*, 224–25; Kerr, *Organized*, 207–10.

21. Clark, *Deliver*, 149–50; Samuel Walker, *Popular Justice: A History of American Criminal Justice* (New York: Oxford University Press, 1980), 180–83; for the scope of organized crime before prohibition, consult Eric A. Monkhonen, ed., *Crime and Justice in American History: Historical Articles on the Origins and Evolution of American Criminal Justice* (Munich: K. G. Sauer, 1992), 8: pts. 1 and 2, "Prostitution, Drugs, Gambling, and Organized Crime."

22. Clark, *Deliver*, 146–47, 151–53, 175–80; Mary Murphy, "Bootlegging Mothers and Drinking Daughters: Gender and Prohibition in Butte, Montana," *American Quarterly* 46 (1994): 174–94, 175, 182.

23. Kerr, *Organized*, 211–74; Sinclair, *Era*, 350–51.

24. The most complete treatment of women against prohibition is Kenneth D. Rose, *American Women and the Repeal of Prohibition* (New York: New York University Press, 1996), 63–147, 67, 72, 141, 143; Gusfield, *Symbolic*, 126–31, 162; Clark, *Deliver*, 200–202; David Kyvig, *Repealing National Prohibition* (Chicago: University of Chicago Press, 1979), 122–27.

25. Charles Merz, *Dry Decade* (New York: Doubleday, Doran and Co., 1931), 221, 242, 293; Sinclair, *Era*, 313, 344–46, 357–58, 370, 414.

26. Jimmie Lewis Franklin, *Born Sober: Prohibition in Oklahoma, 1907–1959* (Norman: University of Oklahoma Press, 1971), 78; Clark, *Deliver*, 162–65; Wayne Wheeler, "The Success and Failure of Prohibition," *Current Opinion* 70 (1921): 37; William G. Brown, "State Cooperation in Enforcement," *Annals of the American Academy of Political and Social Science* 163 (1932): 30–38. On repeal of laws, see Hamm, *Shaping*, 266–67; Kerr, *Organized*, 236; Clark, *Deliver*, 167–69; Brown, "State," 30.

27. Lawrence M. Friedman, *Crime and Punishment in American History* (New York: Basic Books, 1993), 265.

28. In general, for growth of federal law enforcement capabilities, see David R. Johnson, *American Law Enforcement: A History* (St. Louis: Forum Press, 1981), 73–87, 167–76; Friedman, *Crime*, 261–74. On federal liquor law enforcement before national prohibition, see Stephen Cresswell, *Mormons, Cowboys, Moonshiners, and Klansmen: Federal Law Enforcement in the South and West, 1870–1893* (Tuscaloosa: University of Alabama Press, 1991); Wilbur R. Miller, *Revenuers and Moonshiners: Enforcing Federal Liquor Law in the Mountain South, 1865–1900* (Chapel Hill: University of North Carolina Press, 1991). For the enforcement of the oleomargarine tax, see R. Alton Lee, *A History of Regulatory Taxation* (Lexington: University Press of Kentucky, 1973), 12–27, 48–57. For the Harrison Act, see David F. Musto, *The American Disease: Origins of Narcotics Control*, expanded ed. (New York: Oxford University Press, 1973, 1987), 64, 121, 134, 146–47. For the Mann Act and FBI, see David J. Langum, *Crossing over the Line: Legislating Morality and the Mann Act* (Chicago: University of Chicago Press, 1994), 49. For the idea of the patchwork development of the state, see Stephen Skowronek, *Building a New American State: The Expansion of National Administrative Capacities, 1877–1920* (Cambridge: Cambridge University Press, 1982).

29. *Literary Digest*, 17 March 1920, 23, 19 January 1920, 18; Kyvig, *Repealing*, 23.

30. On federal enforcement machinery and efforts, see Albert E. Sawyer, "The Enforcement of National Prohibition," *Annals of the American Academy of Political and Social Science* 163 (1932): 10–29; National Commission on Law Observance and Enforcement, *Report on the Enforcement of the Prohibition Laws of the United States* (Washington, D.C.: Government Printing Office, 1931; reprint Montclair, N.J.: Patterson Smith, 1968); Dorothy M. Brown, *Mabel Walker Willebrandt: A Study of Power, Loyalty and Law* (Knoxville: University of Tennessee Press, 1984), 49–97; Laurence F. Schmeckebier, *The Bureau of Prohibition: Its History, Activities, and Organization* (Washington: Brookings Institution, 1929), 1–62, 50. On the history of federal enforcement, see Sinclair, *Era*, 173–219; Merz, *Dry*; 41 Stat. 305–19 (1919); Kerr, *Organized*, 223–24, 227; Kyvig, *Repealing*; Sinclair, *Era*, 362.

31. Sawyer, "Enforcement," chart between 16–17; Merz, *Dry*, 330–31; Schmeckebier, *Bureau*, 53.

32. Figures derived from Edward Rubin, "A Statistical Study of Federal Criminal Prosecutions," *Law and Contemporary Problems* 1 (1934): 494–508, 497.

33. Brown, *Willebrandt*, 49–80, 50, 54, 72–73.

34. Ibid., 49–80; Mabel Walker Willebrandt, *The Inside of Prohibition* (Indianapolis: Bobbs-Merrill, 1929); Rubin, "Statistical," 507. Willebrandt probably undid all of her publicity work for prohibition by her intemperate attacks on Al Smith during the 1928 campaign and her employment by the California grape industry after she left federal office. Brown, *Willebrandt*, 153–89; Rose, *American*, 124–26.

35. Margaret Werner Cahalan with the assistance of Lee Anne Parsons, *Historical Corrections Statistics in the United States, 1850–1984* (Rockville, Md.: Westat, 1986, for the Department of Justice), 29, 30; Friedman, *Crime*, 269.

36. Cahalan, *Historical Corrections Statistics*, 153, 156; Friedman, *Crime*, 269.

37. Friedman, *Crime*, 269; Brown, *Willebrandt*, 81–97.

38. Sinclair, *Era*, 395. On the nationalization of anticrime efforts, see Friedman, *Crime*, 267–70; Ernest K. Alix, *Ransom Kidnapping in America, 1874–1974: The Creation of a Capital Crime* (Carbondale: Southern Illinois University Press, 1978); and Arthur C. Millspaugh, *Crime Control by the National Government* (Washington, D.C.: Brookings Institution, 1937). On the FBI's ability to ride the waves of public apprehension about crime to prominence in the law enforcement field, see Richard Gid Powers, *G-Men: Hoover's FBI in American Popular Culture* (Carbondale: Southern Illinois University Press, 1983); Max Lowenthal, *The Federal Bureau of Investigation* (New York: William Sloane Associates, 1950); Don Whitehead, *The FBI Story: A Report to the People* (New York: Random House, 1956); Sanford J. Ungar, *FBI* (Boston: Little, Brown and Company, 1975, 1976); and Richard Gid Powers, *Secrecy and Power: The Life of J. Edgar Hoover* (New York: Free Press, 1987). The literature on the FBI, much of it guided by the official line prescribed by the Bureau, gives the impression that the FBI had nothing to do with enforcement of prohibition. Yet many of its antigangster and anticorruption campaigns grew from other agencies' actions in enforcing national prohibition.

39. Rayman L. Solomon, "Regulating the Regulators: Prohibition Enforcement in the Seventh Circuit," and Paul L. Murphy, "Societal Morality and Individual Freedom," in David E. Kyvig, ed., *Law, Alcohol, and Order: Perspectives on National Prohibition* (Westport, Conn.: Greenwood Press, 1985), 81–96, 67–80; Kenneth M. Murchison, *Federal Criminal Law Doctrines: The Forgotten Influence of National Prohibition* (Durham: Duke University Press, 1994); John. J. Guthrie, "Property, Privacy, Police Power, and Prohibition Enforcement: The Judicial Response to the Intoxicating Liquor Laws in Florida, 1885–1935" (Ph.D. Diss., University of Florida, 1993).

40. Murchison, *Federal*, 74–103.

41. Solomon, "Regulating," 88; Guthrie, "Property."

42. Kyvig, *Explicit*, 409, 414, 418.

43. For example, see the proposals by southerners to repeal parts (or all) of the Fourteenth Amendment and the Fifteenth Amendment from 1900 to 1915. Michael A. Musmanno, *Proposed Amendments to the Constitution* (Washington, D.C.: Government Printing Office, 1929; reprint Westport, Conn.: Greenwood Press, 1976), 208–10. The proposal for an unamendable amendment protecting slavery where it existed proposed on the eve of the Civil War presumed that amendments could be re-

pealed; see Kyvig, *Explicit*, 148–53; Sheppard quoted in Kyvig, *Explicit*, 221; Henry L. Mencken, *Prejudices, Fourth Series* (New York: Alfred Knopf, 1924), 161; on the difficulty of the idea of repeal, see Kyvig, *Explicit*, 262; Kyvig, *Repealing*, 53–55.

44. Kyvig, *Repealing*, 71–97, 116–36, 173–77; Clement E. Vose, "Repeal as a Political Achievement," in Kyvig, ed., *Law*, 97–122; Rose, *American*, 63–144; Sinclair, *Era*, 369–99. For a state study of repeal, see Larry Engelmann, "Organized Thirst: The Story of Repeal in Michigan," in Blocker, ed., *Alcohol*, 171–210.

45. Kyvig, *Repealing*, 160–82; Kyvig, *Explicit* 240–67, 275–88; Vose, "Repeal," 100–116; Vose, *Constitutional*, 110–27, 134–35.

46. Kyvig, *Repealing*, 155–57, platform quoted on 155.

47. Ibid., 172–82; Kyvig, *Explicit*, 275–88; Vose, "Repeal," 97–122; David E. Kyvig, "Objection Sustained: Prohibition Repeal and the New Deal," in Blocker, ed., *Alcohol*, 211–34.

48. See Hamm, *Shaping*, 175–226, 235–40, 271.

49. William F. Swindler, "A Dubious Constitutional Experiment," in Kyvig, ed., *Law*, 53–65; Kyvig, *Explicit*, 19–109; Michael Kammen, *A Machine That Would Go of Itself: The Constitution in American Culture* (New York: Knopf, 1986); Sinclair, *Era*, 244–45.

50. Kyvig, *Repealing*, 189–92.

51. Tun-Yuan Hu, *The Liquor Tax in the United States, 1791–1947*, Columbia University Monographs in Public Finance and National Income no. 1 (New York: Graduate School of Business, 1951), 118–19, 132–33; Jay L. Rubin, "The Wet War: American Liquor Control, 1941–1945," in Blocker, ed., *Alcohol*, 250–51; Robert Bader, *Prohibition in Kansas* (Lawrence: University Press of Kansas, 1986), 235; Kyvig, *Repealing*, 188. The second clause was used to shape legislation to aid prohibition states. In 1936 Congress passed a law prohibiting the transportation of liquor into states that banned liquor containing more than 4 percent alcohol by volume. But this law was seldom enforced in prohibition states, and when it was, it sparked backlashes against state prohibition. See Bader, *Prohibition*, 232–33.

52. *State Board of Equalization of California v. Young's Market* 299 U.S. 59 (1936); *Indianapolis Brewing Co. v. Liquor Control Commission*, 305 U.S. 391 (1939); *Hosteteer v. Idlewild Liquor Corp.*, 377 U.S. 324, 330 (1964).

53. *California Retail Liquor Dealers Assn. v. Midcal Aluminum*, 445 U.S. 97, 106–10 (1980); *Bacchus Imports v. Dias*, 468 U.S. 263, 274–76 (1984).

54. *Capital Cities Cable v. Crisp*, 467 U.S. 691, 711–16 (1984).

55. *California v. LaRue*, 409 U.S. 109, 114–19 (1972).

56. *New York State Liquor Authority v. Bellanca*, 452 U.S. 714.

57. *44 Liquormart v. Rhode Island*, 517 U.S. 484, 515–16 (1996); also see *Barnes v. Glen Theatre, Inc.*, 501 U.S. 560 (1991).

58. John C. Burnham, *Bad Habits: Drinking, Smoking, Taking Drugs, Gambling, Sexual Misbehavior, and Swearing in American History* (New York: New York University Press, 1993), 1–49; Friedman, *Crime*, 127; Lawrence M. Friedman, *Total Justice* (Boston: Beacon Press, 1985), 133.

59. Burnham, *Bad*, 50–60, 86–96, 112–20, 146–59, 170–82, 208–18; Friedman, *Crime*, 134–40.

60. Burnham, *Bad*, 60–73, 96–101, 120–45, 160–64, 182–88, 218–23.

61. Ibid., 49, 73–85, 101–11, 164–69, 188–207, 223–92; Friedman, *Crime*, 339. For example, Kenneth Rose asserts that women repealers explicitly sought no such social revolution; see Rose, *American*, 139–40.

7 The Unintended Consequences of the Nineteenth Amendment: Why So Few?

Suzanne M. Marilley

The passage of the Nineteenth Amendment to the Constitution of the United States fulfilled a primary goal for liberal feminists who had struggled for three generations to improve political conditions for women: it gave all women the right to vote and to compete for elective office. By 1920 winning the vote had come to represent the political intentions of middle-class, educated, mostly white feminists in the United States. Unknown at the time but patently clear now is that the suffragists had few, if any, concerted plans to use their new electoral power. Many scholars and political analysts see the lack of a substantial turnout of women voters in national elections, particularly in the 1920s, as a mysterious and even glaring unintentional consequence. Such scholars show how easy it is to forget that those who fought for the Nineteenth Amendment as a single issue disagreed remarkably on their conceptions of the amendment's purpose as well as their intentions for its use. When diverse organized interests unite around a common goal and try to create a powerful coalition, the coalition usually lasts only long enough to achieve a single success. The women and men who supported female enfranchisement were loosely connected. Just as some members of any coalition are dissatisfied with policies that are adopted but fail to achieve their best intentions, so the most egalitarian-minded liberal feminists and some of their progressive allies have pointed to a number of missed opportunities and as yet unrealized expectations for women's use of the vote.

The Nineteenth Amendment was a lasting, meaningful achievement by reformers who possessed multiple intentions and overcame intense resistance. Opposition to female enfranchisement was so strong that woman's rights reformers and suffragists did not and in reality could not publicly state their true intentions. The games that women, as a politically excluded group, found themselves forced to play carried very high costs: men in power assured as far as they could that the right of women to vote would be generally understood in ways that men accepted.

Many scholars consider the compromises made by leading woman suffragists to be unacceptable violations of egalitarian principles. Most criticism has been targeted at woman suffragists for their "failures" to deliver promised policy changes as well as for their accommodations to racism, elitism, and conservatism. These denunciations deny these shrewd and crafty constitutional reformers the standing they deserve. Most recently, historian Sara Hunter Graham thoroughly documented how, in the late 1880s, Susan B. Anthony recast the suffragists' image as respectable and diminished the visibility of Elizabeth Cady Stanton, whose outbursts against black and immigrant male voting were notable features of the retreat from egalitarianism during the quest for woman suffrage.[1] I also lament those compromises, but I see them as necessary political bargains made by the leaders of a powerless group. As a lifelong Roman Catholic, I consider the women who struggled to transform women from a politically excluded group to a politically included group as pioneers who have much to teach similarly situated women. What woman suffragists did for the American polity and other polities I hope can and will be done in the Roman Catholic Church and other patriarchal power structures. The right to vote also carries abundant potential that citizens of the United States have yet to actualize.

Simply from the perspective of change in the Constitution proper, the Nineteenth Amendment appears as a major progressive if not revolutionary change.[2] I agree with David Kyvig that the amendment was legally revolutionary. I also believe that to win passage and ratification the reformers sometimes had to all but deny that woman suffrage would alter the status quo in the slightest. Suffragists faced heavy pressures to compromise, because the Nineteenth Amendment—like the Fourteenth, Fifteenth, and

Eighteenth Amendments—instituted more than an adjustment of basic rules or constitutional procedures for coping with problems such as presidential succession in case of death. Each of these amendments introduced fundamental constitutional reforms in citizenship and political behavior that occasioned intense legislative and electoral debate before passage.

There ends the similarity. Radical Republicans in Congress defined the Reconstruction purpose of the Fourteenth and Fifteenth Amendments to endow African Americans with basic citizenship rights, but white supremacy quickly overwhelmed this aim. The Fourteenth Amendment soon became a tool used by the federal court system for imposing a libertarian vision of free labor markets. Although that use ended in the 1930s, the meaning of the Fourteenth Amendment's due process and equal protection clauses continue to be the subject of major constitutional debates.[3] Although the Eighteenth Amendment was like the Nineteenth in that organized outside pressure groups lobbied for its passage, the former amendment was repealed: support waned after the emergence of grisly crime and massive refusal to observe prohibition. Only the Nineteenth Amendment won acceptance without major calls for repeal or extensive, protracted debate on its meaning.[4] The amendment was written, achieved, and honored as "simple justice," neither more nor less.[5]

When the lack of "real change" engendered by the Nineteenth Amendment is compared with white supremacy's long abnegation of the Fourteenth and Fifteenth and the outright repeal of the Eighteenth, the fate of woman suffrage appears less disappointing. The overwhelming acceptance of women's right to vote, even in states where antisuffragists prevailed until ratification, proves that the suffragists converted many people on the appropriate political standing of women.[6] The Nineteenth Amendment generated less visible, more psychological change than did most of the other amendments.

Although several common purposes united women across this expansive nation during the struggle for woman suffrage, the reformers differed considerably in class, race, ethnicity, gender ideals, and issues of principle. When the 1848 Seneca Falls Convention put votes for women on its agenda, only Frederick Douglass was present to represent African Americans. By the time of ratification, however, the movement's rank and file included African American, Asian American, Catholic, working-class, Socialist, Communist, and southern women. Scholars have yet to discover the long-term intentions that some of these women had for the vote. What we do know is that, in its final stages, the suffrage coalition's leaders, mindful of the diversity in their ranks, allowed for practically no policy aims beyond that of winning the right to vote.[7]

Carrie Chapman Catt, Alice Paul, and their sister leaders fought hard against the injustice that all women suffered regardless of any other social characteristic or political intention: the stigma of political exclusion. After ratification most suffragists returned to their primary communities, and each woman put the vote to the uses she deemed appropriate. The lack of visible change in women's everyday lives or in their political behavior, particularly as voters and contestants for political office, derives mostly from women's choices not to pursue those kinds of transformations as well as the lack of opportunities to pursue them presented by political parties and other electorally influential organized interests.

My positive view of the Nineteenth Amendment, however, derives from my focus on its psychological and potential meaning for each woman, not its immediate electoral consequences. Instead of eminence as a legally "revolutionary" change, the Nineteenth Amendment has earned near notoriety for the lack of noticeable, macrolevel changes that followed. Women did not enter the electorate en masse, or compete for elective office, or win an equal rights amendment, or alter issue priorities on legislative agendas according to their preferences, or lead concerted anticorruption efforts. These "non-developments," as political scientist Theodore Lowi might call them,[8] loom large as betrayals of the 1848 Declaration's purpose—as unintended consequences that make the Nineteenth Amendment a victory more hollow than hallowed.

The widely noted differences between the aims of the suffragists who won the vote and those who pioneered the movement raise a critical question: by whose intentions should we measure the unintended consequences of the Nineteenth Amendment or any other amendment? By current conceptions of equal rights that go well beyond what even the most radical nineteenth-century reformers were willing to conceive? After all, the concrete benefits women received from the right to vote pale when compared with the gains brought by the major achievements of the post–civil rights women's movement of the 1960s. The right to vote did not immediately bring legal reforms such as equal credit opportunity, reproductive rights, and gender equity in hiring and education.

On the other hand, should the impact of the Nineteenth Amendment be measured by the standard of the victorious generation of suffragists? By the original aims of the 1848 Seneca Falls Convention that barely passed the resolution for woman suffrage? By the standard the framers of the Constitution of the United States indirectly set when they wrote the rules for constitutional ratification? If, on this point, the framers of Article V indeed meant to minimize the scope and import of change engendered by constitutional amendments and especially to avoid unintended consequences that might de-stabilize or radically transform government structures, then the Nineteenth Amendment stands as a model for success.[9] The Constitution's requirement of supermajorities for ratification—a congressional majority of at least two thirds and three fourths of the state legislatures has been the most frequently exercised procedure—assured that reforms widely perceived as radical, such as woman suffrage, could not pass until such perceptions markedly changed.

What about the opponents of the Nineteenth Amendment? The antisuf-fragists' misgivings did much to delay and hinder its passage; suffragists had to allay the fears raised by the strongest arguments of their opponents. Did the power of the antisuffragists to sway audiences and stall progress force the suffragists to state intentions that were untrue or partly untrue? If so, then the supposition that one has identified the suffragists' *real* intentions is haz-ardous, because many statements made by the suffragists contradicted egali-tarian ideals in order to accommodate their opponents' intractable racism and ethnocentrism.

Obviously, it is impossible to isolate each of the many true intentions of the suffragists, or those of the framers of Article V, or those of the antisuf-fragists, or even those of the suffragists' contemporary sympathetic critics. It is possible, however, to put the debate over the consequences of the Nine-teenth Amendment into a more elaborate context of political developments to which woman's rights reformers and suffragists had to respond if they wanted to win the vote. In what follows I will (1) review how various schol-ars have interpreted the unintended consequences of the Nineteenth Amend-ment as ironies and suggest that their collective sense of ironic unintended contradictions constitutes an *intended* consequence of the efforts to achieve the Nineteenth Amendment; (2) explain that the resistance to the idea of women voting and the constraints that the rules for constitutional reform put on their strategies forced suffragists to dilute and even to hide their in-tentions and present their goal as a minimalist aim; and (3) propose that if we accept the findings on the less visible changes in political institutions that feminist scholars have made since 1970, we will see that in the long run the intended consequences of the Nineteenth Amendment have outnumbered but not yet overshadowed its unintended consequences.

The concept of "unintended consequences" is itself politically charged and needs some clarification. This idea derives most recently from the pow-erfully influential arguments of distinguished neoconservatives and their assault on the underpinnings of the Great Society programs of the 1960s, including the post-1960s woman's rights movement, its egalitarian ideals, and the idea of affirmative action. Liberals found themselves widely discredited when, in the middle 1960s, neoconservatives pointed out that liberal programs such as busing and poverty relief not only failed to solve the problems for which they were designed but also even seemed to foster new problems (such as welfare dependency and community violence). As journalist E. J. Dionne Jr. points out, affirmative action "hurt" working-class white men, not wealthy white men. Social policy, Johnson style, gradually became understood as "throwing money" at intractable problems and failing to understand problems before "scientifically" designing solutions to those problems.[10]

The "law of unintended consequences," as developed and applied by neoconservatives, encourages negative judgments about liberal reforms, particularly the reforms that have aimed to make the American polity more inclusive. Woman suffrage was such a reform, and when a focus is put on institutional changes for all rather than on the aims of the reformers and the first women voters, plenty of evidence is mustered to show that it changed very little. If we focus on visible macrochanges in political institutions, this neoconservative-inspired perspective certainly carries the day. But such a focus ignores what possession of the right to vote meant to the women who won it and to the female American citizens born after 1920 who never had to consider themselves publicly stigmatized by their disfranchisement.[11] An exclusive focus on the consequences of the Nineteenth Amendment also distracts attention from the steps that were politically necessary for an excluded group to pass a federal constitutional amendment that would include them as voters.

Scholars who esteem liberal ideals and hope for more egalitarian democratic institutions also tend to use those ideals as perfectionist standards that woman suffragists failed to meet. Heavily influenced by the New Left visionaries of the 1960s, a number of insightful scholars have pointed to the American woman suffrage movement as an example of how white middle-class liberals have betrayed equality and inclusivity in order to fortify their political and social privilege. The main hazard of this approach is the use of current expectations about the nature and possibilities of liberalism and democracy to define the intentions of reformers who lived in the previous century. But the limitations, ironies, and outright contradictions pointed out by these scholars positively contribute to the critical thinking essential to the continuation of the liberal and democratic revolutions. Even if they were to argue, as no one bluntly has, that winning the vote in the way it was won became itself an impediment to the achievement of equality for women in the twentieth century, then that realization is partly due to the vision of Elizabeth Cady Stanton and other radical woman's rights reformers.

As Rogers M. Smith observes, suffragists' thinking on the meaning of liberty for all and vision of social change showed more consistencies than that of Thomas Jefferson and other white, male, liberal political thinkers.[12]

Ironies of the Nineteenth Amendment

Many scholars have pointed out ironies in the contradiction between the revolutionary content of the Nineteenth Amendment and the lack of immediately visible change in political institutions, particularly in women's voting behavior and willingness to compete for elective office. Although votes for women was long perceived as a radical goal, it gradually came to be understood as one of the most benign liberal political reforms ever to pass in the United States. Evidence of changing perceptions about woman suffrage emerged as early as 1909, when Helen Sumner (Woodbury) published her social scientific study on the effects of female enfranchisement in Colorado. Sumner concluded that votes for women had had only a "slight" effect on party politics and that "comparatively few [women] have taken an active part in political life."[13] In 1962 the conservative political philosopher Michael Oakshott pointed to female enfranchisement as an example of a reform born out of "intimations" of appropriateness, not out of reason or a quest for justice. Women won the vote because "in all or most other important respects they had already been enfranchised."[14]

The chilling effects of interpretations such as Oakshott's may have prompted William O'Neill to write a humorously ironic account of women's struggles for rights. O'Neill conveys ironies in the movement from start to finish:

> Indeed, it was one of the great ironies in women's history that dress reform, which the early feminists first practiced and then abandoned . . . in the long run proved more valuable than other reforms which seemed essential at the time. Certainly it did women far more good to shed their crippling foundation garments and multi-layered, confining, and unsanitary costumes than to vote. Today the ballot means little to most of them, but with every breath they draw, women have reason to be grateful that capricious fashion did what feminism could not—physically emancipate them from the bonds that taste and custom had forged.[15]

Sara Evans observes irony in the ways in which enfranchisement freed and disbanded the formerly united reformers to pursue diverse goals. "The irony of the vote," she states, "is that what was won with a great collective effort permitted women to confront their newly attained citizenship in the solitude of the voting booth." After the suffrage victory, enfranchised women found themselves more divided from each other than united and closer to the political views of men in their lives on many issues than they were to their suffrage sisters.[16] The victory blurred formerly formalized gender roles and presented feminists with a formidable challenge that Nancy Cott describes as a dilemma: to define "gender consciousness" while aiming "for the dissolution of prescribed gender roles."[17]

Political philosopher Judith Shklar attributed the lack of electoral and other kinds of political change enacted by newly enfranchised women to their heavy conformance with dominant political ideas and practices: "The real irony was that because women had adopted the dominant attitudes of their time and place so completely, their final victory led to no noticeable political change at all." Unlike their forebears who valued natural rights and civic freedom for all, the winning generation of suffragists focused more intently on "self-development" and "nurture of the personality." Thus, most of the victorious suffragists lacked desire for substantial political reform beyond the vote, and "it did not alter their social lives significantly."[18] Political philosopher Carole Pateman finds irony in the coincidence of woman suffrage victories in Western republican democracies at the same time as the ballot decreased in importance and the Soviet revolution threatened similar efforts in the West.[19]

Constitutional scholar Rogers M. Smith similarly observes that the "simple justice" the Nineteenth Amendment instituted was so weak that most Supreme Court justices continued to deny women equal rights on the grounds that women's "special domestic and maternal qualities and needs"—the qualities that suffragists also defined as women's qualifications for voting—should be protected. Thus, perhaps inadvertently, the suffragists conspired in the maintenance of the Court's already formidable battery of arguments against the full political inclusion of women. The justifications that suffragists made for enfranchisement in the last phase of the movement reinforced ideas on female inferiority and the appropriateness of separate spheres that slowed further feminist gains, particularly in the workplace.[20] As Smith points out, the Supreme Court even upheld a Georgia law that exempted a man from paying a poll tax if his wife declined to register to vote.[21]

Was the concern of all these scholars—the lack of change following the ratification of the Nineteenth Amendment—unintended? O'Neill and the founding mothers of the suffrage movement would probably answer in the affirmative. O'Neill openly laments the lack of change engendered by the feminist movement in the United States. Political scientists continue to puzzle similarly over women's lower psychological interest in politics than men's, lower levels of political knowledge, lagging sense of political efficacy, and slightly less active participation in political campaigns.[22] But the emergence of a "gender gap"—women's inclinations to choose liberal issue positions and to vote for Democrats at rates that notably exceed those of men—gives the impression that substantive gender differences have begun to emerge in the electorate. Still, political scientists observe that the gender gap remains weaker than the "marriage gap" and the "class gap." For example, in the 1996 election, "the gender gap was most evident among working women, with 57 per cent of that group voting for Clinton and 34 per cent voting for Dole."[23] And political scientist Roberta Sigel demonstrates that although contemporary women in New Jersey display progressive attitudes on equality for women in the workplace and the right to earn, they continue to tolerate inequality in the division of domestic labor in the home and refuse to organize to improve women's political condition.[24] Americans voice strong egalitarian attitudes but show little evidence of practicing them, at least in the home. By 1998 women citizens in general still had not yet delivered the consciousness or political participation required to generate equality, justice, and liberty for all envisioned in 1848 at the Seneca Falls Convention.

The ironies observed by Shklar, Evans, Cott, and Smith, however, suggest that some blame for the lack of rapid change ought to be cast not only on the aims chosen by the suffragists but also on the inevitable, often protracted postvictory processes of consolidating gains and setting new priorities. Anna Harvey points out that, after women won the vote in New York State, the Democratic and Republican parties mobilized women voters faster and more adeptly than the National League of Women Voters. The New York board of the League found itself hamstrung by the nonpartisan, single-issue strategy developed to promote the vote.[25] Shklar also implies that before women can unify as voters and citizens around common goals beyond the vote, Americans must politically guarantee each citizen the "right to earn," a right that all Americans lack in law.[26] Women need both independent incomes and time to craft new electoral strategies before they can advance politically as an enfranchised group with distinctive interests.

Harvey and Shklar make astute observations about the resources that newly enfranchised women lacked as a group: substantial finances and experience in the running of elections. Female first-time voters entered the electorate as more economically and politically dependent than male voters. In retrospect, it is most striking that the leaders of the major political parties and the Catholic Church—institutions whose prominent leaders had blocked woman suffrage at almost every turn—moved so quickly and successfully to shore up the support of "their" female voters.

What concerns, then, made the suffragists so eager to win the vote and so willing to make costly compromises? Aileen S. Kraditor suggests that intense and widespread resistance forced the suffragists to exaggerate the likely effects of votes for women. "They could afford to state their ideals," she states, "in ringing declarations on democracy that would admit of no qualifications or exceptions. In fact, they had to do so, for only ideals that could inspire a martyr's dedication could sustain these women through the physical violence and almost unbearable ridicule to which they were subjected." But when victories required compromises, the suffragists compromised, "perhaps more than the requirements of the alliances dictated. More often than not they voiced the ideals and advocated the compromises at the same time." [27]

Kraditor reasonably faults the suffragists for overcompromising their ideals. But her observation that they proclaimed and compromised ideals "at the same time" suggests that more attention should be given to such ambiguities. Because so much attention had been given to the inconsistencies between intentions ascribed to the suffragists and the lack of outcomes they originally promised, I decided to study why some middle-class, white, educated women in the late nineteenth and early twentieth centuries so dearly wanted the vote as well as the reasons for the political steps they took. In my effort to understand the passions and interests of the suffragists, I felt a profound obligation to look around and beyond my own preferences and ideals. Eventually I synthesized an interpretative framework that captures much of the variety as well as the unity in the suffragists' liberal feminist ideologies. To complete the synthesis I drew substantially on Shklar's typology of liberal ideologies and Smith's theory of multiple traditions. [28]

Three Kinds of Liberal Feminism

Woman suffragists developed three versions of liberal feminist arguments for the vote: a feminism of equal rights, a feminism of fear, and a feminism of personal development. The feminism of equal rights aimed to gain women political inclusion by winning for women the same legal rights as men. The feminism of fear aimed to persuade women that the vote would liberate them and their children from living in the fear of violent injury or death caused by drunken men. The feminism of personal development aimed to enfranchise women so that each could fully develop her unique potential. Each feminism was liberal because its advocates aimed primarily, as Judith Shklar put it, "to secure the political conditions that are necessary for the exercise of personal freedom."[29] Woman suffragists also, however, esteemed illiberal ideals that distinguish republican and Americanist traditions. They sought freedom for women in the context of diverse communities identified by varied commitments to achieve the common good. Although their liberal goal of winning each woman the right to vote always clashed with republican and Americanist justifications for female disfranchisement, suffragists also readily drew upon illiberal aims and rationales that they could easily attach to woman suffrage. In short, suffragists blended the idea of votes for women with republican motherhood, white supremacy, social democracy, and Americanization.

The 1848 Seneca Falls Declaration, which remains a manifesto for egalitarian feminists, constitutes the touchstone for the feminism of equal rights. For feminists of equal rights, the personal freedom of each woman can only be guaranteed by egalitarian attitudes toward women in general and the making of women equal under the law in particular. The 1848 Declaration presented four kinds of equal rights: the right to political voice, the right to be morally responsible, the right to earn, and the right not to be demoralized. Of these four, only the right to political voice has been guaranteed. The Nineteenth Amendment secured political voice for women in the electorate, but many feminists argue that women still struggle for the right to political voice outside of the electoral arena.

Frances Willard, the temperance leader and rival of Stanton, developed a feminism of fear and put first the aim to liberate women from vulnerability to male cruelty. Willard believed that male violence toward women and children was caused mostly by excessive consumption of alcohol. Willard tried to convince women more traditional than the suffragists to seek the vote as a means of self-protection from the violent attacks of drunken men. Willard inspired hundreds of thousands of women to participate in politics visibly, often militantly, and without apology. Willard's success is proved by the rapid growth of the Woman's Christian Temperance Union (WCTU) under her leadership.

Both the feminism of equal rights and the feminism of fear directly linked the vote with ambitious plans for the transformation of unequal and unjust relations between the sexes. The feminism of personal development, in contrast, portrayed the vote as a much-needed immediate opportunity for each woman to achieve her potential in competitive relations and inegalitarian contexts, including a modernized view of separate spheres. Among woman suffragists, Stanton, Anna Howard Shaw, Charlotte Perkins Gilman, and Carrie Chapman Catt all contributed to the feminism of personal development: the aim to maximize opportunities for each person to develop to her potential. Natural or equal rights mattered to these feminists, but universal rights became subordinated to the achievement of goals for each person in a context where a deeply Americanist social Darwinist *mentalité* dominated. Stanton's acceptance of basic social Darwinist ideas and her exploitation of racialist doctrines evidenced the hold that beliefs about natural inequalities had even on those who espoused the most egalitarian ideals.

Although the feminism of personal development lacked the transformative visions of the earlier feminism, its proponents tolerated each woman's choice of issues, political party, and social vision. Suffragists who mainly espoused a feminism of personal development also accepted varied intentions on how to use the vote. This toleration enabled the reformers to merge together as a "client group" focused exclusively on winning a benefit: the vote. But feminists of personal development promoted almost no consensus on intended consequences beyond ratification. As a result, for them the Nineteenth Amendment brought few if any *unintended* consequences in the way of change in political institutions. Women won the personal right to choose whether to vote; suffragists hoped women would vote, but they made few plans to corral women to the polls en masse.

In fact, the "simple justice" aim that distinguishes Catt's feminism of personal development so exactly met what today might be called the politically imperative "sound-bite" required to win over legislative majorities that I continue to doubt whether she fully subscribed to such a limited view. Still, when the eighteenth-century framers of the Constitution required in Article V such large legislative majorities to enact amendments, they gave much power to defenders of the status quo such as the antisuffragists, and they burdened reformers with formidable mobilization problems. David Kyvig persuasively argues that the framers carefully designed Article V to insure political stability and particularly to guarantee that the tyranny of the majority would not overburden future minority dissenting states. Although many scholars lament the lack of visible institutional change after the passage of the Nineteenth Amendment, Kyvig's explanation enables us to see better how the framers' intentions drive every amendment process. By making amendment proponents persuade supermajorities, narrowly held views and philosophies must be transformed so that many groups share the reformers' goals. In effect, the proponents of a constitutional amendment in the United States must prove that their aim harmonizes with the "public interest" as understood by a supermajority that they must forge—or force— together.

The persuasion process—shepherding the amendment through both houses of Congress, garnering supermajorities in Congress, state legislatures, or state conventions—forces proponents to prove their aim merits inclusion and to articulate a rationale acceptable to a maximum number of citizens. Any reform that excites pronounced opposition such as woman suffrage and the equal rights amendment can be easily blocked by organized opponents.[30] Because it was a liberal aim, woman suffrage, like conservative-backed proposals to balance the budget, permit prayer in public schools, and make flag burning illegal, excited substantial opposition.

When they were widely perceived as radical in the nineteenth century, woman suffragists simply could not garner supermajorities in Congress or among state legislatures. Before 1910 only four states had enfranchised women. The high hurdle Article V set could only be cleared after reformers made arguments acceptable to such supermajorities and weakened their image as threatening radicals. Moreover, the liberal feminism of the suffragists included manipulative arguments that unfortunately have contributed to some grave misunderstandings of the suffragists' ideals.

Misconceptions about Suffragists' Aims

The Nineteenth Amendment had few unintended consequences mainly because woman suffragists actually held less radical aims—especially for the vote—than their opponents assumed.[31] Indeed, the antisuffragists designed more elaborate visions of egalitarian change—portrayed, of course, as highly undesirable—than the suffragists presented. Despite woman's rights reformers' strong egalitarian vision of social change—portions of which had yet to be realized by the 150th anniversary of the 1848 Declaration—they disagreed on the prudence of claiming the vote. The 1848 Declaration set ambitious goals such as the elimination of separate spheres, equal access to "wealth and distinction," and encouragement and praise to women who become public figures rather than entertainers. But the fears of some reformers that the idea of women voting "would defeat others they deemed more rational, and make the whole movement ridiculous" made female enfranchisement the woman's rights goal with the weakest consensus.[32]

As early as 1851 woman's rights reformers took special pains to deemphasize the egalitarian reforms that might easily be associated with winning the vote. In her celebrated article "The Enfranchisement of Women," Harriet Taylor claimed that the enfranchisement of women entailed "their admission, in law and in fact, to equality in all rights, political, civil, and social, with the male citizens of the community," and she insisted that equality was the appropriate ideal for woman's rights reformers to promote and profess.[33] In the fall of 1851, members of the Second Annual Woman's Rights Convention, which met in Worcester, Massachusetts, tried to distinguish their aims as different from and less ambitious than Taylor's. Their first convention resolution stated: "That while we would not undervalue other methods, the Right of Suffrage for Women is, in our opinion, the corner-stone of this enterprise, since we do not seek to protect woman, but rather to place her in a position to protect herself."[34] Perhaps anticipating that the kind of egalitarian reforms Taylor envisioned would require more of an interventionist national government than they could accept, the suffragists in the United States narrowed the concept of political enfranchisement to winning the right to vote. They explained why they limited their goal to the achievement of women's political liberty: "It is enough for our argument that the natural and political justice, and the axioms of English and American liberty, alike determine that rights and burdens—taxation and representation— should be co-extensive; hence women, as individual citizens, . . . have a self-evident and indisputable right, identically the same right that men have, to a direct voice in the enactment of those laws and the formation of that government."[35]

The members of the 1851 Worcester Convention focused on winning the vote and defended that goal as limited, with no implications for egalitarian reforms. Less fearful than some of the older woman's rights reformers, Elizabeth Cady Stanton, Susan B. Anthony, and Lucy Stone professed egalitarian ideals that were similar to Taylor's (and they temporarily donned the bloomers), but each still considered the franchise as one of many necessary reforms. In fact, Lucy Stone decided just before her marriage that political enfranchisement was one of the least radical goals the movement professed. In a letter to Antoinette Brown (later the Reverend Antoinette Brown Blackwell) Stone wrote that although she thought that it was too early to raise "the marriage question" at the national convention, "it is clear to me, that question underlies, this whole movement. . . . It is very little to me to have the right to vote, town property & c. if I may not keep my body, and its uses, as my absolute right."[36] Stanton and Anthony pressed hard for the vote, but when audiences of women in upstate New York showed a preference for property rights reform, they compliantly put their energies into winning it.[37] After ratification of woman suffrage, Carrie Chapman Catt also remarked that the vote never was the ultimate or only goal of the movement.[38]

The endurance for over forty years of the divisive split that emerged between proponents of the first equal rights amendment and the early defenders of protective legislation was perhaps the most obvious unintended consequence of the Nineteenth Amendment victory.[39] Certainly Florence Kelley could not have intended that the Child Labor Amendment would fail to pass less than ten years after women had won the right to vote. Carrie Chapman Catt herself also disappointed some suffragists when she abandoned her insistence on nonpartisanship to campaign openly for the Democratic ticket in the fall of 1920. Catt, an intense supporter of the League of Nations, probably lost much support among her Republican colleagues. Most former suffragists undoubtedly found themselves unprepared when Catt—disillusioned with political bargaining—decided soon after the vote was won to struggle for peace instead of equal representation for women in political parties.[40]

Participants in the 1848 Seneca Falls Convention presciently anticipated that public opinion and various authorities would resist the idea of women voting. Despite the early consensus that female enfranchisement meant only simple inclusion, the right to a "direct voice" in lawmaking and elections, the opponents of woman's rights and woman suffrage repeatedly portrayed the vote as a radical reform that would introduce inappropriate and dangerous egalitarian relations between the sexes. At an 1853 woman's rights convention in New York City, Dr. H. K. Root, an opponent of woman's rights, explained why women should not vote: (1) God commanded that man should rule because it was Eve who tempted Adam in the Garden of Eden and thereby created original sin; (2) "because man's [physical] strength is greater than woman's"; and (3) because voting would bring woman into "the field of competition with man," leading "not only to domestic unhappiness, but a great many other ill feelings."[41] Antisuffragists such as Root rejected the idea that women could be endowed with the same rights as men; woman suffrage represented a relinquishment of rights and responsibilities to the sex of imprudent Eve.

Suffrage opponents perceived and feared radical changes that went beyond what most suffragists publicly divulged to have been their greatest hopes. Moreover, Stanton, Anthony, and Stone professed egalitarian ideals at a time when they were still young women equally committed to radical Garrisonian antislavery reform and winning women rights. The aftermath of the Civil War changed the character of the movement from a unified quest for equal rights to separate civil rights movements by different groups. The gender exclusivity of the Fourteenth Amendment precipitated sharp segmentations that Stanton, Anthony, Stone, and other equal-rights Garrisonians never intended. The priority put on winning votes for women and reformers' determination to achieve it owes much to these women's feelings of betrayal and desires to redress their grievance.[42]

During the ratification of the Fourteenth and Fifteenth Amendments, which enfranchised black men but not women, these about-to-become leaders of two national woman suffrage associations used racist concepts to condemn the federal government's enfranchisement of black men only. Stone begrudgingly accepted the Fifteenth Amendment as a poor half-loaf of progress on the franchise but added that "the safety of the government would be more promoted by the admission of woman as an element of restoration and harmony than the [N]egro." Stanton more fiercely betrayed the egalitarian principles she had tenaciously promoted when she denounced the "aristocracy of sex" introduced by the Reconstruction Amendments. In her address to the National Woman Suffrage Convention in January 1869, Stanton angrily asked her audience how the women who already bore "the oppressions of their own Saxon Fathers, the best orders of manhood" would endure rule by "the lower orders of foreigners now crowding our shores."[43]

After the Civil War no major suffragist leader put egalitarian visions ahead of the formulation of arguments that would persuade the audience at hand to accept votes for women. Of course, some egalitarian arguments were made for suffrage by reformers who identified themselves primarily as radical populists, socialists, and trade union leaders as well as by suffragists to such audiences.[44] The quest for the Nineteenth Amendment, however, became a struggle to redress the explicit exclusion of women from the vote manifested by the constitutional protections given explicitly to men in the Fourteenth Amendment and the elaborate endorsement of that meaning by the Supreme Court in *Minor v. Happersett* (1874) soon thereafter.

As Rogers Smith explains, Chief Justice Morrison Waite's opinion strengthened the opposition to female political inclusion in the *Minor* case. Although Waite admitted that women were citizens, he contended that suffrage had never been a "privilege of citizenship." He thereby reinforced the republican tradition of states' rights over electoral laws as well as the liberal view that "political participation is inessential to citizenship." As Smith points out, Waite considerably strengthened Americanist rationales for keeping the vote out of women's hands, and he introduced a legal distinction that enabled the Court to endow other groups with ambiguous citizenship.[45] The *Minor* decision effectively closed the federal court system as an avenue for winning woman suffrage.

Waite's concession that women already possessed appropriate equal rights with men—after all, they *were* citizens (that is, if they met residency and marriage requirements)—induced the suffragists to avoid egalitarian arguments and to concentrate on proving why women deserved the right to vote. After Reconstruction Stanton never entirely discarded the liberal claim that guarantees of rights to all made female enfranchisement necessary, but she preferred to defend the rights of educated women. In fact, Stanton contributed just as much thought and careful argument to the feminism of personal development as she had devoted to the feminism of equal rights.[46]

Willard directly attacked Waite's logic as well as the antisuffragists' contentions that God had not made women to vote. As I have argued elsewhere, Willard's aims went beyond winning Maine laws and other prohibitionist legislation: she wanted men and women alike to traverse the separate spheres so that "mother-love," God's most powerful gift, would become the dominant authority in government as well as the home. To win members for the WCTU and support for her radical vision, Willard began most of her speeches with the claim that all women were vulnerable to injury and even violent death caused by the uncontrolled physical outbursts of drunken men. Citizenship under such conditions had little meaning for women. The ballot, however, offered women release from this tyranny as well as a means to protect themselves and their children from future injury. Furthermore, she argued, women's campaigns for temperance, suffrage, and multiple social reforms constituted a fair portion of their duty to "God, home, and native land."[47]

Willard's rhetorical vision of Christian women transforming the polity succeeded as a means for the mobilization of large numbers of traditionalist women into the WCTU. In the late nineteenth century the main task for woman's rights reformers was to encourage women to participate in public life. Severe proscriptions of such participation, many taken verbatim from the Bible, were regularly cited by antisuffragists and ministers fearful of how women's stepping out of the domestic sphere would affect social structures. Willard and other leaders did their best to counteract these proscriptions because they correctly perceived that social and political problems such as widespread alcoholism, poverty, prostitution, and ineffective government demanded women's attention.

Frances Willard made some exaggerated promises for how enfranchised Christian women would transform the polity from a male-dominated society ruled by vice and self-interest into a woman-led community of conscience and love. Nonetheless, she was nominally a temperance leader and as such campaigned for the vote as more of a means than an end. In fact, much the same can be said of Harriet Stanton Blatch, the suffragist concerned about the livelihood of working women, Jane Addams, the social reformer, and Florence Kelley, leader of the campaign against child labor. Willard, Blatch, Addams, and Kelley each hoped most for changes of attitude on the part of elected and appointed officials, not immediate transformations of the public institutional structures. Only their shared assumption that enfranchised women would pressure concertedly for such change was proven wrong.

Despite the suffragists' best efforts, the antisuffragists did not disband or weaken their resistance to the idea of women voting. Indeed, their arguments became predictable. Enfranchised women would destroy the family structure, disrupt the natural or God-given division of labor, and upset the political system. Several award-winning antisuffrage cartoons published in the *New York Times* in 1911 portrayed suffragists in turn as sexless, naive, and dangerous.[48] In fact, it is truly ironic that so little attention has been paid to overcoming the persistent resistance to woman suffrage. Only the antisuffragists, with their court challenges of the Nineteenth Amendment and continued efforts to discredit suffragists such as Catt and Addams, considered the Nineteenth Amendment as an unintended outcome, the consequences of which had to be curbed sharply.[49] After the ratification of the Nineteenth Amendment, the antisuffragists rechristened themselves Woman Patriots and proceeded to portray the former suffragists as Communists. Such organizations helped to defeat the Child Labor Amendment.[50]

Overcoming Persistent Resistance

During the final years of struggle for the vote, the leaders of the two different national suffrage organizations designed and presented ambiguous collective representations of their demands. Sharp contrasts emerged between the disciplined and respectful lobbying techniques developed with the blessing of Catt and the National American Woman Suffrage Association (NAWSA) and the defiant protests followed by hunger strikes led by Alice Paul and the National Woman's Party (NWP). The lobbyists became "friendly nags," and they cast themselves in the image of benevolent, respectable, middle-class beggar women.[51] The suffragists who picketed the White House under the auspices of the NWP presented themselves as defiant revolutionaries. These different images reveal much about the divergent intentions of suffragists just before victory.

Eleanor Flexner portrays the NAWSA reformers as self-consciously respectful and deferential to President Wilson during his speech at their 1916 convention in Atlantic City. President Wilson obliquely expressed support for female enfranchisement by announcing that he had "no quarrel in the long run" with how the vote would be achieved. After Anna Howard Shaw politely responded, " 'We have waited so long, Mr. President, for the vote —

we had hoped it might come in your administration,' the entire audience of women rose silently and turned toward him (quite spontaneously)." After the Nineteenth Amendment passed the House in early 1918, someone started to sing "Old Hundred," and others joined in.[52] These respectful images of self-control appealed to those citizens who valued traditional, peaceful means of change.

Flexner argues that the NWP pickets and hunger strikes by defiant women were overemphasized as contributors to or delayers of woman suffrage. She also rightly observes that "the pickets were actually among the earliest victims in this country of the abrogation of civil liberties in wartime."[53] The accounts of these women's acts and experiences reveal the vigorously liberal or radical intentions of an influential minority of woman suffragists and their sympathizers who rejected what Eileen McDonagh labels "a maternal albatross"[54] and stood as defenders of basic rights, particularly the rights of political prisoners and others against the arbitrary coercive powers of the state.

For example, Dorothy Day, the social justice leader and cofounder of the Catholic Worker Movement, vividly describes the agony she suffered in 1917, at age twenty, during a ten-day hunger strike at the Occoquan, Virginia, prison workhouse with women mobilized by Alice Paul's NWP. First she endured the cat-and-mouse games prior to arrest and jail. Soon after the women were imprisoned, a suffragist announced the plan for a hunger strike. Two guards immediately seized each woman and dragged her out of a holding room. Day tried to resist the rough handling: "It was a struggle to walk by myself, to wrest myself loose from the torture of those rough hands. We were then hurled onto some benches and when I tried to pick myself up and again join Peggy in my blind desire to be near a friend, I was thrown to the floor. When another prisoner tried to come to my rescue, we found ourselves in the midst of a milling crowd of guards being pummeled and pushed and kicked and dragged, so that we were scarcely conscious, in the shock of what was taking place." Day, who had joined the protest at the White House not as a suffragist but simply to "uphold the rights of political prisoners," found herself incarcerated in an institution that made her think of herself as "if in a zoo."

Day's recollections of this hunger strike are worth recounting at length because numerous influential, if not powerful women such as "the wife of the president of the board of trustees of Bellevue Hospital, . . . society women of Philadelphia, Baltimore and Boston . . . schoolteachers, writers, [and] ardent champions of feminism"[55] undoubtedly shared such anecdotes with their friends and relatives, who must have reacted with shock. In the first stage of the strike, Day writes that she "lost all consciousness of any cause. I had no sense of being a radical, making protest against a government, carrying on a nonviolent revolution. I could only feel darkness and desolation all around me." Later she spoke of losing any sense of being free "when I knew that behind bars all over the world there were women and men, young girls and boys, suffering constraint, punishment, isolation and hardship for crimes of which all of us were guilty." She then began to identify with "those around me."

> I was that mother whose child had been raped and slain. I was the other who had borne the monster who had done it. I was even that monster, feeling in my own breast every abomination. Is this exaggeration? There are not so many of us who have lain for six days and nights in darkness, cold and hunger, pondering in our heart the world and our part in it. If you live in great cities, if you are in constant contact with sin and suffering, if the daily papers print nothing but Greek tragedies, if you see on all sides people trying to find relief from the drab boredom of their job and family life, in sex and alcohol, then you become inured to the evil of the day, and it is rarely that such a realization of the horror of sin and human hate can come to you. . . . It was one thing to be writing about these things, to have the theoretical knowledge of sweatshops and injustice and hunger, but it was quite another to experience it in one's own flesh.

This memory of the brutal suffering endured by the NWP suffragists and their allies testifies not only to how affluent women intensely felt the stigma of political exclusion but also to how threatened the white men in power felt by suffragists' demands. Day and her cohort were told that Occoquan had "a whipping post and bloodhounds wandering through the grounds to terrorize the prisoners." It is worth speculating whether the experience of this torture chamber successfully terrorized most of the women prisoners enough to keep them from subsequently engaging in protests over the denial of their civil liberties. But they must have shared their revulsion and horror at the conditions of the jail and their treatment with many others. For Dorothy Day, this time in jail became a landmark in the journey that led her to Communism, then to God, Catholicism, and the formation of the Catholic Worker Movement.[56] Her chronicle offers a valuable reminder of the resistance the suffragists faced and the kind of pain that is easy for us to forget.

Day and many other radical women suffered the suppression of their newspapers and more time in jail during the Palmer raids, which coincided with the woman suffrage victory. The first major Red Scare was an unexpected development that probably did more than most other events to quash socialist, egalitarian reform efforts in the United States.

The Resistance of the Catholic Church

From the beginning of the woman suffrage movement, many Catholic priests and especially the Church's leaders resisted, if they did not oppose outright, the idea of women voting. Between 1909 and 1920 most articles and editorials on suffrage printed in *America* magazine, published by the Jesuits, conveyed skepticism, nervousness, and profound discomfort over woman suffrage. The earliest articles simply summarized recent developments with the addition of occasional quips. To the news that woman suffrage had made the governmental agenda in Italy, for example, the magazine's editor added: "Signor Giolitti thinks that the granting of female parliamentary suffrage in the South would be a surrender of many seats to the Clericals."[57] Other articles regularly included an insistent disclaimer that the pope and clergy did not see women as inferior, just different. The key difference, however, was a divinely mandated responsibility to put charity first and particularly to protect women and children. One editorial rhetorically queried, "What broader or higher mission could one ambition?"[58] At the 17 June 1909 St. Joseph's College commencement, Cardinal Gibbons asserted, "I am entirely opposed to woman suffrage, not because I hate the women, but I love them and want them to fulfill the mission for which God intended them."[59]

Such affirmations of women's worth formed some of the strongest resistance to female enfranchisement. The editors of *America* magazine published many similar arguments. Beginning in 1915, Martha Moore Avery, an antisuffragist, published a regular column in which she painted woman suffrage as a socialist idea, a threat to the "rights of the family," and a likely harbinger of public disorder.[60] Although in 1909 an unnamed subscriber had dissented from the "very one-sided presentation of the suffrage movement" in the magazine and asked for articles that addressed "both sides of the question,"[61] the editors of *America* demurred. But from 1914 until the federal amendment passed, letters from suffragists appeared periodically. These letters and the slight modification of editorial opinion reveal the kinds of concessions the suffragists made to win a modicum of support among liberal (read "open-minded") Catholics.

One of the first of suffragists' letters to *America*, written by M. X. Hedrick of White Plains, New York, excoriated the author of an article titled "The

Becoming in Womanhood" for its exaggerations and distortions of women's virtue in England, where "laws see to it that English mothers, as parents, do not exist." Hedrick also denied outright that suffragists "spurned the assistance or counsel of male companions"; she claimed instead that liberal men—including prosuffrage priests—deserved much credit for the suffragists' success.[62]

Two letters from suffragist Bertha Hopkins of Baltimore drew attention to the needs of working women from the factory to the cranberry bogs of Cape Cod to the "tobacco-laden basements of cigar manufactories." She questioned whether one antisuffragist columnist could tell her "that these women are there from choice." In the mills of Massachusetts alone, she stated, "there are 200,000 women and children and only four women inspectors to look after the interests of these slaves. In New York a wife is not entitled to her own earnings. Men have made the law that the joint earnings belong to the husband, who may drink them and let wife and children starve."[63] Hopkins passionately insisted, "The cry for woman suffrage is the cry of the working, broken mother, the cry of the hungry, bloodless child. It [is] a cry from our slums, where disease and crime, born of poverty, rot and fester together. Can any evils of Feminism be worse? Why then, at least, not try for some amelioration by giving women more power and influence?"[64] Mary Gertrude Lawlor of Utica, New York, put the struggle for woman suffrage in the context of Western world history and urged Catholics to accept the issue as one of many "economic agitations" that was a consequence of the inclusion of women in "the shops and colleges."[65] Lawlor opined that "the woman in industry" ought to have "the same protection that is accorded to the workingman, the ballot."[66]

The arguments made by Hopkins and Lawlor fell mostly but not entirely on deaf ears. Hints of compromise with modernity appear in a 1919 article, "The Woman Worker," by Joseph Husslein, S.J. In this article Husslein conceded that many women earn; "woman's place . . . is wherever Providence has given her duties to perform." But, he was quick to add, it is "in her normal duty as wife and mother" that "she can render to society her greatest service, unless indeed she choose for her sole Spouse Christ the Lord, that she may become the spiritual mother of souls." In this capitalistic world, Husslein asserted, the state should enable women to be mothers first, male and female earners should practice thrift, and "every man should be assured a family wage." And he surmised, "the wage-labor of countless women is to a great extent unnatural, because unnecessarily enforced upon them through capitalistic greed, through inadequate legislation and through personal habits of thriftlessness and excess." Husslein looked forward to "a future reconstruction in which woman will be given ampler opportunities to promote her own happiness and that of the race."[67]

Faced with opposition such as that posed by the Catholic Church with its defense of family and already overburdened women, the suffragists could hardly afford *not* to appropriate and develop progressive maternalistic appeals. Without regular, forceful, and sincere affirmations of women's identities *as women* and women's unique talents, the suffragists would not have made much headway. Middle-class women possessed the time to fight for suffrage (and in our time to enter the labor force in increasing numbers) because working-class women performed servile work.[68] Moreover, current liberal social policy makers continue to assume that the private sector will create viable remedies to the problem of dependent care.[69] The suffragists and proponents of protective legislation should be credited for bringing the issue to the table even if their remedies have become unacceptable.

After the New York State and federal amendment suffrage victories, the editors of *America* tried to conciliate women. In a 1918 editorial they applauded the "Catholic women of New York" for establishing a course of lectures on American citizenship and suggested that a similar course for men would be appropriate.[70] In a summary of an address of Pope Benedict on women's roles and responsibilities the magazine underscored the message that "changed conditions" and new rights conferred on women do not "remove woman, conscious of her mission, from her natural center, which is the family." *America*'s editors preferred to see women in a "widened" sphere, the "natural center" of which "must be the home. Whatever tends to disturb that center, weakens woman's best influence."[71] Just before the federal amendment victory *America*'s editors lamented the change as more undermining of republican government: "the form of government ordained by the Constitution is fast changing into a bureaucratic organization in practical control of forty-eight departments."[72] But soon after victory they began to mobilize women voters:

In questions of mere politics there will always be the widest divergence of opinion. But in matters of clear right or wrong, of enlightened democracy or menacing autocracy, of the common good or the assumption of unwarranted special privilege, of religious liberty or oppressive bigotry, Catholics, like all true patriots, can have no choice. They must cast a solid vote. Strenuous times call for strenuous action. Where woman suffrage is an accomplished fact, Catholic women must take the lead in the use of the power accorded them. Not the weight of the sword, but the weight of the ballot will decide the nation's fate. Again we look to woman to help in the world's salvation.[73]

In an ironic turn of events, later that fall *America* reported that Alice M. Robertson, an antisuffragist, had become the second woman to win a seat in Congress.[74]

The firm opposition voiced by the Catholic hierarchy to votes for women followed by concessions to the vote but a reaffirmation that women's natural and first-order priority was the home provide additional clues to the slow pace of change after the Nineteenth Amendment passed. Prior to victory many if not most of the powerful Catholic clergy were opponents; after victory they became competitors. Winning the vote did not lighten women's familial responsibilities; it added to them in ways hoped for by Frances Willard but in ways for which many women were probably not prepared. The clergy remained powerful moral authorities for Catholic women; it is quite possible that clergy in other denominations as well as other male leaders quickly proclaimed similar messages. The coincidence of the first Red Scare at home and the emergence of fascism abroad, particularly in Italy, undoubtedly fortified the pressures traditional patriarchal authorities put on women in church and on girls still in school.[75]

Unsung Intended Consequences

The widespread resistance to the idea of women voting enabled antisuffragists to reap many successes. To cope with this formidable opposition and overcome enough resistance to win the vote, woman suffragists became skilled employers of all arguments in favor of the measure. When she mobilized trade union women in New York City, Harriet Stanton Blatch emphasized how political equality for women would enhance the resources of American workers.[76] When southern suffragists cultivated support among southern women, they usually endorsed white supremacy.[77] During the final five years of struggle for the vote, the touchstone of Catt's Winning Plan was an insistence that victory be put above all other goals and that internal conflicts on ideals and issues be silenced. Although this posture surely was authoritarian and intolerant, it is difficult to fault it or imagine another way to circumvent the many possible ways the Nineteenth Amendment could have been blocked and defeated.

Because woman suffragists in the United States weathered so many defeats, they gradually learned to expect slow change and accept small gains. Those scholars who consider the acceptance of incremental advances as a sellout of egalitarian ideals make strong arguments. At the same time, however, it is possible to see the reformers as heroic because they were unwilling to relinquish their commitment to win the vote no matter how long the struggle took or how hard the defeats. The tough standards for victory set by Article V taught the suffragists to demand the vote with arguments that struck majorities of elected officials as reasonable and in accord with the Constitution.

A close study of the strategies woman suffragists in the United States designed to win the vote reveals the turning points after which reform leaders gradually stopped planning day by day and articulating ideologies based on intensely held beliefs beyond the justice of political inclusion. The first turning point occurred during the 1850s, when the opposing arguments to suffrage became so fierce that leaders worried the quest for other woman's rights would suffer. Reform leaders publicly demoted the vote to a second- or third-place concern regardless of how each felt about its importance. The second and more critical turning point came during the agonized debates over the Reconstruction Amendments among Garrisonians. During these debates the egalitarian-minded woman's rights reformers articulated a quite different and racist ideological aim: the view that women deserved political inclusion ahead of black men. After 1870 a widely shared determination to "get even" and to redress the humiliation of explicit political exclusion drove the quest for woman suffrage as much or more than their previous commitment to egalitarian ideals. Ultimately the overriding intention behind the Nineteenth Amendment was women's need to "feel equal" regardless of what men thought about women. And ratification easily fulfilled this intention.

The third turning point occurred during the much-repeated learning process on how to expect unexpected campaign outcomes. Many times the suffragists' precampaign assessments of likelihood for success were wrong. For example, in late 1892 Stone and Anthony confidently assumed that the upcoming opportunity to win a suffrage referendum in Kansas was far better than the chances in Colorado. But unforeseen developments in the following months proved them wrong: Colorado passed its referendum in the fall of 1893, but the measure was defeated in Kansas the next year. After several decades of struggle, the reformers anticipated the hazards of prediction in electoral politics. As suffragists continued to struggle, they realized that they had to prepare to exploit every kind of opportunity and defend themselves on all fronts. Catt's almost pure strategy of campaigning everywhere in 1916 so that the real focus of energy would not be detected "where the real battles were" emerged after such political learning.[78]

The passage, ratification, and shortcomings of the Nineteenth Amendment stand as the "textbook case proof" for Kyvig's explanation of the democratic purposes behind Article V. During the final push the main goal was to pass and ratify the amendment. Little else mattered. Still, few would deny that the subsequent decline in voter turnout and more recent erosion of traditional voluntary participation signal fundamental threats to the survival of even the highly imperfect, rudimentary democratic elements in our political institutions. Whose actions and whose inactions are to blame for this snail-paced change?

Rather than placing so much blame on women's failure to create or even demand fuller change, I suggest we take a hard look at the political hospitality practiced by male political leaders. Imagine, for just a moment, what changes might have occurred in the 1920s if the leaders of major political parties and organized interests had practiced political hospitality according to democratic and liberal principles. What if these leaders had suddenly felt an obligation to compete for women's allegiance not by token representation at the top but by inviting women to meetings held in their own neighborhoods? What if they had decided that women should contribute half of the ideas to the party platforms? What if these leaders played so consistently according to democratic rules that they put a high priority on educating women about parliamentary procedure and on the reasons for their rules so that women could suggest changes in those rules? I suggest that if the white men in power had actively encouraged women's participation and modified their organizations to make women truly welcome, electoral behavior in the United States would have been visibly and permanently altered.

Of course, the men who held power reacted in less hospitable ways. They made less visible, almost imperceptible changes in their organizations and strategies. The lack of visible change so overshadowed less visible adjustments that only a few scholars have studied what actually changed after women won the vote. In a recent eye-opening study, political scientist Kristi Andersen carefully documents numerous small steps that brought women directly into political parties and legislative politics, steps that could not have occurred in the 1920s and 1930s without the Nineteenth Amendment. Most notable among the changes Andersen identifies are that (1) electoral candidates had to consider women's opinions and preferences, (2) prominent women in political parties and public office helped sustain "progressive impulses" to extend and fortify the welfare state, and (3) by conducting surveys focusing on issues instead of personalities and continuing to extract politics from party machines, women accelerated "the transformation of the act of voting from a male ritual to a good citizen's obligation."[79] Most of these changes brought elite women's influence into centers of political power and undermined exclusionary practices without destabilizing the system. It is this kind of change that the framers of Article V surely favored. And in light of the early fears of what women's votes would bring into politics, it is ironic that the struggle for the Nineteenth Amendment facilitated the evolution of an issue-based and more inclusive democratic politics without violence, all of which actually *strengthened* the American political system. Women did not vote in large numbers, but as potential voters they appear to have upgraded debate and deliberation on political policy.

Because the passage of the Nineteenth Amendment followed some kind of suffrage legislation in many states, a number of the changes Andersen points to (changing the polling places, innovative tactics, and new political issues) had become modi operandi well before 1920. Still, she reminds us that once women had the right to vote, party leaders could not afford to sidestep women during campaigns. Andersen's study helpfully redirects attention to women's political innovations during the struggle for the vote and other reform efforts.

After the 1920s women continued to make some headway against resistance to a more complete political inclusion of women. In 1931 Emily Blair called for a revival of women's organizations to pressure male leaders of political parties.[80] Women played effective roles in the administration of Franklin Delano Roosevelt but lacked the power necessary to achieve much of their agenda.[81] They sought to move from "margin to mainstream" in the Democratic and Republican parties.[82] Women's organizations "survived the doldrums" and sustained pressure for women's advances in the 1940s.[83] Scholars of these developments concur with theorists of collective action who argue that successful persuasion—conversion of supporters and sustaining hope for improvement—constitutes a mark of achievement for a movement however invisible it may become for a time.[84]

The leaders of the women's liberation movement revived the egalitarian ideals of the early suffragists and made strides that have gone well beyond the vision of the 1848 Declaration. Women now vote at practically the same rate as men, and increasing numbers of women run for political office and win. Survey data suggest that women would promote more egalitarian social policies than men, particularly when it comes to helping persons who need relief.[85] One striking influence of the suffragists, however, has been on visions for global reform.

The Mission Statement and Critical Areas of Concern from the Platform for Action of the United Nations Fourth World Conference on Women includes egalitarian liberal aims and calls for challenges to existing inequalities across the globe. Among other purposes, the Mission Statement declares:

> equality between women and men is a matter of human rights and a condition for social justice and is also a necessary and fundamental prerequisite for equality, development and peace. A transformed partnership based on equality between women and men is a condition for people-centered sustainable development. A sustained and long-term commitment is essential, so that women and men can work together for themselves, for their children and for society to meet the challenges of the twenty-first century.

Critical areas of concern in the conference platform include "inequalities and inadequacies and unequal access to education, training, and health care." Other concerns were inequalities in economic structures and policies, in all forms of productive services, and in the sharing of power and decision making between women and men at all levels. The conference also targeted the stereotyping of women and "persistent discrimination against and violation of the rights of the girl child" as global impediments for women's equality.[86]

A monumental change, literally speaking, also bears mention. In her first edition of Century of Struggle, published in 1959, Eleanor Flexner sadly observed that the Wesleyan Chapel, the site of the Seneca Falls Convention of 1848, was "marked only by a signpost on the sidewalk. In the 1950s it did service as a filling station and garage; more recently it served as a laundromat. Any day a bulldozer could obliterate it for a parking lot." In her 1975 revised edition, Flexner reported that she had "written to the village clerk in Seneca Falls for information on the present status of the building. She replied that during her twenty-three years in the post of village clerk, no person or organization had made any attempt to set aside the site for commemorative or historical purposes."[87] It is a great relief that some American women and the federal government, probably with Flexner's urging, have finally rectified this situation. Two partial brick walls of the Wesleyan Chapel now stand gracefully in the Women's Rights National Park in Seneca Falls, on streets decorated with American flags, next door to a museum that includes splendid photographs and creative technology for learning about the struggles of all American women. The Stanton home has been partially restored; efforts are also under way to restore Mary Ann McClintock's home, the site of the drafting of the 1848 Declaration.

The Nineteenth Amendment to the Constitution of the United States guaranteeing women the right to vote was achieved after nearly seventy-five years of protracted struggle. Two generations of leaders led the struggle, and there are many reasons for its long duration. First, in total numbers, antisuffragists' successes dwarfed those of the suffragists. Numerous antisuffrage victories derived mostly from intense psychological resistance to the idea that women should be politically included, resistance that survives today. The psychological drives behind sexism, as Elisabeth Young-Bruehl carefully explains, aim less to harm women per se than to sustain a narcissistic "ideology of desire" for oneness that can be expressed either as a determination to create sameness or to define female sexual characteristics as other but inferior to—which in Young-Bruehl's framework also means similar to—male sexual characteristics.[88] When women demanded the vote, they disturbed the "fantasy structure" that most men and women relied on to make sense of their lives.[89]

Carole Pateman names the "sexual contract" as a core fantasy that makes the separation of the public and private spheres logically necessary in social contract theory. As Pateman explains, to obtain physical protection for themselves and their children, women "agreed" to provide men with sexual service (as well as other forms of support). This "sexual contract," Pateman observes, establishes civil society, and it must logically precede the social contract, because Hobbes, Locke, and Rousseau each assume that only men create the social contract. As a result, women are included in civil society but as subordinates, excluded from full citizenship. Although some women may interpret enfranchisement as a liberating step out of the sexual contract, men may well not see it the same way. Only a fuller reevaluation and challenge of women's subordination as women and the ways women consent to this subordination offer hope for a real political revolution for women.[90] Moreover, demands for enfranchisement, like demands for equal rights in the late 1960s and 1970s, divided women against women. Building a stronger consensus and solidarity among all women across race, class, and region remains the major challenge for future feminist leaders.[91]

Woman suffragists could not have won the vote without assuring most citizens that they did not intend to alter the separate spheres or fundamentally alter what appear to be necessary "fantasy structures." They succeeded largely because between 1915 and 1920 they persuaded enough citizens and, more importantly, legislators that women had unique resources that were politically useful and thus ought to be included.[92] That aim may appear as a highly limited kind of "simple justice" today, but winning the vote was no simple effort.

Not all of the arguments that worked for the suffragists should be expected to further the political integration of women in the twenty-first century. At the same time, the arguments women made to win the vote fit the suffragists and their purpose. We should not blame these arguments and those women for the slow pace of change. It is more appropriate to look beyond the arguments and keep in mind the enormously difficult task of transforming women from a politically excluded group to an included group.

NOTES

1. Sara Hunter Graham, *Woman Suffrage and the New Democracy* (New Haven, Conn.: Yale University Press, 1996), 1–10, 43–52.

2. David E. Kyvig, *Explicit and Authentic Acts: Amending the U.S. Constitution, 1776–1995* (Lawrence: University Press of Kansas, 1996), 238–39.

3. The debate between Felix Frankfurter and Hugo Black over the intentions of the designers of the Fourteenth Amendment in *Adamson v. California*, 332 U.S. 46, 67 Sup. Ct. 1672 (1947) continues to challenge the Supreme Court. These intense and prolonged disagreements focused on the goals of a small group of radical Republican federal legislators who wrote the Fourteenth Amendment.

4. Some states did impede women from voting and won the blessing of the Supreme Court. See Rogers M. Smith, "'One United People': Second Class Female Citizenship and the American Quest for Community," *Yale Journal of Law and the Humanities* 1 (1989): 280.

5. Susan W. Fitzgerald, "Women in the Home," in Anne Firor Scott and Andrew MacKay Scott, *One Half the People: The Fight for Woman Suffrage* (Urbana: University of Illinois Press, 1982), 115.

6. Rogers M. Smith correctly observes that acceptance of women's right to vote did little to undo related attitudes on women as second-class citizens. See Smith, "One United People," 274–93.

7. Eleanor Flexner, *Century of Struggle: The Woman's Rights Movement in the United States*, enlarged ed. (Cambridge, Mass.: Belknap, 1996), 272–85; Scott and Scott, *One Half the People*, 38–41, 129–36, 142–44, 147–48, 155–60; *The History of Women in the United States: Historical Articles on Women's Lives and Activities*, ed. Nancy F. Cott, 20 vols. (New York: K. G. Sauer, 1992), 19: pts. 1 and 2; Glenda Elizabeth Gilmore, *Gender and Jim Crow: Women and the Politics of White Supremacy in North Carolina, 1896–1920* (Chapel Hill: University of North Carolina Press, 1996); Rosalyn Terborg-Penn, "Discontented Black Feminists," in Mary Beth Norton, ed., *Major Problems in American Women's History* (Lexington, Mass.: D. C. Heath, 1989), 341–49, and *African American Women in the Struggle for the Vote, 1850–1920* (Bloom-

ington: Indiana University Press, 1998); *African American Women and the Vote, 1837–1965*, ed. Ann D. Gordon et al. (Boston: University of Massachusetts Press, 1997).

8. Theodore J. Lowi, "Political History and Political Science," in *The Dynamics of American Politics: Approaches and Interpretations*, ed. Lawrence Dodd and Calvin Jillson (Boulder, Colo.: Westview, 1994), ix–xvii.

9. Kyvig, *Explicit and Authentic Acts*, 42–65.

10. E. J. Dionne Jr., *Why Americans Hate Politics* (New York: Simon and Schuster, 1991), 55–76.

11. For a similar perspective on assessing the consequences of the achievements of the Chicago Housing Authority in the 1940s, see Jim McNeill, "The Conscienceless Conservative and the Decline of Public Housing," *In These Times*, 12 July 1998, 29–30.

12. Rogers M. Smith, *Civic Ideals* (New Haven, Conn.: Yale University Press, 1997), 231.

13. Helen L. Sumner, *Equal Suffrage: The Results of an Investigation in Colorado Made for the Collegiate Equal Suffrage League of New York State* (New York: Harper, 1909), 258–59.

14. Michael Oakeshott, *Rationalism in Politics and Other Essays* (London: Methuen, 1962), 124.

15. William O'Neill, *Everyone Was Brave: A History of Feminism in America* (Chicago: Quadrangle, 1971), 270.

16. Sara Evans, *Born for Liberty: A History of Women in America* (New York: Free Press, 1989), 173; Aileen S. Kraditor, *The Ideas of the Woman Suffrage Movement, 1890–1920* (Garden City, N.Y.: Anchor, 1971), 217–18.

17. Nancy F. Cott, "The National Woman's Party," in Norton, ed., *Major Problems*, 340, and *The Grounding of Modern Feminism* (New Haven, Conn.: Yale University Press, 1987), 53–81.

18. Judith N. Shklar, *American Citizenship: The Quest for Inclusion* (Cambridge, Mass.: Harvard University Press, 1991), 60.

19. Carole Pateman, "Women, Nature, and Suffrage," *Ethics* 90 (July 1980): 574.

20. Smith, "One United People," 274–93, and *Civic Ideals*, 454–59.

21. Smith, "One United People," 280.

22. Nancy E. McGlen and Karen O'Connor, *Women, Politics, and American Society*, 2d ed. (Upper Saddle River, N.J.: Prentice-Hall, 1998), 65–67.

23. Barbara Bardes et al., *American Government and Politics Today: The Essentials* (Belmont, Calif.: Wadsworth, 1998), 213.

24. Roberta Sigel, *The Politics of Accommodation: How Women View Gender* (Chicago: University of Chicago Press, 1996), 105–21, 192–94.

25. Anna L. Harvey, "The Political Consequences of Suffrage Exclusion: Organizations, Institutions, and the Electoral Mobilization of Women," *Social Science History* 20 (Spring 1996): 97–132, and "Women, Policy, and Party, 1920–1970: A Rational Choice Approach," *Studies in American Political Development* 11 (Fall 1997): 292–325.

26. Shklar, *American Citizenship*, 63–101.

27. Kraditor, *Ideas of the Woman Suffrage Movement*, 212.

28. Judith N. Shklar, "The Liberalism of Fear," in Nancy Rosenblum, ed., *Liberalism and the Moral Life* (Cambridge, Mass.: Harvard University Press, 1989), 21.

29. Ibid., 21–38; Smith, *Civic Ideals*, 2–12, "Beyond Tocqueville, Myrdal, and Hartz: The Multiple Traditions in America," *American Political Science Review* 84 (1993): 549–66, and "The 'American Creed' and American Identity: The Limits of Liberal Citizenship in the United States," *Western Political Quarterly* 41 (1988): 225–51.

30. Janet K. Boles, *The Politics of the Equal Rights Amendment: Conflict and the Decision Process* (New York: Longman, 1979), 61–99, 184–89; Jane J. Mansbridge, *Why We Lost the ERA* (Chicago: University of Chicago Press, 1986), 90–117, 149–64, 187–99; Donald G. Mathews and Jane Sherron DeHart, *Sex, Gender, and the Politics of ERA* (New York: Oxford University Press, 1990), 54–90, 152–80.

31. The following section of this essay includes several excerpts from my book, *Woman Suffrage and the Origins of Liberal Feminism in the United States* (Cambridge, Mass.: Harvard University Press, 1996), 52–54, 57–62, 82–83, 104–14.

32. "The Declaration of Sentiments," in Elizabeth Cady Stanton, Susan Anthony, and Mathilda Joslyn Gage, eds., *The History of Woman Suffrage*, 6 vols. (1881; reprint New York: Arno and the *New York Times*, 1969), 1: 72–73.

33. Harriet Taylor, "The Enfranchisement of Women," *Westminster Review* 55 (1851): 289–93.

34. Stanton, Anthony, and Gage, eds., *History of Woman Suffrage*, 1: 825.

35. Ibid.

36. Lucy Stone to Antoinette Brown, 11 July 1855, in Carol Lasser and Marlene Deahl Merrill, eds., *Friends and Sisters: Letters between Lucy Stone and Antoinette Brown Blackwell, 1846–93* (Urbana: University of Illinois Press, 1987), 143–45.

37. Marilley, *Woman Suffrage*, 58, 62–65.

38. Jacqueline Van Voris, *Carrie Chapman Catt: A Public Life* (New York: Feminist Press of the City University of New York, 1987), 153–54, 171, 178.

39. Susan M. Hartmann, *From Margin to Mainstream: American Women and Politics since 1960* (New York: Knopf, 1989), 20–21; Christine A. Lunardini, *From Equal Suffrage to Equal Rights: Alice Paul and the National Woman's Party, 1910–1928* (New York: New York University Press, 1986), 165–68.

40. Van Voris, *Carrie Chapman Catt*, 162–65, 184–88. Van Voris observes that Catt's antiwar activism brought her accusations of "taking orders from Moscow" leveled by the Daughters of the American Revolution (189).

41. "Summary and Minutes of the Mob Convention in New York," 6 and 7 September 1853, in Stanton, Anthony, and Gage, eds., *History of Woman Suffrage*, 1: 560.

42. Ellen Carol Dubois, *Feminism and Suffrage: The Emergence of an Independent Women's Movement in America, 1848–1869* (Ithaca, N.Y.: Cornell University Press, 1978), 92–104; McDonagh, "The 'Welfare Rights State' and the 'Civil Rights State,'" 247–51.

43. Marilley, *Woman Suffrage*, 80.

44. Ibid. On Populists, see 125–31, 134–35, 141–50; on Socialists, see Mari Jo Buhle, *Women and American Socialism, 1870–1920* (Urbana: University of Illinois Press, 1981), 214–45; on suffragists' connections and breaks with socialists and trade unions, see Meredith Tax, *The Rising of the Women: Feminist Solidarity and Class Conflict, 1880–1917* (New York: Monthly Review Press, 1980); and Nancy Schrom Dye, *As Equals and as Sisters: Feminism, Unionism, and Women's Trade Union League of New York* (Columbia: University of Missouri Press, 1980).

45. Smith, *Civic Ideals*, 347–52, and "One United People," 229–31.

46. Elizabeth Cady Stanton, "The Solitude of Self," in Ellen C. DuBois, ed., *Elizabeth Cady Stanton/Susan B. Anthony: Correspondence, Writings, Speeches* (New York: Schocken, 1981), 246–54.

47. Marilley, *Woman Suffrage*, 100–123.

48. Ibid., see inset illustration no. 4.

49. Susan E. Marshall, *Splintered Sisterhood: Gender and Class in the Campaign against Woman Suffrage* (Madison: University of Wisconsin Press, 1997); Jane Jerome Camhi, *Women against Women: American Anti-Suffragism, 1880–1920* (Brooklyn, N.Y.: Carlson, 1994).

50. Kristi Andersen, *After Suffrage: Women in Partisan and Electoral Politics before the New Deal* (Chicago: University of Chicago Press, 1996), 1–19, 160–70.

51. Maud Wood Park, *The Front Door Lobby* (Boston: Beacon, 1960); Flexner, *Century of Struggle*, 270–85, 300–317; Graham, *Woman Suffrage and the New Democracy*, 81–127.

52. Flexner, *Century of Struggle*, 271–72, 284.

53. Ibid., 277.

54. McDonagh, "The 'Welfare Rights State' and the 'Civil Rights State,'" 247.

55. Dorothy Day, *The Long Loneliness: The Autobiography of Dorothy Day* (New York: Harper, 1952), 98.

56. Ibid., 72–79.

57. "News Notes," *America*, 24 April 1909, 41.

58. "What the Pope Did Not Say," *America*, 8 May 1909, 102.

59. "Platform and Pulpit," *America*, 26 June 1909, 303.

60. Martha Moore Avery, "Genesis of Woman Suffrage," *America*, 16 October 1915, 5–6.

61. "Letters to the Editor," *America*, 15 May 1909, 138.

62. M. X. Hedrick, "A Voice from the Suffragist Camp," *America*, 6 June 1914, 180.

63. Bertha Hopkins, "Woman's Place," *America*, 11 September 1915, 541.

64. Bertha Hopkins, "Woman Suffrage," *America*, 9 October 1915, 637.

65. Mary Gertrude Lawlor, "Woman's Place," *America*, 11 September 1915, 541.

66. Mary Gertrude Lawlor, "Woman Suffrage," *America*, 9 October 1915, 637.

67. Joseph Husslein, S.J., "The Woman Worker," *America*, 7 September 1918, 521–23.

68. Elsa Barkley Brown, "'What Has Happened Here': The Politics of Difference in Women's History and Feminist Politics," *Feminist Studies* 18 (Summer 1992): 298–302.

69. Mona Harrington, "The Care Equation," *American Prospect* (July–August 1998): 61–67.

70. "Catholic Women Voters," *America*, 5 October 1918, 626.

71. "Words of the Pope," *America*, 6 December 1919, 143.

72. "Votes for Women," *America*, 7 August 1920, 375.

73. "The Duty of Woman Suffrage," *America*, 28 August 1920, 448.

74. "Woman Elected to Congress an Anti-Suffragist," *America*, 13 November 1920, 95.

75. Van Voris, *Carrie Chapman Catt*, 173–80, 189–97; Cott, *Grounding of Modern Feminism*, 260–61.

76. Ellen Carol DuBois, *Harriet Stanton Blatch and the Winning of Woman Suffrage* (New Haven, Conn.: Yale University Press, 1997), 88–181.

77. Marjorie Spruill Wheeler, *New Women of the New South: The Leaders of the Woman Suffrage Movement in the Southern States* (New York: Oxford University Press, 1993).

78. Kyvig, *Explicit and Authentic Acts*, 230.

79. Andersen, *After Suffrage*, 170, and "After Suffrage," *Clio: Newsletter of Politics and History* 8, no. 2 (1998): 33.

80. Estelle Freedman, "What Happened to Feminism in the 1920s?" in Norton, ed., *Major Problems in American Women's History*, 329–32.

81. Susan Ware, *Beyond Suffrage: Women in the New Deal* (Cambridge, Mass.: Harvard University Press, 1981) and *Partner and I: Molly Dewson, Feminism, and New Deal Politics* (New Haven, Conn.: Yale University Press, 1987), 175–244.

82. Hartmann, *Margin to Mainstream*, 1–22.

83. Leila J. Rupp and Verta Taylor, *Survival in the Doldrums: The American Women's Rights Movement, 1945 to the 1960s* (Columbus: Ohio State University Press, 1990).

84. Ralph H. Turner and Lewis M. Killian, *Collective Behavior* (Englewood Cliffs, N.J.: Prentice-Hall, 1987), 158–61, 171–72, 178–80, 190–91, 209–10, 212–13, 291–303. For an innovative comparative study of what the American and Swiss suffrage movements contributed to social movement theory, see Lee Ann Banaszak, *Why Movements Succeed or Fail: Opportunity, Culture, and the Struggle for Woman Suffrage* (Princeton, N.J.: Princeton University Press, 1996).

85. "If Women Were in Charge, a Kinder and Gentler Nation?" in Susan Welch et al., eds., *American Government*, 6th ed. (Belmont, Calif.: Wadsworth, 1998), 102.

86. Florence Howe, ed., "Beijing and Beyond: Toward the Twenty-first Century of Women," *Women's Studies Quarterly* 24 (Spring–Summer 1996): 160–61, 141–53.

87. Flexner, *Century of Struggle*, 72, 352, n. 15.

88. Elisabeth Young-Bruehl, *The Anatomy of Prejudices* (Cambridge, Mass.: Harvard University Press, 1996), 31–32, 130–36, 419–35.

89. Ibid., 420.

90. Carole Pateman, *The Sexual Contract* (Palo Alto, Calif.: Stanford University Press, 1988).

91. Young-Bruehl, *Anatomy of Prejudices*, 118–19.

92. See my book, *Woman Suffrage and the Origins of Liberal Feminism in the United States.*

Afterword

David E. Kyvig

In the winter of 1998 the sudden eruption of a fierce political tempest made it apparent that unintended consequences of constitutional amendment remain at least potentially powerful influences on the political culture of the United States. In the thirteenth month of his second term, President Bill Clinton's ship of state appeared to be sailing along on a high tide of economic prosperity and public approval. Unexpectedly, it struck the late twentieth century's equivalent of an iceberg, widely publicized allegations of sexual and legal misconduct involving a subordinate. The hull of the good ship *Clinton* suffered damage that appeared capable of forcing the captain overboard. In the superheated partisan and media atmosphere of the day, the purported improprieties brought talk of presidential resignation or impeachment. Overlooked in the tumult of suppositions, speculations, rumors, allegations, and denials was the effect of three post-1930 constitutional amendments in weakening Clinton's capacity to defend himself against a congressional onslaught and rendering likely, especially if he were to be driven from office before the midpoint of his second term, protracted difficulty for the office of the presidency. As Clinton's problems evolved into a prolonged political-legal battle, the constitutional implications receded deeper than ever into the shadows, but not so far as to escape notice altogether. The episode in fact underscored the potential significance of unintended consequences of constitutional amendment.

The Twenty-second Amendment, adopted between 1947 and 1951, limited a president's stay in office. The Twenty-fifth Amendment, added to the Constitution between 1965 and 1967, provided a system of vice presidential replacement if for any reason the office became vacant between elections. Both amendments had already shown themselves individually to possess significant unintended consequences. The Clinton tempest put on display more unanticipated results when the two amendments worked in tandem.

The Eightieth Congress, elected in 1946 with a Republican majority for the first time in eighteen years, entered office determined to undercut the legacy of Franklin Roosevelt. It intended, among other things, to prevent another popular Democrat from repeating FDR's long tenure in the White House. Within five weeks the House of Representatives approved an amendment limiting a president to two terms in office. Scarcely a month later the Senate, after making some revisions in the measure, concurred.

The adoption of the presidential term limit amendment by Congress and its subsequent ratification by the necessary three fourths of the states provided further evidence that, contrary to the framers' intent, the supermajority requirements of Article V did not guarantee the sort of consensus they had considered appropriate for amendment. The Twenty-second Amendment showed, in fact, that two congressional factions, Republicans and southern Democrats, each sizable but quite distinct, pursuing different goals, and separately far smaller than the proportion of the population deemed adequate to set the Constitution's terms, could coalesce to secure constitutional change. Likewise, the support of all but one of the twenty-six state legislatures then in Republican hands was insufficient to win ratification for the proposed amendment. Not until southern Democrats, alarmed by rising sentiment for civil rights within the northern wing of their party, joined the anti–third term campaign could the amendment achieve success.[1]

The presidential term limit amendment produced an ironic outcome almost certainly unintended by its conservative supporters. Based on their recent experience, they anticipated having to deal with a parade of liberal presidents in the mold of Franklin Roosevelt. Over the next half century, however, only Republicans Dwight Eisenhower, Richard Nixon, and Ronald Reagan were elected to second terms. Thus only social and political conservatives found themselves in a position to be barred from seeking a third term. Meanwhile, changes in race relations went steadily forward.

The sponsors of the Twenty-second Amendment would have been surprised and, in light of who it hamstrung, might well have been dismayed by the measure's other notable and indeed more profound unforeseen consequence: the substantial diminution of the effective power of second-term presidents. Denied the option of running again and thus the capacity to affect the fate of other political leaders, not to mention bureaucrats and even judges, second-term presidents lost influence over government during their final quadrennium in office. In its attempt to prevent another FDR, the Eightieth Congress undermined the position of later presidents by turning them into four-year lame ducks. Eisenhower and Reagan in particular might have achieved unrealized conservative objectives had they not been hobbled by the Twenty-second Amendment. Arguably, the term-limit amendment also emboldened some of those who turned against Richard Nixon and helped shorten his second term.

When the Twenty-second Amendment was under consideration in the Eightieth Congress, the question arose as to whether a vice president who assumed the presidency in the midst of a term should thereafter be limited to one elected term. For a variety of reasons, including a Republican desire not to appear unfair to Harry Truman (who at the moment seemed an extremely weak political opponent unlikely to win one term of his own, much less contest for two), the final version of the Twenty-second Amendment exempted Truman and stipulated that future vice presidents who succeeded to less than half of a presidential term could subsequently serve two full elected terms.

Another amendment affecting the presidency was adopted in the aftermath of the assassination of John Kennedy. The Twenty-fifth Amendment, among other things, dealt with the problem of presidential or vice presidential departure in the midst of a term by establishing a system of vice presidential replacement. Should the vice presidency be vacated by the incumbent's elevation to the presidency or for any other reason, the president was authorized to nominate a replacement who would take office if confirmed by majorities of both the House and Senate.[2]

The legislators who crafted the Twenty-fifth Amendment never anticipated that the procedure it established for vice presidential replacement might be called upon more than once in a single term. Despite the premature departure from office of seven presidents and vice presidential vacancies totaling thirty-eight years, not once in over 175 years had both a president and vice president left office within a single term. The most obvious unintended consequence of the Twenty-fifth Amendment arose when precisely such events occurred less than a decade after its adoption. The resignation of Vice President Spiro Agnew, followed less than a year later by the resignation of President Richard Nixon, produced circumstances in which neither the country's chief executive nor his deputy and potential successor had been conventionally chosen by the American electorate. A vice president chosen by the Twenty-fifth Amendment system succeeded to the presidency and in turn chose a new vice president. Gerald Ford and Nelson Rockefeller provided the country with the most unexpected and odd couple of national executives in its history.

Less evident at the time was the related unintended consequence of the Twenty-second Amendment. The two-term limit, along with his own problems, hobbled second-term incumbent Richard Nixon as he faced the need to nominate Spiro Agnew's successor in October 1973. His own authority under severe test, Nixon could ill afford a congressional rejection of his nominee and further erosion of his already diminished stature. Had he not been a lame duck, he might well have had more flexibility in his choice. As it was, he felt compelled to choose a new vice president certain to be acceptable to the Congress, a figure of greater stature in Congress and with greater independence from the administration than Nixon might have liked. Perhaps the Watergate crisis was too far along for Nixon to have done otherwise, but had he not been a lame duck he might have been able to gain confirmation of a vice president that Congress would have been less happy to contemplate as an alternative to the wounded Nixon. Nixon's earlier ability to select Agnew as his running mate in 1968 and 1972 despite (or perhaps precisely because of) widespread lack of enthusiasm for the former Maryland governor as Nixon's potential successor suggests what a less handicapped Nixon might have been able to achieve.

Gerald Ford, the first vice president named under the provisions of the Twenty-fifth Amendment, was also the first to take over the presidency limited to one further term by the conditions of the Twenty-second. Lyndon Johnson had become president in 1963 with less than fourteen months remaining of John Kennedy's elected term; Johnson therefore was eligible to serve two full terms, although ultimately he did not seek to do so. Since Ford assumed the presidency before the midpoint of Nixon's second term, he was restricted by the Twenty-second Amendment to one full elective term. Had he been elected president in 1976, he would have become a lame duck at the very moment that his hold on the office was first confirmed by a direct vote of the American people. Only his loss to Jimmy Carter spared him and the nation from that unprecedented and problematic situation.

Early in 1998, when Clinton's ship began, at least momentarily, to list,

Vice President Albert Gore found himself in a situation potentially the same as Ford confronted. The possibility arose that, like Ford, Gore might have to serve more than half of his departed predecessor's presidential term. Given his all-but-announced intention to seek the presidency in his own right in the year 2000, his lack of connection to the scandal that threatened to sink Clinton, and his prominence in an otherwise popular administration, Gore could be presumed to have a reasonable chance to win the millennial election. In that case, the Twenty-second Amendment would constrict his destiny. Under its provisions, if Gore assumed the presidency before 20 January 1999, he would be limited to one elected term. Whether or not this would reduce his attractiveness or appetite for the office was impossible to predict, but a half-century's experience suggests that the constraints of the Twenty-second Amendment would hamper his ability to function as president.

The abundant evidence since the adoption of the Twenty-second Amendment that a president unable to run again suffers reduced influence and effectiveness suggests how Gore might be hobbled. What nearly occurred in the 1970s but for Gerald Ford's narrow loss to Jimmy Carter in the 1976 election nevertheless remained unprecedented when faced by Gore in 1998: the possibility of two consecutive presidential terms weakened by the term limit provision. Neither the drafters of the Twenty-second Amendment who were most hostile to the presidential power of Franklin Roosevelt nor the bipartisan proponents of the Twenty-fifth Amendment appeared to have contemplated imposing upon the office of the president such an extended period of potential weakness. Even before various unintended consequences of the Twenty-second Amendment had come to light, some congressional Republicans who had voted for the amendment in 1947 agreed with Harry Truman in 1959 when the former president declared that "Roosevelt haters [had] sold the country a bill of goods."[3]

A third twentieth-century constitutional amendment proved in the 1998 Clinton crisis to have unintended consequences diametrically opposed to the desires of its proponents. The Twentieth Amendment was approved by Congress in March 1932 and ratified less than eleven months later during the time between Franklin Roosevelt's election as president and his assumption of office. This amendment sought to eliminate a well-recognized problem of lame ducks, not those yet to be created by presidential term limits but those long a feature of the Congress. The existence of congressional lame ducks was itself an unintended consequence of the Constitution's original design.[4]

"I do not believe there are 2 percent of the American People who know that a Member of Congress is elected one year and does not take his office until 13 months afterwards," lamented Representative Fiorello La Guardia in

1927.[5] He and other proponents believed that an amendment to deal with lame ducks was necessitated by an unexpected and otherwise uncorrectable flaw in the founders' work. The Philadelphia convention, unable to predict exactly when the new Constitution might be ratified, could not establish a precise schedule for putting it into effect. The framers did, however, stipulate that Congress would convene annually on the first Monday in December. After ratification of the Constitution was completed in the summer of 1788, the expiring Articles of Confederation Congress determined that, given the time needed for elections beforehand, the new government could not be ready to function before March 1789. Thus the two-, four-, and six-year terms of representatives, presidents, and senators would start on 4 March. The combination of specified term lengths, the date for their commencement, and the annual meeting of Congress in December produced a governmental calendar with serious inherent problems.

With the old Congress not expiring until the March after a November election, the new Congress would not be scheduled to meet until the December thirteen months after the balloting. Presidents could and often did summon special sessions. Expiring Congresses sometimes arranged for their successors to convene early, as was done during Reconstruction to prevent Andrew Johnson from having a free hand to act without congressional supervision. While an early convening of a newly elected Congress was both attractive and feasible by the 1930s, the continuation of an old Congress beyond the national election subsequent to the one at which it was chosen proved a much more serious problem. Indeed, the second regular session of each Congress did not even begin until after its successor had been selected.

Under the constitutional calendar, officials repudiated at the polls continued to exercise authority from November until March. Defeated office holders might be inclined to self-serving acts. The behavior of Republican lame ducks currying favor with the Harding administration following the 1922 election dramatically raised awareness of this constitutional problem. Nebraska senator George Norris proposed to eliminate the lame-duck session and advance the commencement of congressional and presidential terms through a constitutional amendment. On the first Monday in January, congressional terms would begin and the annual meeting of Congress would commence. Presidential terms would start two weeks later, leaving the newly elected Congress time to resolve any disputed election. The choices made at an election would be more promptly realized, while rejected alternatives would be far less likely to be implemented.

The House of Representatives long delayed approval of the Norris amendment as its leaders fought to retain the tactical advantage of a short post-election session with a definite terminal date as a means of exerting political leverage and resolving issues before all legislative opportunities expired. The congressional tide turned after the 1930 elections as victorious Democrats reacted against a system that allowed President Hoover to avoid confronting the new Congress until December 1931. As finally approved, the Twentieth Amendment provided that congressional terms would begin on 3 January following an election and presidential terms would start on 20 January. Congress would assemble on 3 January unless it appointed a different day to avoid being compelled occasionally to convene on Sunday. State ratification was not only prompt, it was unanimous. To say that state legislatures welcomed the chance to do away with lame-duck sessions of Congress would be a considerable understatement.

In the November 1998 congressional elections, American voters, seemingly unimpressed by intense criticism of President Clinton, elected a Congress more sympathetic than its predecessor to the beleaguered chief executive. The expiring House of Representatives, containing thirty-nine lame ducks who had either declined to seek reelection or suffered defeat at the polls, ignored the post–Twentieth Amendment pattern of not meeting at all. The expiring 105th Congress convened for a bitter debate over the president's conduct. The lame-duck House voted by a narrow margin along party lines to impeach Clinton for allegedly lying under oath and obstructing justice in response to an investigation into his sexual behavior. The U.S. Senate then ignored arguments by constitutional scholars that such lame-duck actions were precisely what the Twentieth Amendment sought to prevent and, furthermore, would die with the end of the congressional session that spawned them.[6] Whether the 106th Senate would have liked to escape the need to deal with an impeachment trial but found the technicalities of the congressional calendar too arcane to use as a basis for ignoring the final act of the 105th Congress or whether a Senate Republican majority's partisan hostility to Clinton overrode constitutional scruples, the intent of the Twentieth Amendment was brushed aside. The expansion of congressional authority at the expense of executive power, if not entirely unwelcome to the framers of the Twenty-second Amendment and not even contemplated by supporters of the Twenty-fifth Amendment, stood out as a consequence decidedly unintended and unwelcome to the architects of the Twentieth Amendment. All that hinged on these unintended consequences was the fate of a popular president, the future balance of executive and legislative power, and the degree of legislative responsiveness to the electorate.

In recent decades constitutional reformers have been no more prescient than their predecessors in anticipating all the eventualities that might confront the American republic. When the 105th House reconvened after the 1998 elections to impeach President Clinton, for example, it acted within the framework of the revised congressional calendar. The December 1998 action of the House, which most observers concluded ran contrary to the will of the electoral majority, was precisely the type of behavior that the designers of the Twentieth Amendment had sought to preclude. It did not, however, violate the technical requirements established by the Twentieth Amendment. In their reluctance to provide for an instant transfer of authority to newly elected officials (reasonable though that hesitancy may have been given the specter of unsettled electoral outcomes), the drafters of the Twentieth Amendment left open the possibility, albeit much reduced, of the very sort of lame-duck action they were trying to eliminate. The last act of the 105th House of Representatives provides a spectacular example of how an imperfect constitutional amendment can have the most decidedly unintended consequences.

The essays in this volume have illuminated multiple episodes of formal U.S. constitutional reform from the eighteenth, nineteenth, and twentieth centuries. Profound repercussions of constitutional revision, whether undeniably major or apparently minor, have been brought into sharper focus. Unexpected outcomes of amendment, both positive and negative, some quickly apparent and others slow to surface, have been made evident. Those who read these historical assessments must consider whether the essays are merely interesting vignettes to be safely ignored or whether their insights should provide a foundation upon which to build with care and caution.

Since the 1930s at least, the framers' intention that the fundamental terms of government responsibilities and limits be defined in formal constitutional language has receded as a national priority. On the one hand, numerous attempts have been made to reformulate the Constitution without amendment, slipping its restraints through majoritarian political pressure and judicial acquiescence or by the same means making its provisions more restrictive. For a time this benefited progressives and then with a turn of the tide it favored conservatives, but in both cases it provided less certainty of stability than offered by a stricter adherence to constitutionalism. On the other hand, there have been multiple attempts to trivialize the Constitution by inserting into it measures incongruous, if not incompatible, with its grand structure. The framers' intentions for their constitutional republic would appear to have been eroded from both directions.

The framers would not have been likely to regard their constitutional intentions to have been compromised by modern judicial readings of the Bill of Rights occasioned by completely unanticipated developments. They had, after all, placed in the hands of federal courts the authority to adjudicate disputes as to the law. Their desire, as David Bodenhamer has pointed out, was to secure individual liberties from unwarranted government intrusion while providing for a government that functioned effectively in their interest. The framers would probably be comfortable with this generation's interpretation of provisions of the Constitution to protect free speech on the Internet and limit the right of citizens to bear automatic weapons with firepower equivalent to a small eighteenth-century army. They might understand and tolerate the judicial decisions of the 1920s in support of the Eighteenth Amendment, pointed out by Richard Hamm, that granted police authority to wiretap telephones and conduct warrantless searches of automobiles, though they would likely be more comfortable with the subsequent constraints placed on government exercise of such authority.[7] They would not likely find anything amiss in the modern shift in values leading to the regard of some of their normal practices as cruel and unusual punishment.

Without question the framers would accept as a proper exercise of sovereign power the outcome of Article V actions to reduce the vice presidency, end slavery, tax incomes, directly elect senators, create and then dismantle alcohol prohibition, and expand the suffrage to blacks, women, and eighteen-year-olds. Despite their preference for rotation in office, they might doubt the wisdom of absolute presidential term limitation, especially in light of its consequence of constricting presidential effectiveness in a second term, but they would have no doubt that it was the right of mid-twentieth-century Americans to adopt such an amendment if they chose. Their intention was always to allow each generation, if supermajority agreement could be reached, to define the terms of government as it wished. The amendments discussed by David Bodenhamer, David Currie, Mary Farmer and Donald Nieman, and Suzanne Marilley would all, most likely, have seemed proper in form and substance to the framers. It is decidedly less clear what they might have thought about time limits on amendment ratification, an innovation mentioned by Richard Hamm. Even more problematical are the tactics employed by the Fourteenth Amendment's framers and noted by Richard Aynes in which a variety of measures were combined into one amendment, thus assuring that endorsement of one element meant the adoption of the whole package.

The framers would, however, most likely consider their intentions regarding constitutional change to have been frustrated by much that has occurred from the 1930s onward. They might well conclude that their notion of the Constitution as a set of clear statements of government principles had been compromised. They would no doubt find most notable the failure of the

New Deal generation and its successors to articulate a modern declaration of the social and economic obligations of the central government. They would certainly not find it surprising that the absence of such an amendment led to a long, contentious, and unproductive debate, continuing to this day, over the proper role of the federal government in dealing with issues of public welfare, race, health, and education.[8]

The framers might well also be disappointed by some uses of the amending process that fell below the standards they set for constitutional draftsmanship and articulation of principle. The Twenty-third Amendment, completed in 1960 and recognized from the outset as at best a partial solution to the issue of representation for the District of Columbia, granted the federal district three electoral votes rather than the five to which its population was then arguably entitled and provided it no congressional representation. This ill-considered, hastily approved amendment, called by some a second three-fifths compromise on slavery, had the effect of thwarting a full, not to mention more equitable, resolution of the District of Columbia problem, which, as a result, is ongoing.

Even more likely to be thought unsatisfactory by the founders would be the Twenty-seventh Amendment. Adopted by the First Congress along with the amendments that became the Bill of Rights, this restriction on the power of Congress to increase its pay long languished unratified. Its failure to gain ratification appears connected to fears in some states that it would have the consequence, unintended or otherwise, of restricting congressional service to a wealthy elite not dependent on a salary to serve in Congress. Then in the 1980s a campaign for its ratification began, based on the argument that no time limit on its completion had been stipulated. The completion of ratification in 1992, although accepted by Congress, paid no heed to the founders' presumption that supermajority congressional and state support for an amendment would be reasonably contemporaneous, not separated by two centuries. The adoption of the Twenty-seventh Amendment, irrespective of its contents, was certainly an unintended consequence of constitutional amendment.

The framers of 1787 and the ratifiers of 1788 would most definitely be uncomfortable with the strength shown in recent decades by amendment efforts designed to undercut though not directly confront other constitutional principles. In their own discourse they sought to probe every implication they could foresee of proposed constitutional terms. Whatever fiscal views they might have held, the framers would surely have had reservations about proposals for a balanced budget amendment that would undermine the principle of legislative majoritarianism. Requiring a 60 percent vote of Congress to unbalance an annual budget or a two-thirds vote to raise taxes would no doubt have disquieted them. They intended that enduring constitutional terms, difficult to renegotiate international treaties with the force of law, and legislation approved over presidential objection be approved by supermajorities, but otherwise they stood steadfast for majority rule, recognizing that departures from that standard placed a veto power in the hands of a minority. Proposed school prayer, flag desecration, and political campaign financing amendments, designed to reduce the sweep of the First Amendment, and a victims' rights amendment, intended to modify the Fifth and Sixth Amendments' definition of a fair trial, would almost certainly have distressed them as well.

No doubt the framers would also be disturbed by a notable phenomenon of recent decades that they would hardly have anticipated: the practice of proposing constitutional amendments less as a means of achieving a reform for which a consensus might be rallied than as a device to strike a distinguishing partisan political posture. At least some of the amendments addressed by the 105th Congress fell into this category. As members of a generation that treated constitution making with the utmost seriousness, the framers would be hard pressed to fathom the modern tendency to embrace constitutional measures without apparent attention to their consequences. What would they have thought, for instance, of a symbolic vote by a majority of the House of Representatives on 15 April 1997, and again on 15 April 1998, the day on which the previous year's federal income tax returns were due, for an amendment to require two-thirds congressional approval to increase taxes? The measure's advocates offered no explanation or even acknowledgment of the measure's effect of giving a veto over tax increases to a legislative minority. The framers would likely have been baffled as well by inattention or indifference to the consequences of other highly publicized amendment proposals, the balanced budget amendment's likely stymieing of social welfare initiatives, the school prayer amendment's preservation of white Protestant cultural hegemony, or the flag-burning amendment's suppression of criticism of the federal government. Questions remain unanswered as to why present-day politicians wish to insert such measures into the Constitution. Have advocates of these amendments simply failed to contemplate the possibility of unintended consequences? Do the proponents intend consequences not perceived by others? Are sponsors not willing to call known consequences of amendment to the attention of those they ask for support? Or are they indifferent to the possibly corrosive effects of such measures on the very notion of constitutionalism?

Clearly the framers of Article V of the Constitution intended that any changes in the fundamental law would be carefully considered and discussed at both the federal and state levels as well as endorsed by a substantial supermajority consensus before taking effect. They would not have had any problem in principle with political campaigns built around rigid commitment to one or more constitutional amendments. The electoral expression of the popular will was, after all, an important component of their political philosophy. But the essence of the system of republican government so valued by the framers called upon elected representatives to exercise considered judgment in making political decisions. The founders created a system that called for the exercise of care in designing reform, both because a high degree of consensus was required to achieve it and because correcting mistakes would subsequently be so difficult. In essence, the founders were saying in Article V, "Be careful what you ask for, because you may get it."

The procedures of the 105th Congress in dealing with the balanced budget amendment in March 1997 would no doubt have left the framers aghast. In debating this hardy perennial, the Senate did not arrange for speakers supporting and opposing the measure to alternate, as is customary. Rather, it allotted lengthy periods of time to first one side, then the other, so that senators would be freed from having to listen to the other side's arguments.[9] James Madison and George Mason would certainly have been horrified. Despite or indeed because of their strong differences, they felt it necessary to address each other at length at the Philadelphia convention of 1787 and again during the Virginia ratifying convention the following summer. No doubt their fellow convention delegates likewise would have been dismayed by an approach to constitutional reform that places so little value on serious, thoughtful, and open-minded exploration of its potential effects.

The unintended consequences of the system of constitutional amending created in the late eighteenth century are in many cases the unavoidable result of political and social changes that could not be foreseen. Yet in other instances they represent choices made and practices adopted without due respect for the core principles of the Constitution's framers. In dealing with public policy matters as significant as constitutional reform, there is merit in reflecting on the beliefs of the creators of the system regarding the purposes of constitutions, not to mention the purpose of their amendment. Likewise, there is value in considering the various episodes of amendment over the life of the United States Constitution, some of which have contributed the results intended and others of which produced unintended consequences. Having contemplated those past intentions and experiences, citizens are free to take whatever actions they choose, but at least those choices will then be well informed. They may even, perhaps, be enlightened.

NOTES

1. A fuller discussion of the adoption of the Twenty-second Amendment can be found in my *Explicit and Authentic Acts: Amending the U.S. Constitution, 1776–1995* (Lawrence: University Press of Kansas, 1996), 325–36.

2. See ibid., 357–63.

3. Harry S Truman, "Excerpts of Statement before the Subcommittee on Constitutional Amendments of the Senate Committee on the Judiciary on Repeal of the 22nd Amendment," 4 May 1959, Post-Presidential Files, Harry S Truman Library, Independence, Missouri.

4. For an extended discussion of the Twentieth Amendment, see Kyvig, *Explicit and Authentic Acts*, esp. 268–75.

5. U.S. House of Representatives, Committee on Elections, *Proposed Constitutional Amendments: Hearings*, 70th Cong., 1st sess., 1927, 2.

6. Bruce Ackerman, in testimony before the House Judiciary Committee, and Anthony Lewis, in his syndicated column, both made this point. See *New York Times*, 9 December 1998, 5 January 1999.

7. See Kenneth M. Murchison, *Federal Criminal Law Doctrine: The Forgotten Influence of National Prohibition* (Durham: Duke University Press, 1994).

8. This core argument of my *Explicit and Authentic Acts* is explored in detail in chapters 13, 18, and 19.

9. *New York Times*, 5 March 1997, A12.

Contributors

RICHARD L. AYNES is dean and professor of law at the University of Akron School of Law. He has written "On Misreading John Bingham and the Fourteenth Amendment," *Yale Law Journal* 103 (1993); "Constricting the Law of Freedom: Justice Miller, the Fourteenth Amendment, and the Slaughter-House Cases," *Chicago-Kent Law Review* 73 (1994); and "Felix Frankfurter, Charles Fairman, and the Fourteenth Amendment," *Chicago-Kent Law Review* 73 (1995).

DAVID J. BODENHAMER, professor of political science and director of the POLIS Research Center at Indiana University–Purdue University at Indianapolis, is the author of *Fair Trial: Rights of the Accused in American History* (New York: Oxford University Press, 1992).

DAVID P. CURRIE is Edward H. Levi Distingished Service Professor of Law at the University of Chicago Law School. His many publications include *The Constitution in the Supreme Court,* volume 1, *The First Hundred Years* (Chicago: University of Chicago Press, 1985) and volume 2, *The Second Century* (Chicago: University of Chicago Press, 1990) as well as *The Constitution in Congress: The Federalist Period, 1789–1801* (Chicago: University of Chicago Press, 1995).

MARY J. FARMER, a Ph.D. candidate in American history at Bowling Green State University, is preparing a dissertation on "Freedwomen and the Freedman's Bureau: Gender, Race, and Public Policy in the Age of Emancipation."

RICHARD F. HAMM is associate professor of history and public policy at the University at Albany, State University of New York, and author of *Shaping the Eighteenth Amendment: Temperance Reform, Legal Culture and the Polity, 1880–1920* (Chapel Hill: University of North Carolina Press, 1995).

DAVID E. KYVIG is Presidential Research Professor at Northern Illinois University. His most recent book is *Explicit and Authentic Acts: Amending the U.S. Constitution, 1776–1995* (Lawrence: University Press of Kansas, 1996).

SUZANNE M. MARILLEY, assistant professor of history and government at Capitol University, Columbus, Ohio, wrote *Woman Suffrage and the Origins of Liberal Feminism, 1820–1920* (Cambridge, Mass.: Harvard University Press, 1997).

DONALD G. NIEMAN, professor of history at Bowling Green State University, organized the 1997 Bowling Green conference on the unintended consequences of policy decisions. He is the author of *Promises to Keep: African Americans and the Constitutional Order, 1776 to the Present* (New York: Oxford University Press, 1991).

Index

www.ingramcontent.com/pod-product-compliance
Lightning Source LLC
Chambersburg PA
CBHW010114270326
41929CB00023B/3351